D1562392

Robert Greene

Twayne's English Authors Series

Arthur F. Kinney, Editor

University of Massachusetts, Amherst

TEAS 416

Robert Greene

By Charles W. Crupi

Albion College

Twayne Publishers • *Boston*

Robert Greene

Charles W. Crupi

Copyright © 1986 by G. K. Hall & Co.
All Rights Reserved
Published by Twayne Publishers
A Division of G. K. Hall & Co.
70 Lincoln Street
Boston, Massachusetts 02111

Copyediting supervised by Lewis DeSimone
Book production by Elizabeth Todesco
Book design by Barbara Anderson

Typeset in 11 pt. Garamond
by Modern Graphics, Inc., Randolph, Massachusetts

Printed on permanent/durable acid-free paper
and bound in the United States of America

Library of Congress Cataloging in Publication Data

Crupi, Charles W., 1939–
    Robert Greene.

    (Twayne's English authors series; TEAS 416)
    Bibliography: p. 169
    Includes index.
    1. Greene, Robert, 1558?–1592.
2. Authors, English—Early modern, 1500–1700—Biography.
I. Title. II. Series.
PR2546.C78   1986   828'.309 [B]   85–16374
ISBN 0–8057–6905–6

Contents

About the Author

Born in Ohio in 1939, Charles W. Crupi received a B.A. from Harvard University, an M.A. from the University of California at Berkeley, and a Ph.D. from Princeton University. He has taught at Princeton and, since 1974, at Albion College, where he is presently professor and chairman of the Department of English. In 1980 he was a visiting lecturer at Stockholm University. He has published articles on Elizabethan drama and is presently working on Shakespeare's comedies. He is also coauthor (with Russell Aiuto) of two plays.

Editor's Note

A major reassessment of the life and works of Robert Greene is long overdue. Now, drawing on new genealogical and sociological research as well as the best extant European and American scholarship of the past 200 years, Charles W. Crupi has done just that. In a significant study for Twayne's English Authors Series, he challenges nearly every commonplace concerning Greene. Crupi argues, with considerable care, that the received story of Greene's relatively low birth and life of dissolution is based more in myth than in available documentation; that Greene's prose romances, forging a poetics of emblematic fiction new to English literature, are important investigations of human will and depravity that explore the relationships of experience and story, delusion and fantasy in fresh and important ways; and that Greene's drama, far from merely anticipating some of the best comic techniques in Shakespeare, stood on its own with Elizabethans as complex, sophisticated, and artistically structured studies in the human need to reconcile the self and the world. Greene here emerges as a writer whose deliberate interplay of type-figures and conventional situations continually confronts the conflicting attitudes of men and women and their difficulties of describing human experience. His art, Crupi claims, disorients because it denies easy resolutions; Greene is an author who insists on importing fables into the concrete world of Tudor experience. This is an important work, intended to initiate a full-scale revaluation of one of the most important Elizabethan writers.

—Arthur F. Kinney

Preface

Although Robert Greene has not lacked for readers through the years, his name most often arises in three connections: he called Shakespeare an upstart crow, he is seen as the most prolific and most shameless of Elizabethan literary hacks, and he is said to have stumbled onto a dramatic form that could be put to better use in Shakespeare's comedies. These perhaps dubious accomplishments may serve to introduce the three chapters that make up the body of this study. That is, the attack on Shakespeare is one episode in Greene's life (chapter 1), Greene's literary professionalism is most clearly evident in his many prose works (chapter 2), and his helping to prepare a way for Shakespeare reflects his own career in drama (chapter 3).

The first chapter, treating Greene's life, is longer and more thorough than perhaps might be expected in view of the familiarity of the main outlines of the story. Greene's melodramatic descent to depravity and his struggles to repent have been described many times, especially in the later nineteenth century, when, as Willard Thorp writes, "the Victorian enthusiasts for the Elizabethan drama dropped silent tears over the fate of Robert Greene."[1] Yet this well-known tale is nothing like as straightforward as some of its many retellings suggest. The evidence is tangled and ambiguous, and no simple listing of the major facts is possible; any serious attempt to deal with what is known of Greene's life must inevitably turn into an essay on our sources of information. It has been almost fifty years, moreover, since the biographical material has been systematically drawn together, and a number of new facts have been discovered and new conjectures advanced in that time. Chapter 1, then, addresses these issues, attempting the first comprehensive review of Greene's life in a generation and attempting also a careful evaluation of what has been said about him. A very cautious chapter results, but I hope it is not plodding or overly fussy.

The prose works treated in the second chapter present problems of a different sort. We know what Greene wrote well enough, but we sometimes think we know that he wrote too much: we have trouble taking seriously works that streamed so rapidly from his pen and that appealed so directly to a large audience. As John Clark Jordan wrote in 1915, "we must be careful . . . not to regard as necessarily deliberate art what may be only shrewdness."[2] Jordan's comment reflects a bias toward popular literature that must be left behind for the appreciation of Greene (as, indeed, it must be left behind for the appreciation of Shakespeare), and there are some other biases to leave behind with it: whether we like it or not, Greene writes in an emblematic, "nonrealistic" mode, he shares his contemporaries' love of rhetorical display, and he makes extensive use of conventional motifs. To see Greene in his own terms, however, is to find that the prose works in fact reward close critical attention. I try to make that point in chapter 2, taking the works seriously as products of their era, and I have found no occasion to substitute the dismissal of a work as hackwork for an attempt to analyze it. Some works seem more important to me than others, of course, and some of the best of them are among the least known. One of my purposes has accordingly been to arouse new interest in *Alcida, Planetomachia, Philomela,* and other works, some of which have received little or no serious critical attention; there is more to attract us in Grosart's fifteen-volume edition of Greene than *Pandosto* and the coney-catching pamphlets. I have been guided by the implications of what C. H. Herford told the New Shakspere Society a century ago: Greene produced "the most considerable body of English narrative which the language yet contained."[3]

One very specific problem in dealing with Greene's prose works perhaps requires a brief comment. Greene's reputation as a hackwriter rests partly on the fact that he borrows freely from other writers and from his own earlier works, a tendency that would seem to make difficult any attempt at close reading. Three factors permit such an attempt, however. First, Greene's borrowings have often been exaggerated. Although a few works are indeed largely secondhand, most of them are original in major respects. Second, the great majority of the borrowings discovered by diligent scholars through the years follow the pattern defined by Norman Sanders: Greene's "main borrowings are for illustrations and exemplary anecdotes with which to pad out his narration, or for citations from classical history and mythology to give authority to the points he is making."[4] That is, both the "narration" and the "points" remain Greene's. Third, when Greene uses a passage from another work, we must at the least concede that he is making a conscious choice, and that the choice which he makes can be discussed in relation to the structure and purpose of the work at hand. For all three reasons, I have felt free to analyze the prose works as they stand, and I have noted the source of a passage only if the use of the source raises a point of particular interest.

The plays discussed in chapter 3 present still a third kind of problem: moving Greene out from under the shadow of Shakespeare. Although Greene's plays have been read and appreciated as a result of his relation to Shakespeare, the search for "fore-gleams of the Shakespearian drama . . . in Greene's works"[5] has tended to focus attention on only some aspects of the plays. In chapter 3 I have accordingly tried to see Greene on his own. Parallels to Shakespeare are noted, of course (indeed, some new ones are suggested), but I have emphasized them only when they illuminate Greene's own plays. I hope that I have avoided the impression that Greene is chiefly of interest as a harbinger and focused attention instead on his dramatic achievement. At the center of that achievement, I argue in chapter 3, is the use of emblematic characters and situations in plays unified by the ideas which they treat. What Alan S. Downer says of the double-plot of *Friar Bacon and Friar Bungay* seems to me relevant to all of Greene's plays: "two fully developed plots with apparently no unity beyond the mechanical use of characters common to each merge into a single whole with a *unity of theme.* The structure is, therefore, of greatest importance to the development of panoramic drama and repays close analysis."[6]

Finally, I offer a word of explanation for a subject that I do not take up in a systematic way: Greene as a poet. The poetry scattered throughout the prose works has been praised by critics from Alexander Dyce ("Greene chiefly claims our notice as a poet") to C. S. Lewis ("as a poet he has permanent claims").[7] I certainly agree with those who have found in Greene an authentic lyric gift and with those who point to the wide variety of meters, styles, and subjects that he uses.[8] At the same time, the poetry seems to me to be notably straightforward: rarely is there depth and complexity in language, rarely is there paradox and tension in structure. All of Greene's poems were written as songs or speeches delivered by characters in his fiction, and, for me, the chief interest of the poetry lies in its dramatic function. I therefore deal with a number of poems in chapter 2 as aspects of the works in which they occur, but nowhere do I attempt to evaluate the quality or significance of the poems independent of context.

What is true of the poetry is true of Greene's work in general: his significance as a writer is most clear not in individual parts of his works, but in the relation of parts; his best effects are structural, and his most complex and interesting works make great use of these effects. I hope that the chapters which follow illuminate Greene's methods, both in prose and drama, and that they go at least part of the way toward disproving what Ernest A. Baker asserted many years ago: "Robert Greene is an interesting case in literary history rather than a writer of literary importance."[9]

* * *

It is a pleasure to record my gratitude to the institutions and individuals who have helped me to complete this project. A grant from the Andrew W. Mellon Foundation gave me a summer in which to commute to the University of Michigan Library and the Michigan State University Library, and a second grant allowed a trip to the Harvard University Library. Albion College awarded me sabbatical leave in the fall of 1983. Colleagues in the English Department helped make both the sabbatical and coming back from it productive, and I especially thank Delores Goodall. The staffs at the libraries I used were universally helpful, and I appreciate in particular the efforts of Judy Johnson of Albion College. Dr. Brenda Richardson of the Queen's University of Belfast read a draft of chapter 1 and generously shared some of her own research with me, rescuing me from a variety of errors. Other parts of the manuscript were read by Richard Schrader of Boston College and David Konstan of Wesleyan University; I thank both for their suggestions. Richard Schrader also helped make a visit to Boston a fruitful one. My debts to Russell Aiuto only begin with the support he has given in his capacity as vice-president for academic affairs at Albion College. Finally, I thank Tamara, Kate, Michael, and David, and I dedicate the book to my parents.

Charles W. Crupi

Albion College

Chronology

Stationers' Register (S.R.) dates are from Edward Arber, ed., *A Transcript of the Registers of the Company of Stationers of London: 1554–1640*, 5 vols. (London, 1875–94). "Earliest ed." means earliest surviving edition.

1558 Baptized at St. George's of Tombland, Norwich (11 July).

1573 A Robert Greene, possibly the writer, enters Corpus Christi, Cambridge.

1575 Enters St. John's, Cambridge (26 November).

1580 Receives B.A. from St. John's, Cambridge (22 January). Travels on Continent at this time or soon afterward? *Mamillia* (S.R., 3 October; earliest ed. 1583).

1581 A ballad of repentant youth, possibly by Greene, in S.R. (20 March).

1583 Receives M.A. from Clare Hall, Cambridge (7 July). *Mamillia II* (signed 7 July; S.R., 6 September; earliest ed. 1593).

1584 Marries, according to most conjectures, sometime in 1584–86. *Gwydonius (Carde of Fancie)* (S.R., 11 April; earliest ed. 1584). *Arbasto* (S.R., 13 August; earliest ed. 1584). *Myrrour of Modestie* (not in S.R.; earliest ed. 1584). *Morando (Tritameron)* (S.R., with pt. 2, 8 August 1586; earliest ed. 1584).

1585 *An Oration or Funerall Sermon* (not in S.R.; earliest ed. 1585). *Planetomachia* (not in S.R.; earliest ed. 1585).

1586 *Tritameron II* (S.R., with pt. 1, 8 August; earliest ed. 1587).

1587 Dramatic career begins, according to many conjectures. (*Farewell to Folly?*—see 1591). *Penelopes Web* (S.R., 26 June; earliest ed. undated). *Euphues His Censure* (S.R., 18 September; earliest ed. 1587).

1588 Receives M.A. from Oxford (July). *Perimedes the Blacke-Smith* (S.R., 29 March; earliest ed. 1588). (*Orpharion?*—see 1590). *Pandosto* (not in S.R.; earliest ed. 1588). *Alcida* (S.R., 9 December; earliest ed. 1617).

1589 *Spanish Masquerado* (S.R., 1 February; earliest ed. 1589). *Menaphon* (S.R., 23 August; earliest ed. 1589). *Ciceronis Amor* (not in S.R.; earliest ed. 1589).

1590 Richard Harvey's *Lamb of God. Orpharion* (S.R., 9 January; earliest ed. 1599; written 1588?). *The Royal Exchange* (S.R., 15 April; earliest ed. 1590). *Never Too Late* (not in S.R.; earliest ed. 1590). *Francescos Fortunes (Never Too Late II)* (not in S.R.; earliest ed. 1590). (*Greenes Vision?*—see 1592). *Greenes Mourning Garment* (S.R., 2 November; earliest ed. 1590).

1591 *Farewell to Folly* (S.R., 11 June 1587?; earliest ed. 1591). *A Maidens Dreame* (S.R., 6 December; earliest ed. 1591). *Notable Discovery of Coosnage* (S.R., 13 December; earliest ed. 1591 o.s.). *Second Part of Conny-Catching* (S.R., 13 December; earliest ed. 1591 o.s.).

1592 *Thirde Part of Conny-Catching* (S.R., 7 February; earliest ed. 1592). Dedication to *Euphues Shadowe* (S.R., 17 February; earliest ed. 1592). *Defence of Conny Catching* (S.R., 21 April; earliest ed. 1592) (by Greene?). *Philomela* (S.R., 1 July; earliest ed. 1592) ("written long since"). *A Disputation* (not in S.R.; earliest ed. 1592). *Quip for an Upstart Courtier* (S.R., 20 July; earliest ed. 1592). *Blacke Bookes Messenger* (S.R., 21 August; earliest ed. 1592). Robert Greene dies (3 September, according to *Repentance*); buried near Bedlam (4 September, according to Gabriel Harvey). *Groats-Worth of Wit* (S.R., 20 September; earliest ed. 1592). *Repentance of Robert Greene* (S.R., 6 October; earliest ed. 1592). *Greenes Vision* (not in S.R.; earliest ed. 1592; written 1590?). Gabriel Harvey's *Foure Letters* (S.R., 4 December). Henry Chettle's *Kind-Hartes Dreame* (S.R., 8 December). Nashe's *Pierce Penilesse* (2d ed., late 1592, mentions Greene's death).

1593 Nashe's *Strange Newes* (S.R., 12 January). B. R.'s *Greenes Newes* (S.R., 3 February). Harvey's *Pierces Supererogation* (S.R., 27 April). Harvey's *A New Letter of Notable Contents* (S.R., 1 October). Fortunatus Greene buried in Shoreditch (12 August).

1594 R. B.'s *Greenes Funeralls*. T. B.'s *Second Part of the French Academie*.

1596   Nashe's *Have with You to Saffron-Walden.*

Note: None of Greene's plays can be dated with certainty. In the following list they are arranged in the order most commonly suggested, with all known contemporary records of them added. Performance dates are from *Henslowe's Diary,* ed. R. A. Foakes and R. T. Rickert (Cambridge: Cambridge University Press, 1961).

Alphonsus, King of Aragon

1599   Earliest edition.

Orlando Furioso

1592   Performed by Lord Strange's Men (21 February).

1592   Referred to in *Defence of Conny Catching* (S.R., 21 April).

1593   S.R. (7 December).

1594   S.R. (28 May).

1594   Earliest edition.

A Looking Glasse for London and England

1592   Performed by Lord Strange's Men (8 and 27 March, 19 April, 7 June).

1594   S.R. (5 March).

1594   Earliest edition.

Friar Bacon and Friar Bungay

1592   Performed by Lord Strange's Men (19 February, 25 March, 26 April, 6 May).

1593   Performed by Lord Strange's Men (10, 17, and 30 January).

1593   Performed by Queen's and Sussex's Men (1 and 5 April).

1594   S.R. (14 May).

1594   Earliest edition.

1602   Prologue and epilogue written by Thomas Middleton for court performance.

ROBERT GREENE

James IV
1594   S.R. (14 May).
1598   Earliest edition.

Chapter One
Greene's Life

In *An Account of the English Dramatic Poets* (1691), Gerard Langbaine began his section on Robert Greene by describing his doubts about his source—and then proceeded to quote the source verbatim as the basis of his survey of Greene's life and career.[1] Langbaine here set a pattern that has continued into the twentieth century: generations of scholars express uncertainty, for example, about the authenticity of the autobiographical pamphlets published just after Greene's death while relying on them for details about Greene's life; or they deplore the irresponsible attribution of anonymous plays to Greene while adding others to the list; or they argue for skepticism toward what Greene's contemporaries said of him while using their comments to analyze his character. For perhaps no other Elizabethan writer, even Shakespeare or Marlowe, do fact and conjecture so tightly intertwine. On the surface is a clear image of Greene, passed on from book to book for the past four centuries. Beneath the surface lie important questions that remain unanswered, and perhaps unanswerable. The sources of Greene's life are both unusually rich and unusually untrustworthy; too suspicious to be used without reservations, they are also, for us as for Langbaine, too suggestive not to be used at all.

The biographical puzzles have implications beyond antiquarianism, for Greene stands out among Elizabethan writers in the apparent closeness of relation between his life and his work. Whether, for example, Greene actually wrote the posthumous repentance pamphlets affects our attitude toward the claims of moral purpose running throughout his career. Indeed, Greene himself often insists on the connection of his works to his life and opinions, demanding a regard for authorial intentions that not all modern readers will concede willingly. At the same time, Greene's life has taken on independent interest. Although the works will survive without that interest—*Friar Bacon and Friar Bungay, Menaphon, Pandosto,* and some of the others are among the common coin of Elizabethan scholarship—it is not literary achievement that has made Greene the hero of novels and plays[2] and the subject of an endless stream of biographical notes and queries. Anyone who knows Greene's name at all knows something of his life, if only the image of his last days summarized by Felix E. Schelling early in this century: "Degraded with sin, pinched with want, starving and dying in the street, except for the charity of a shoemaker's wife, almost a beggar like himself, he had reached the end of a short and wasted life, and now too late lay repentant in the agony of hopeless humiliation."[3]

Greene himself founded the tradition upon which Schelling's description rests, and the examination of Greene's life must begin with his own proclaimed version of it. Many of the works published before his death contain biographical information, including descriptions of a developing intellectual and moral life. We may sometimes doubt Greene's accuracy or honesty, but at least we know that he wrote what we are reading. Such is not the case with the repentance pamphlets that appeared shortly after his death as the products of his last illness: *Greens Groats-worth of Wit, The Repentance of Robert Greene,* and *Greenes Vision.* Although many readers have seen these works as Greene says the Romans saw Ovid's—they "that heard his loues beleeued his penance" (9:123)[4]—others have questioned them from their first publication down to the present day. Especially important is a section of the *Repentance* called "The life and death of Robert Greene Maister of Artes," for it offers a brief, but quite detailed, autobiography. A third source of information consists of what was said by those who knew Greene. Both friends and enemies wrote about him, most notably in works of attack and defense following his death; Gabriel Harvey in particular gives many significant details. Here again, however, is uncertainty: these writers had their own selves to serve and Greene was not alive to respond. Finally, of course, there are the findings of modern scholarship, sometimes the result of the patient searching out and interpreting of documents but just as often the result of whimsical conjecture.

Sorting through these various sources is a difficult task indeed. Accounts must be set beside each other and carefully evaluated at every point, with the result, all too often, of the verdict "not proven." And yet there are some certainties in the end. If we will never know the truth of everything said about Greene and by Greene, we can have confidence in our knowledge of the larger outlines of his life and in at least some of the important elements of his character.

Norwich to London

Birth, youth, and education. Greene signed himself "R. Greene, *Nordouicensis*" on one occasion (14:300) and *"Rob. Greene. Norfolciensis"* on another (1:258), and records of several Greene families have been found in Norwich. In the very thorough biographical introduction to his 1905 edition of Greene's plays, John Churton Collins concluded from the records that a 1558 baptismal entry at St. George, Tombland probably refers to Greene: "Robtus Grene filius Robti Grene xj Julii 1558 baptizatus fuit" (*PP*, 1:12). Of possible Robert Seniors, Collins thought a saddler of that name most likely, ending earlier speculation that Greene was born into the landed gentry.[5] This interpretation of the Norwich records stood unchallenged until very recently, with Brenda Richardson's argument that Greene's father is more likely to have been another Robert Greene, a cordwainer turned innkeeper who probably spent a period in Yorkshire.[6] Because of the significant differences between the Norwich and Yorkshire environments, the identity of Greene's father bears on an approach to his works. Following Collins in setting Greene's boyhood in a saddler's shop at Norwich, René Pruvost, author of the most substantial book on Greene yet written, finds as formative on his character the active religious climate of Norwich, particularly its progressive and iconoclast elements. He sees Greene growing up in a Puritan hotbed fed by refugees from the Low Countries, a setting that not only affected his attitudes toward religion but also influenced his temperament with its instability and tendency toward enthusiasm.[7] At the same time, this world of "martyrs and rebels" was a world of self-indulgence in drama, shows, and feasts, providing the young Greene with a contrast between Renaissance and Reformation that drew him simultaneously toward prodigality and repentance.[8]

The case is altered if the young Greene spent time in Yorkshire— less populous, more conservative, and more clearly dominated by local aristocratic families than his birthplace. Here he could have made contact with a well-established landed gentry, members of which not only later received dedications from Greene but responded with laudatory poems prefixed to his works. Indeed, Pruvost's image of a Greene with roots urban, bourgeois, and radical in religion fits rather awkwardly with the clearly traditionalist elements of some of his works. In *A Quip for an Upstart Courtier,* for example, Greene warmly praises one Thomas Barnabie as a true *"maintayner of Cloth breeches (I meane of the old and worthie customes of the Gentilitie and yeomanrie of* England*)"* (11:210). As Richardson says, "if Greene grew up in an environment where the conservative values of the gentry were within sight and only just out of reach, his instinct to preserve and conserve becomes comprehensible."[9]

Beyond these efforts to measure the influence of his early environment, little can be said of Greene's youth and family. The wills of the various Greenes who may have been related to him contain nothing of interest in approaching the works. The "Life and Death of Robert Greene" describes the "grauitie and honest life" of Greene's parents (12:171), but attempts to link Greene's father to the various fathers of prodigals in his works run up against the conventionality of the figure of the patriarch dispensing sage advice. And we need to be wary, certainly, of assuming that the unusual energy of Greene's apparent revolt from traditional morality reflected unusual narrowness in its presumed spokesman, Greene's father. In fact, even the posthumous pamphlets do not so portray his father, although they portray a devoted mother who "pampered" a child already given to selfishness and rebellion and thus helped him to grow "prone to all mischiefe" (12:172).

Greene describes his education on the title-pages of several of his books. At various points he is "Robert Greene Graduate in Cambridge" (2:3), "Robert Greene Maister of Arts, in Cambridge" (2:139), and "R. Greene. *Vtriusq. Academiae in Artibus Magister"* (9:117). A further clue is provided by part 2 of *Mamillia,* entered in the Stationers' Register on 6 September 1583, in which Greene signed the epistle "From my Studie in Clarehall the vij. of Iulie" (2:143). With these various references set against university records, a Robert Greene has been found who entered St. John's, Cambridge, on 26 November 1575 as a sizar (a poor student assigned miscellaneous tasks). This Robert Greene received a B.A. degree early in 1580. Assuming that this is the correct Robert Greene, he changed colleges, entering Clare Hall, where he received an M.A. on 7 July 1583 (the date of the preface to *Mamillia*). Five years later, in July of 1588, a Robert Greene received an M.A. at Oxford; presumably this Greene was again the writer, granted the degree not after a course of study but as a privilege traditionally extended by one university to graduates of the other. Greene could now call himself *"Vtruisq. Academiae in Artibus Magister."*[10]

Of Greene's university years beyond these basic facts, nothing is verifiable. His undistinguished class ranking indicates little: for the B.A., 38th of 41 at St. John's and 115th of 205 at the University; for the Cambridge M.A., 5th of 12 at Clare Hall and 29th of 129 at the University. We do not know why Greene moved from St. John's to Clare Hall, although changing colleges was not unheard of, nor the extent to which he was actually in residence. Poems later prefixed to his works identify certain of his university friendships, but whether he came into contact with people who influenced his development as a writer is unknown. Several young men who went on to literature had university careers that overlapped with his. Brian Melbancke, for example, who, like Greene, imitated Lyly in the early 1580s, was in Greene's class at St. John's, but no university friendship with him can be documented—or with Marlowe, Lyly, or other writers of the day who had been at Cambridge.[11]

Perhaps most interesting, we do not know whether university life began the descent to depravity described in the posthumous pamphlets. Certainly late sixteenth-century Cambridge presented Greene with a turbulent environment of religious controversy and rowdy students. As the university historian writes, "it will be difficult to find any testimony in the half-century that follows upon the year 1570 which describes the general condition of the students as satisfactory"; moreover, he writes elsewhere, the "spirit of insubordination appears to have been exceptionally rife" at St. John's.[12] The effect of such an atmosphere on Greene is readily conjectured. More specifically, Cambridge students included the studiously idle rich, so devoted to fashionable dress that a number of ordinances were issued in the last two decades of the century. In 1578, for example, a decree of Lord Burghley, chancellor of the university, forbade such enormities as "excessyve ruffs" and "hoses of unsemely greatnes or disguised fashion." Burghley expressed special concern about the influence of young nobles' extravagance on students of limited means, who might be induced "to change and cast away ther modesty and honest frugallitie, to overcharging of ther frends: and namely, to the attempting of unlefull meanes to mayntean them in ther sayd wastful disorders."[13] It is not difficult to imagine Greene, a sizar, among those vulnerable to the imitation of social superiors. Indeed, such imitation was perhaps among the functions of university education for young men of Greene's background. Here the son of a cobbler (Marlowe), grocer (Lodge), or clerk (Peele) could turn his back on tradesmen's concerns and explore a larger world. The experience was no doubt unsettling for many, leading into a kind of social vacuum, a sense of placelessness in a rigidly structured society. As Alfred Harbage comments, "a Marlowe or a Greene is a young man uprooted."[14] For those who went on to write literature, literature may accordingly have served the cause of social aspiration, helping to explain, perhaps, Greene's fulsome addresses to potential patrons and gentlemen readers and his portrayals of leisured nobles debating definitions of love and the like. Greene's search for an aristocratic literary mode may thus reflect rejection of his origins and emulation of the many young men at Cambridge who were "ruffeled out in . . . silks," as Greene himself is described in the "Life and Death of Robert Greene" (12:172).

The same work claims that university friends led Greene to Italy and Spain, where he "sawe and practizde such villainie as is abhominable to declare" (12:172). Here the young man's corruption flowered, and he returned that Elizabethan stereotype scorned in a famous passage in Roger Ascham's *The Scholemaster* (1570), the Italianate Englishman: frivolous, vice-ridden, atheistical. Greene himself has Cloth Breeches in the *Quip* describe the coming from Italy of Velvet Breeches "accompanied with multitude of abhominable vices," including "vaine glory, selfe loue, sodomie and strange poisonings" (11:226). Unfortunately, evidence for travel is very slim beyond the "Life and Death." Only one work published before Greene's death makes explicit reference to continental travel, and there a sweeping claim to know by observation the customs of Italy, Spain, France, Germany, Poland, and Denmark is difficult to take very seriously (10:6). Greene several times portrays young men who fall to vice while traveling, but never with concrete detail. Indeed, most critics find all of his references to continental customs and landscapes brief and conventional.[15] One would perhaps not expect the contrary from a writer who had traveled, given Elizabethan narrative styles, but knowing the truth of the matter might still bear on the reading of Greene's works: a continental journey would again indicate Greene's identification with a higher social stratum than his Norwich origins suggest.

Once back in England, according to the "Life and Death," Greene immersed himself wholly in vice: "Yong yet in yeares, though olde in wickednes, I began to resolue that there was nothing bad that was profitable: whereupon I grew so rooted in all mischiefe, that I had as great a delight in wickednesse, as sundrie hath in godlinesse: and as much felicitie I took in villainy, as others had in honesty. . . . From whordome I grew to drunkennes, from drunkennes to swearing and blaspheming the name of God, hereof grew quarrels, frayes, and continual controuersies" (12:173–74). The "Life and Death" also describes, however, a crisis of conscience induced "in Saint Andrews Church in the Cittie of Norwich, at a Lecture or Sermon then preached by a godly learned man" (12:175). The Greene of this work promised amendment and prayed for grace, but "this good motion lasted not long," for, he says, "my copesmates . . . fell vpon me in ieasting manner, calling me Puritane and Presizian, and wished I might haue a Pulpit, with such other scoffing tearmes, that by their foolish perswasion the good and wholesome lesson I had learned went quite out of my remembrance: so that I fel againe with the Dog to my olde vomit, and put my wicked life in practise" (12:176). Again a story in a work of questioned authenticity rests uncorroborated in other works or in independent evidence. Collins found that a powerful "Lecture or Sermon" could have been delivered by John More, at St. Andrew's throughout the 1570s and 1580s and a man "of remarkable accomplishments and eloquence who was known as the Apostle of Norwich" (*PP,* 1:18). This finding perhaps makes the episode more plausible, but it adds nothing in the way of verification. Nevertheless, the conversion has appealed to many commentators as an emblem of Greene's divided nature. It reveals a Greene well-intentioned but weak-willed, capable of conscience but easily tempted by bad company and the pleasures that bad company offers.

Marriage and desertion to London. In addition to what it might reveal of Greene's character, the Norwich conversion involves two other biographical questions. First, if it happened as described, the copesmates' success in appealing to anti-Puritan snobbery again shows Greene adopting an aristocratic pose, a pose consistent with his mockery in the *Farewell to Folly* of "our deare English breethren that measure their praiers by the houre glasse" (11:230). Second, the account places Greene back in Norwich sometime during his university years. Just when is unknown, and his movements are impossible to trace. At some point during these years, however, Greene married, for the evidence, though ambiguous in some respects, consists of more than passages in the posthumous pamphlets.

The "Life and Death" (12:177–78) says that "soone after" Greene's
relapse from conversion he married "a Gentlemans daughter of good
account" who drove him away, despite the birth of a child, by her
attempts to persuade him from his "wilful wickednes." Having spent
her dowry, Greene went to London, and his wife and child went
into Lincolnshire. Greene never saw her again, says the "Life and
Death," but the tale ends with a moving address to her: "But oh
my deare Wife, whose company and sight I haue refrained these
six yeares: I aske God and thee forgiuenesse for so greatly wronging
thee, of whome I seldome or neuer thought untill now. Pardon mee
(I pray thee) wheresoeuer thou art, and God forgiue mee all my
offences." This account shares some details with the story of Roberto's marriage in the *Groats-worth of Wit*. Roberto, "a Scholler,"
marries "a proper Gentlewoman" (12:103) but deserts her for the
courtesan Lamilia. "How often," says the narrator, "his wife la-
boured vainely to recall him, is lamentable to note: but as one giuen
ouer to all lewdnes, he communicated her sorrowful lines among
his loose truls, that iested at her booteless laments" (12:135). The
same passage describes the "shamefull ende of sundry his consorts,"
one of whom, "brother to a Brothell he kept, was trust vnder a tree
as round as a Ball." Here is an apparent allusion to the thief Cutting
Ball and his sister, an allusion that gives the story of Roberto a
London reference and makes it in fact the story of Greene. Indeed,
later in the pamphlet the fiction is melodramatically abandoned:
"Heere (Gentlemen) breake I off *Robertos* speech; whose life in most
parts agreeing with mine, found one selfe punishment as I haue
doone. Heereafter suppose me the said *Roberto*" (12:137). A few
pages later comes one further reference to Greene's marriage: "if
thou be married, forsake not the wife of thy youth, to follow strange
flesh; for whoremongers and adulterers the Lord will iudge. The
doore of a Harlot leadeth downe to death, and in her lips there
dwels destruction; her face is decked with odors, but shee bringeth
a man to a morsell of bread and nakednesse: of which myselfe am
instance" (12:140). While neither of these pamphlets can be proved
authentic, Greene portrays desertion analogous to what they describe
in several earlier works, though never with a claim of autobiographical implication. The plays *James IV, Friar Bacon and Friar Bungay,*
and *Orlando Furioso* all include portraits of faithful women suffering
male betrayal patiently, and the motif runs throughout the prose
works, sometimes involving fascination with a courtesan. Closest

in details to the posthumous pamphlets is the desertion of wife and son in *Never Too Late* (1590) by Francesco, lured on by a courtesan during a visit to Troynovant. In the second part of this work Francesco returns to his wife after six years, abandoning his new career as a playwright.

Such incidents can be read two ways. They may reveal Greene drawing on his own experience for his fiction before going on to dramatize it directly in repentance pamphlets, or they may only show him using a narrative situation found in other works of the day but in the process providing inspiration to a later forger. Most scholars have found the first of these hypotheses the more attractive, partly because of the evidence provided shortly after Greene's death by Gabriel Harvey's *Foure Letters and Certeine Sonnets* in an attack on Greene that contains a reference to Greene's "forsaking of his owne wife, too honest for such a husband."[16] Harvey's attack (its occasion is discussed below) also describes Greene's "keping of . . . Balls sister, a sorry ragged queane,"[17] in apparent agreement with the reference to Ball and his sister in the *Groats-worth*. Perhaps the same woman was the Em Ball at whose house the actor Richard Tarlton had died in 1588, described as "a woman of verye bad reputacion" in a contemporary court record.[18] Further credibility is lent by one other detail: Harvey claims that Ball's sister bore Greene a "base sonne, *Infortunatus Greene*,"[19] and a Fortunatus Greene was buried in Shoreditch on 12 August 1593, less than a year after Greene's own death.[20] If this was indeed Greene's son, Harvey's turning of Fortunatus into Infortunatus is perhaps no more a tasteless feature of the sad tale than Greene's own choice of the infant's name.

Although these pieces of information cohere well enough, no date for the marriage has ever been determined. The reference to a six-year separation in the "Life and Death" of 1592 sets the desertion in 1586, with marriage at least long enough before to allow for the child Greene left behind. Conjectures have thus focused on the years 1584–86.[21] The question bears on the consideration of autobiographical elements in Greene's works, the first of which, *Mamillia,* was registered in 1580. This work already centers on a faithless hero, portraying Pharicles's betrayal of a virtuous gentlewoman and ending with his sudden disappearance, much to the confusion of the gentlewoman, now his betrothed. This anticipation of Greene's later works, understandably slighted by biographical interpreters, calls seriously into question simple assumptions about Greene's rendering of his own life in fiction. At the same time, *Mamillia* would acquire additional interest if Greene were known to have married earlier, and an earlier date has indeed been recently proposed: Greene may have married one Isabell Beck in November 1579 in Long Bennington, Lincolnshire.[22] If so, events connected with the marriage might conceivably have inspired the story of wooing, winning, and deserting told in *Mamillia*.

Here the matter of Greene's marriage rests, with a reading of *Mamillia* or any other of the works remaining hypothetical; too little is known to separate the autobiographical from the fictional in Greene's treatment of love. That Greene's relation to his wife is entirely without use in approaching his works does not follow, however. As Richard Helgerson has argued in *The Elizabethan Prodigals,* the Elizabethan writer-prodigals wrestled in their own lives with the revolt against convention which they depicted in fiction. A kind of autobiography can thus be seen in Greene's works whatever the dates of his marriage and separation. Greene's youths, torn between respectable and unrespectable women, are conventional figures of Elizabethan literature, but they became conventional because they embodied genuine moral and emotional issues for Elizabethan readers and writers, including Greene himself.

Links between life and art perhaps help explain the fact that surviving accounts of Greene's life in London once he had left his wife behind, whether early or late in the 1580s,[23] have a conventional ring. The accounts emphasize not simply dissoluteness but also a deliberateness in prodigality, a self-consciousness in rejecting bourgeois values. Most notable of these accounts is Gabriel Harvey's, which needs to be quoted at length:

who in London hath not heard of his dissolute, and licentious liuing; his fonde disguisinge of a Master of Arte with ruffianly haire, vnseemely apparell, and more vnseemelye Company: his vaineglorious and Thrasonicall brauinge: his piperly Extemporizing, and Tarletonizing: his apishe counterfeiting of euery ridiculous, and absurd toy: his fine coosening of Iuglers, and finer iugling with cooseners: hys villainous cogging, and foisting; his monstrous swearinge, and horrible forswearing; his impious profaning of sacred Textes: his other scandalous, and blasphemous rauinge; his riotous and outragious surfeitinge: his continuall shifting of lodginges: his plausible musteringe, and banquetinge of roysterly acquaintaunce at his first comminge; his beggarly departing in euery hostisses debt; his infamous resorting to the Banckeside, Shorditch, Southwarke, and other filthy hauntes: his obscure lurkinge in basest corners: his pawning of his sword, cloake, and what not, when money came short; his impudent pamphletting, phantasticall interluding, and desperate libelling, when other coosening shifts failed: his imployinge of Ball (surnamed, cuttinge Ball) till he was intercepted at Tiborne, to leauy a crew of his trustiest companions, to guarde him in daunger of Arrestes: . . . particulars are infinite: his contemning of Superiours, deriding of other, and defying of all good order?[24]

Throughout the passage runs an element of public display—in eccentric dress, in bragging and swearing, in blasphemy and atheism. Even Greene's "ruffianly haire" seems to score a point against a Cambridge statue condemning "long lockes of Hayre" on students[25] as Greene dramatizes himself as a rebel against the traditional values that Harvey expresses with such outrage.

Harvey admits that he was "altogether vnacquainted" with Greene and "neuer once saluted him by name,"[26] and he was, moreover, given to vituperation and hyperbole by temperament. At the same time, other writers confirm much of what he says. Cuthbert Burby, printer of the *Repentance,* concedes that Greene's "loose life was odious to God and offensiue to men," and describes him as "forsaking all godlines, & one that daily delighted in all manner of wickednes" (12:155–56). Henry Chettle, friendly enough to assist, he says, in the publication of a manuscript Greene left behind, confirms one small detail in Harvey's account (Greene's hair) while describing Greene's appearance in a dream, but pointedly evades assessing his character: "a man of indifferent yeares, of face amible, of body well proportioned, his attire after the habite of a schollerlike Gentleman, onely his haire was somewhat long, whome I supposed to be Robert Greene, maister of Artes: of whome (howe euer some suppose themselues iniured) I haue learned to speake, considering he is dead, *nill nisi necessarium.*"[27] More overtly sympathetic is one R. B., who calls himself Greene's friend in *Greenes Funeralls,* a curious work consisting of fourteen awkwardly written poems that praise Greene extravagantly two years after his death. Despite professed adulation, R. B. admits in his sonnet 12 that Greene's life was "a loathsome / Puddle of filthynes, inly poluted, / With all abuse, that can be deuised."[28] Another anonymous writer, B. R., calling up Greene's ghost for a journey to heaven and hell, casually exploits his reputation by having Greene recall the "lyquour, which I was wont to drinke, with my

Hostesse, at the Redde lattesse in *Tormoyle streete.*"[29] Further testimony is provided by Thomas Bowes, who, in the preface to his translation of the second part of the *French Academy,* offers up the recently dead Greene as an example of the "desolute life" and atheistical opinions of Machiavelli's followers in England.[30]

Bowes has been taken as a valuable witness because he took an M.A. at Clare Hall the same year that Greene did and may have known him.[31] One other commentator on Greene's life in London, Thomas Nashe, certainly knew him. Responding to Harvey's attack on Greene in one phase of his own quarrel with the Harveys (discussed below), Nashe denies some of what Harvey says but hardly attempts a whole-scale defense of Greene's memory: "he might haue writ another *Galataeo* of manners, for his manners euerie time I came into his companie: I saw no such base shifting or abhominable villanie by him."[32] Nashe claims here no more than never having seen the Greene Harvey describes, an evasion he immediately makes explicit: "Something there was which I haue heard, not seene, that hee had not that regarde to his credite in, which had been requisite he should." In passing, Nashe perhaps gives substance to Harvey's charge of vanity by describing Greene's beard as "a iolly long red peake, like the spire of a steeple," which "hee cherisht continually without cutting, whereat a man might hang a Iewell, it was so sharpe and pendant."[33] Nothing Nashe says bears on Greene's wife or Ball's sister, but he echoes Harvey's description of Greene's appetites in redefining them as marks of conviviality: Greene "made no account of winning credite by his works . . .: his only care was to haue a spel in his purse to coniure vp a good cuppe of wine with at all times."[34] Nashe presents Greene as "a good fellowe," balancing his carelessness against Harvey's prudence: Greene "would haue drunke with thee for more *angels* then the Lord thou libeldst on *gaue thee in Christs Colledge;* and in one yeare hee pist as much against the walls, as thou and thy two brothers spent in three."[35] It is Nashe, again attempting to define a Greene reckless but not vicious, who tells the well-known story of Greene's making "an Apparriter once in a Tauern eate his Citation, waxe and all, very handsomly seru'd twixt two dishes."[36] Finally, however, although Nashe "neuer knew him tainted" by "any notorious crime," he can only plead the excuse of human frailty for Greene's vices: "Debt and deadly sinne who is not subiect to?"[37]

Nashe and other witnesses, then, may show Harvey guilty of wrath and exaggeration, and perhaps of puritanical finickiness, but not of fundamental misrepresentation. Indeed, there is sad justness in Harvey's assertion that Nashe's defense is "a more biting condemnation, then my reproofe."[38] These writers all attest to the life in London described in the posthumous pamphlets. Moreover, even if those pamphlets were forged, no forger would invent a Robert Greene entirely at odds with reality. There is little reason, in short, to doubt the portrait in the pamphlets of a man deeply immersed in "a battaile between the spirite and the flesh" (12:170).

Writer by Profession

Prose writer. At times, of course, the spirit seems to have prevailed, most spectacularly, if the repentance pamphlets are genuine, as Greene lay on his deathbed. By the time of those famous last days, however, Greene was well established as a writer. Whatever the expense of spirit in a life of dissipation, he sent a steady stream of pamphlets to the press, with over thirty appearing before his death at age thirty-four. As Nashe said of him in 1592, "in a night & a day would he haue yarkt up a Pamphlet as well as in seauen yeare."[39] Indeed, Nashe had already applauded Greene's facility in 1589 in his preface to *Menaphon:* "giue me the man, whose extemporall vaine in anie humor, will excell our greatest Art-masters deliberate thoughts; whose inuention quicker than his eye, will challenge the proudest Rethoritian, to the contention of like perfection, with like expedition" (6:11). Greene's "yarking up" of pamphlets was not always scrupulous by modern standards, for he freely pieced out some of his works with unacknowledged translations, borrowings from other writers, and repetitions from his own earlier works. Still, he moved from genre to genre with remarkable fluency and, apparently, remarkable success. In Nashe's words, "glad was that Printer that might bee so blest to pay him deare for the very dregs of his wit."[40] Harvey scorned Greene's prolificity—"Is this *Greene* with the running Head, and the scribling Hand, that neuer linnes putting-forth new, newer, & newest bookes of the maker?"—and lamented the sale of his works: "I would, some Buyers had either more reason to discerne, or less Appetite to desire such Nouels."[41] More sympathetic, the author of *Greenes Newes* has the ghost of Greene introduce himself in terms of his popularity:

"I am the spirite of *Robert Greene,* not vnknowne vnto thee (I am sure) by my name, when my wrytings lately priuiledged on euery post, hath giuen notice of my name vnto infinite numbers of people that neuer knewe me by the view of my person."[42]

Greene's many prose works went through several distinct phases, as will be considered in chapter 2 below. To review the purely biographical aspects of his career here, Greene's first work, *Mamillia,* was perhaps written before he left Cambridge[43] and was entered in the Stationers' Register in 1580. Whether it was printed that year is not known, since no edition before 1583 survives. The second part was not registered until 1583 and Greene apologizes for its having *"bene so long in penning"* (2:145), allowing conjectures that in the years 1580–83 he was otherwise occupied. The second part began a quick succession of titles published by the end of 1584, all of which, like *Mamillia,* imitate John Lyly's *Euphues* in several respects. Then a second unexplained gap occurs, with only three works appearing in 1585 and 1586, before a renewal of activity in 1587. The works that follow move away from the imitation of Lyly and make use of the livelier and more complicated plotting of romance, and in this period come such well-known works as *Menaphon* and *Pandosto.*

In 1590, although with no interruption in the flow of rapidly written works, the tone of Greene's epistles and dedications changes: he begins to admit that his writing so far has been immoral and to claim that henceforth he will write solely for edification. Greene's statements to this effect are often taken as a major turning-point, with the works to come read accordingly—as more clearly autobiographical and more consistent in their moral framework than the earlier works. The evidence for a change of heart is easily oversimplified, however. A number of problems emerge from close inspection of the works in question, beginning with *Never Too Late,* probably written in 1590. Greene does not describe this work as a new departure, but links it directly to earlier works in the preface: *"if I presume to present you as hethertoo I haue done with friuolous toyes; yet for that I stretch my strings as hie as I can"* (8:8). Moreover, in announcing a sequel he admits that more "toyes" will follow: "And therefore assoone as may bee . . . looke for *Francescoes* further fortunes, and after that my *Farewell to follie,* and then adieu to all amorous Pamphlets" (8:109). In the sequel, *Francescos Fortunes,* Greene again says that he is renouncing tales of love, but again the work at hand does not yet represent a new mode: he writes it only because he has promised it and now plans to go on to "more deeper matter" (8:118). In short, Greene labels the two works normally seen as beginning a new phase of his career as examples of the old phase.

Further confusion arises in the next of the works, *Greenes Mourning Garment:* the dedication calls it an attempt to "wean" young men "from wanton desires" (9:121), but in the end Greene calls it "the last of my trifling Pamphlets" (9:222). Again a gap between Greene's definition of the work and his definition of his own condition of mind exists. He describes the latter at length in the dedication. Hearing "with the eares of [his] heart *Ionas* crying, *Except thou repent,"* Greene has "changed" the "inward affectes" of his mind and turned his "wanton works to effectuall labours" (9:119–20). As a further problem for biographical interpretations, the "inward metamorphosis" (9:122) is exclusively literary. Comparing himself to the young Ovid as an author of "amorous fancies" (9:121), Greene loathes his role as "Loues Philosopher" (9:122) but makes no statement of spiritual transformation; he renounces only "publishing . . . wanton Pamphlets, and setting forth Axiomes of amorous Philosophy" (9:119). The same revulsion from tales of love is the central theme of *Greenes Vision,* published after Greene's death but probably written about this time (discussed below), and it too eschews all comment on Greene's own behavior. In addition to this puzzling isolation of literary repentance from broader moral commentary there is the fact that Greene had by no means written exclusively about love; when he did, moreover, he did so with a highly moralistic tone, often condemning "amorous fancies." It is difficult to conceive why Greene should wish to present himself to the public as "Loues Philosopher." Gabriel Harvey would soon make the same change, but Harvey admits—or perhaps boasts—that he had never read Greene's works.[44]

These contradictions make the matter of Greene's change of heart in 1590 obscure. Perhaps, of course, there was no change; perhaps Greene simply found that *Never Too Late* was well received and so followed it up by presenting more exaggerated claims of reform in his next few works, giving them as title-page motto a Latin echo of *Never Too Late:* "sero sed serio" (late but in earnest). As for the awkwardness of a repentant Greene continuing to publish unrepentant works while promising fruits of reform to come, we know that he was, at least in part, clearing his desk of projects. He published two old manuscripts at just this point, one of which, the *Farewell to Folly*, became the next work in the series proclaiming reformation.[45] Its content is consistent with Greene's earlier works (as discussed in chapter 2) and its dedication again links it to the past as "the last I meane euer to publish of such superficiall labours" (9:229). Greene adds a new note, however, to previous dedications by going much farther in describing his state of mind. For the first time, explicitly at least, he claims to repent not simply his earlier literary efforts but also his earlier life, urging readers to "lay open my life in your thought and beware by my losse" (9:231). In this "vltimum vale to al youthful vanities" he looks toward his fellow prodigals: "Such wags as haue been wantons with me, and haue marched in the Mercers booke to please their Mistris eye with their brauerie, that as the frolike phrase is haue made the tauern to sweat with riotous expences, that haue spent their wits in courting of their sweete-hearts, and emptied their purses by being too prodigall, let them at last looke back to the follies of their youth, and with me say farewell vnto all such vanities" (9:231–32). While this passage at last seems to describe general moral transformation, it hardly answers all questions, and the evidence for a significant change in Greene's outlook around 1590 remains ambiguous. The prefaces cannot be used to interpret the works of the period in terms of a fundamentally altered purpose which makes them more clearly or consistently didactic than earlier works.

Whatever its real nature, the proclamation of new purpose continues into the next phase of Greene's prose: his exposure of the London underworld in the coney-catching pamphlets that occupied the last year of his life. In the first of them, Greene declares that *"my younger yeeres had vncertaine thoughtes, but now my ripe daies cals on to repentant deedes, and I sorrow as much to see others wilful, as I delighted once to be wanton"* (10:5). An assertion of moral and social purpose runs throughout the sequence (their title-page motto is *nascimur pro patria*—"we are born for our country") and Greene claims it his duty to report his observation of crime in London. Whether he actually had firsthand experience has been debated. Gabriel Harvey, as noted earlier, makes Greene the comrade of Cutting Ball and other criminals, and Greene admits as much, though denying a part in crimes, when he describes *"the odde mad-caps I haue been mate too, not as a companion, but as a spie to haue an insight into their knaueries, that seeing their traines I might eschew their*

snares" (10:5—6). In the first of the pamphlets he claims to be able
to name names, and in one of the sequels he promises that his next
work will contain a list of receivers of stolen goods and a "Bed-roll
or Catalogue" of London's criminals (10:236—37). He uses names
or initials and he fills the works with references to London streets.
Once he claims to have portrayed a London prostitute who "hath
sworne to weare a long Hamborough knife to stabbe mee" (10:236).
Such threats of reprisal run throughout the pamphlets, beginning
with the preface to the first. At one point Greene describes how,
at supper in "the Saint Iohns head within Ludgate," he was set upon
by "some fourteene or fifteene" and rescued when "the curteous
Cittizens and Apprentices" took his part (10:236). Such details may,
of course, be intended simply to lend authenticity, and there is no
independent evidence for evaluating the pamphlets. A point against
Greene's assertions is the fact that some of the material in the
pamphlets results not from personal observation at all, but from the
reading of earlier exposés. At the same time, much of the material
exists nowhere else, and many critics have taken it at face value.
Opinions run a gamut from J. Churton Collins ("Greene certainly
went in danger of his life") to John Clark Jordan (instead of "comrade
of the disreputable," Greene should be called "literary liar").[46]

Whatever his sources, Greene worked on the coney-catching pamphlets and related works until the illness that led to his death
interfered. They represent the last clear phase of his career, and they
show him a member of a newly developing class in England: authors
dependent on the public at large, not on patronage or court ap-
pointment. As Cibber said, he was "amongst the first of our poets
who writ for bread."[47] Cambridge had taken Greene beyond his
provincial origins, but not into one of the traditional learned professions. He became what Nashe, speaking in *Strange Newes* of Greene's
role among London writers, called "chiefe agent for the companie
(for hee writ more than foure other)."[48]

Dramatist. While writing the prose works Greene also wrote
plays; as Burby said, his "pen in his lifetime pleased you as well
on the Stage, as in the Stationers Shops" (12:155). We do not know,
however, when his involvement with the theater began, how long
it lasted, how many plays he wrote, or in what order he wrote the
plays now assigned to him. Collins may overstate the claim that
"we have no certain evidence that he was engaged in dramatic
composition before 1592" (*PP,* 1:38),[49] but it is true that Greene

himself makes no unambiguous reference to writing plays before
the repentance pamphlets. Problems begin with Greene's comments
on drama in *Perimedes the Blacke-Smith,* published in 1588:

I keepe my old course, to palter vp some thing in Prose, . . . although
latelye two Gentlemen Poets, made two mad men of Rome beate it out
of their paper bucklers: & had it in derision, for that I could not make
my verses iet vpon the stage in tragicall buskins, euerie worde filling the
mouth like the faburden of Bo-Bell, daring God out of heauen with that
Atheist *Tamburlan,* or blaspheming with the mad preest of the sonne: but
let me rather openly pocket vp the Asse at *Diogenes* hand: then wantonlye
set out such impious instances of intolerable poetry. . . . If I speake
darkely Gentlemen, and offend with this digression, I craue pardon, in
that I but answere in print, what they haue offered on the Stage.
(7:7–8)

This obscure passage may mean that Greene had been satirized on
the stage either for not writing plays or for writing a bad one. Most
scholars have thought the latter, finding the most likely candidate
for a failed play to be *Alphonsus, King of Aragon,* printed a decade
later (1599) with "Made by R. G." on its title page.[50] Certainly
this play invites satire, and its obvious imitation of *Tamburlaine* can
be reconciled with Greene's scorn for Marlowe's style in the *Perimedes*
passage. That is, the argument runs, Greene's attempt to follow in
Marlowe's wake led only to failure and ridicule, and he responded
by attacking what he himself could not achieve. Such a sequence
has struck many commentators as plausible and in keeping with
Greene's temperament. Moreover, the poor reception of *Alphonsus*
might explain the lack of a record of Greene's ever having written
the sequel promised at the end of the play.

    Greene did write other plays, however, although none follows
Alphonsus in imitating Marlowe's rhetoric so extensively. In addition
to the several generally attributed to him today, many more have
been proposed through the years, for Greene has been a favorite
subject for conjectural authorship (with well over forty plays assigned
to him at one time or another). One play has special relevance to
the study of Greene's life: *Orlando Furioso,* referred to in a curious
passage in *The Defence of Conny Catching.* This work appeared as an
answer to Greene's coney-catching pamphlets, its author calling
himself Cuthbert Cunny-Catcher and claiming to be one of the
criminals whose methods Greene had exposed. Some have believed,

however, that Greene himself wrote the *Defence,* their case resting
partly on the fact that it states little that genuinely damages Greene's
reputation.[51] The main point is simply that "we Conny-catchers are
like little flies in the grasse, which liue on little leaues and doe no
more harme: whereas there bee in *Englande* other professions that
bee great Conny-catchers and caterpillers, that make barraine the
field wherein they baite" (11:47). Demonstrating the roguery of
various trades and professions, the *Defence* attacks Greene himself
only twice, once for neglecting "the part of a Scholler" to write
"triuiall trinkets and threedbare trash" (11:49) and once for double-
dealing in the sale of *Orlando:* "Aske the Queens Players, if you sold
them not *Orlando Furioso* for twenty Nobles, and when they were
in the country, sold the same Play to the Lord Admirals men for
as much more. Was not this plaine *Conny-catching* Maister R. G.?"
(11:75–76). No basis exists for evaluating the accusation or for
determining whether Greene himself wrote it, although its details
are consistent with what is known of the dramatic companies named
and the textual history of the play.[52]

True or not, the story of the double-sale of *Orlando* nicely links
Greene to the commercial element in Elizabethan drama and indicates again the professionalism of his career. Greene himself describes a young man turning to the stage in desperation in *Never
Too Late,* the same work that portrays a marriage perhaps parallel
to his own. Cheated by a courtesan, ashamed to return to his wife,
threatened with prison for his debts, and stripped of articles to
pawn, Francesco meets a company of players who promise they will
"largelie reward him for his paines" if he can "performe anything
worth the stage." Trying his hand, Francesco "writ a Comedie,
which so generally pleased all the audience, that happie were those
Actors in short time that could get any of his workes, he grewe so
exquisite in that facultie. By this meanes his want was releeued,
his credit in his hosts house recouered, his apparell in greater brauerie
then it was, and his purse well lined with Crownes" (8:128–29).
Even if the story is autobiographical, Francesco's quick popularity
does not necessarily reflect Greene's own career, for he may well
have portrayed an alter ego more successful than himself. At the
same time, Francesco's story agrees in essential details with the story
of Roberto in the *Groats-worth.* Cheated by a courtesan, Roberto
asks a friendly stranger "how he might be imployed" (12:131). The
stranger turns out to be an actor, and he urges Roberto to try his

hand at writing plays. Again the motive is purely commercial. The actor's evident prosperity impresses Roberto: "A Player, quoth *Roberto*, I tooke you rather for a gentleman of great liuing, for if by outward habit men should be censured, I tell you, you would be taken for a substantiall man. So am I where I dwell (quoth the player) reputed able at my proper cost, to build a Windmill. . . . my very share in playing apparell will not be solde for two hundred pounds" (12:131). The actor promises that Roberto "shall be well paied" (12:132) and, indeed, he proves successful in his new career: "*Roberto* now famozed for an Arch-plaimaking-poet, his purse like the sea somtime sweld, anon like the same sea fell to a low ebbe; yet seldom he wanted, his labors were so well esteemed" (12:134). The "Life and Death of Robert Greene" includes a similar tale of turning to literature in time of need, told more briefly and in the first person: "I left the Vniuersitie and away to London, where (after I had continued some short time, & driuen my self out of credit with sundry of my frends) I became an Author of Playes, and a penner of Loue Pamphlets, so that I soone grew famous in that qualitie, that who for that trade growne so ordinary about London as *Robin Greene*" (12:172–73).

None of these accounts of writing plays for profit suggests that Greene took drama seriously. He makes no reference to the content of his plays, although he several times comments on the content of his prose, and no play published before his death with his name on it survives. Every indication is that Greene, like most other writers of his day, saw play scripts as paid labor, not literature; it is perhaps significant that in *Never Too Late* and the *Groats-worth* the writing of plays parallels the feeding of swine in the story of the prodigal son. Greene's references to drama take for granted its low social status and sometimes show particular scorn for playwrights' lack of his own university education. As he writes in the *Farewell*, "he that can not write true Englishe without the helpe of Clearkes of parish Churches, will needes make him selfe the father of interludes" (9:233). In the same spirit, Thomas Nashe in his preface to *Menaphon* mocks those who "busie themselues with the indeuors of Art, that could scarcelie latinize their necke-verse if they should haue neede," contrasting them to Greene, a "scholler-like Shepheard" worthy the attention of "Gentlemen Students *of both Vniuersities*" (6:15, 9). Like Greene's scornful reference to *Tamburlaine*, Nashe's preface attacks the language that ignorance speaks in playwrights that "bodge vp a blanke verse with ifs and ands" (6:16) and rely on "swelling bumbast" to "outbraue better pens" (6:10). If Greene indeed saw the theater as beneath his intellectual and social aspirations, it is not surprising that he said so little about his plays or that attempts to establish a canon and a chronology have achieved no consensus. All that can reasonably be said is that Greene became at some point one of the many London writers who supplied the stage with its daily fare. Any literary pretensions of a more modern sort were reserved, like his explicit claims of moral purpose, for his prose works.

Friend and enemy. As a writer for both press and stage, then, Greene spent the end of his life in a world of literary professionals, among whom he made both friends and enemies. We have already seen Henry Chettle and Thomas Nashe. Some ten years younger than Greene, Nashe knew him by 1589, when his preface to *Menaphon* appeared as his own first published work. Indeed, Harvey called Nashe Greene's "sworne brother" and "inwardest companion"[53] and accused him of imitating Greene's style. Nashe denied both assertions after Greene's death, with special anger, in *Have with You to Saffron-Walden,* about the latter: "and where, like a iakes barreller and a *Gorbolone,* [Harvey] girds me *with imitating* of Greene, let him vnderstand, I more scorne it than to haue so foule a iakes for my groaning stoole as hys mouth; & none that euer had but one eye, with a pearle in it, but could discern the difference twixt him & me."[54] As for being Greene's friend, Nashe answers in *Strange Newes,* "neither was I *Greenes* companion any more than for a carowse or two."[55] Although he attacks Harvey for attacking Greene, he does not do so on the grounds of friendship: he would "do as much for any man, especially for a deade man, that cannot speake for him-selfe," and, he says, "a thousand there bee that haue more reason to speak in his behalf than I, who, since I first knew him about town, haue beene two yeares together and not seene him."[56] Nashe may accurately report the nature of the relationship or he may exaggerate in order to separate himself from Greene's reputation—a likely possibility if association with Archbishop Whitgift had led Nashe into new circles.[57] Friendship with Greene for at least some period, however, is suggested not only by the *Menaphon* preface but also by his admission in *Strange Newes* that he had discussed writing with Greene: "Not *Tarlton* nor *Greene* but haue been contented to let my simple iudgement ouerrule them in some matters of wit."[58]

Harvey's linking of Nashe and Greene, moreover, cannot have been entirely gratuitous and, indeed, it may have been the friendship that led to Harvey's hatred of Greene.

The complicated story of Harvey's hatred can be only briefly summarized. In 1590 Harvey's brother Richard, in the epistle to his work *The Lamb of God,* chided Nashe for "peremptorily censuring his betters at pleasure" in the *Menaphon* preface.[59] Nashe's preface was indeed a bold attack for a young man, and the Harveys might have objected as well to Nashe's description of the decline of Cambridge (6:17–20), where Gabriel Harvey had become a leading scholar. Richard Harvey named both Nashe and John Lyly, presumed author of *Pappe with an Hatchet,* one of the answers to Martin Marprelate, the anonymous Puritan writer of 1588–89. As Nashe describes it in *Have with You to Saffron-Walden,* "he and his Brother . . . scummerd out betwixt thē an *Epistle to the Reader* against all Poets and Writers; & M. *Lilly* & me by name he beruffianized and berascald, cōpar'd to *Martin,* & termd vs *piperly make-plaies and make-bates.*"[60] He tells the same story in *Strange Newes,* and then goes on to describe Greene's entering the quarrel: "Hence *Greene,* being chiefe agent for the companie (for hee writ more than foure other, how well I will not say: but *sat citò, si sat benè*) took occasion to canvaze him a little."[61] The reply Nashe describes is a brief but highly inflammatory passage in Greene's *Quip* mocking not only Richard and Gabriel Harvey but also their father and brother. The passage was excised after the first printing, but Gabriel Harvey was nonetheless furious, particularly since one of his brothers had died just before the publication of the *Quip.* Greene's death prevented legal redress, and instead Harvey fell on the dead Greene with savage scorn, within days of Greene's burial vilifying him in what Pruvost calls an "espèce de danse du scalp."[62] Nashe's answer began an exchange of pamphlets with Harvey which stopped only when the authorities forbade the printing of further works by either writer. Harvey's description of Nashe's attacks as "pestilent & Virulent sheetes of wast-paper" might well be applied to both sides of the quarrel which thus came to an end.[63]

Various elements in this affair remain obscure. Why did two years pass, for example, between Richard Harvey's provocation and the retaliation in the *Quip?* On what grounds did Gabriel Harvey link Greene to Nashe?[64] Did Nashe and Greene share Lyly's anti-Martinism?[65] Does the *Quip* passage sufficiently explain Harvey's wrath or do other references to the Harveys, now unrecognized, lie buried in Greene's works? Why was the attack on the Harveys removed from the *Quip*?[66] Such questions may not be answerable, but two points can perhaps be made about Greene himself. First, in attacking the eminently respectable Harveys, Greene expressed the same revolt against convention visible in other aspects of his life. Harvey's condemnation of Greene records shock and outrage in addition to personal resentment of insult. He reacts with moral zeal against the "straunge, & almost incredible Comedies of [Greene's] monstrous disposition: wherewith I am not to infect the Aire, or defile this paper."[67] A clergyman, a physician, and a scholar—the Harvey brothers gave Greene a paradigm of conventional respectability in the offending passage in the *Quip;* in it, a ropemaker (such was the elder Harvey) describes his three sons. The clergyman, a "vaine glorious asse," kisses his parishioners' "wiues with holy kisses, but they had rather he should keep his lips for madge his mare." The second son is a "Physitian or a foole" who "had proued a proper man if he had not spoiled himselfe" with astrological predictions. The third is "a Ciuilian, a wondrous witted fellow" but once "orderly clapt in the Fleet."[68] The passage attacks the Harveys where most vulnerable, undercutting their dignity and suggesting that their respectability was hollow. Its effect resembles the affront Nashe offers to sobriety in the train of scatological imagery running throughout his contributions to the quarrel.

While the Harveys represented comfortable adherence to convention, they were also social upstarts. Greene may well have seen these ropemaker's sons as pretentious social climbers of the sort described elsewhere in the *Quip:* "Yet as the peacocke wrapte in the pride of his beautious feathers is knowne to be but a dunghill birde by his foule feete: so though the high lookes and costly suts argue to the eies of the world they were Caualiers of great worship, yet the churlish illiberality of their mindes, bewraide their fathers were not aboue three poundes in the kinges bookes at a subsidie" (11:215). So R. B. McKerrow analyzes the dispute. The "very head and front of [the Harveys'] offending," he writes, was "that they did not recognize their proper station," and, indeed, Nashe calls Harvey "this mud-borne bubble, this bile on the brow of the Vniuersitie, this bladder of pride newe blowne."[69] Greene and Nashe could thus have it two ways, attacking from both bohemian and aristocratic perspectives. As at other points, Greene seems to escape his Norwich

origins both by defying bourgeois attitudes in his personal life and
by identifying with the older attitudes of nobility and gentry in his
writing.

On both scores, Greene wrote on behalf of himself and also the
professional writers whom Richard Harvey had called *"piperly make-
plaies and make-bates,"* and he had ties to various of those writers in
addition to Nashe. Greene saw to the publication of Thomas Lodge's
Euphues Shadowe in 1592, when Lodge was away on a voyage, calling
him "my absent friend" in introducing the work (1:258). Three
years before, Lodge had called Greene *"mon doux ami"* in a French
sonnet prefixed to Greene's *The Spanish Masquerado* (5:240), and the
two collaborated in writing *A Looking Glasse for London and England.*
Either Nashe or Lodge (the point remains unsettled despite a great
deal of conjecture)[70] is probably "young *Iuuenall,*" one of three
*"Gentlemen his Quondam acquaintance, that spend their wits in making
Plaies,"* who are addressed in the posthumous *Groats-worth* (12:141–
46). One of the other two may be George Peele, whose place in
Greene's circle is also suggested by Nashe's extravagant praise of
him in the *Menaphon* preface (6:26).[71] The third is universally taken
to be Christopher Marlowe, called "thou famous gracer of Trage-
dians" in the passage and urged to recant atheism. Greene's relations
with Marlowe are obscure, however. Here he refers, if the *Groats-
worth* is authentic, to Marlowe as "my friend," and he had received
a dedicatory poem from Marlowe's close associate Thomas Watson
(8:103). On the other hand, Greene mocks *Tamburlaine* in the passage in *Perimedes* quoted above, and an uncomplimentary allusion
to Marlowe may be intended in *Menaphon* (6:86). The contradiction
cannot be accounted for on the basis of facts now known, and no
more can safely be said than that Marlowe and Greene were alike
members of a circle of London writers small enough to breed both
loyalties and antagonisms. There were writers to supply the laudatory poems prefacing works of the period, but there were also
writers whom Greene described in the Epistle to *Pandosto* as "currish
backbiters [breathing] out slaunderous speeches" (4:229).

The bohemian flavor of the life of Greene and his fellow writers
is a familiar chapter in literary history. Greene's life in London we
have seen, and Marlowe's reputation for atheism and violence of
temper was as widespread in his own day as in ours. Thomas Watson
killed a man in a street skirmish,[72] and Peele's life is a record of
debts, lawsuits, and illnesses before he died, if Francis Meres is

accurate, of syphilis.[73] Nashe, who admitted to having been imprisoned for debt, was accused by Harvey of haunting "infamous, or suspected houses, tauernes, lewd company, and riotous fashions"; he also tried his hand at erotic verse.[74] Lodge, according to Charles J. Sisson, "ran through approximately a thousand pounds . . . between the ages of twenty-one and twenty-five"—a "magnificence of waste" appropriate to a man described by Stephen Gosson in these terms: "the person whom I touch is (as I heare by hys owne frendes, to hys repentance if he can perceiue it) hunted by the heauy hand of God, and become little better than a vagrant, looser than liberty, lighter than vanity it selfe."[75] Such behavior required a price. In 1590 these six writers ranged in age from twenty-five to thirty-three. By 1595, four were dead, and a fifth (Nashe) died sometime before 1601. Only Lodge survived, and he had abandoned literature and London to study medicine in 1597.

Lives so careless may help explain the intensity of Gabriel Harvey's anger; he must have felt contempt not only for Greene's attack in the *Quip* but also for the environment from which it had sprung. Greene himself perhaps captures Harvey's attitude in the comments on a poet that he gives Cloth Breeches in the *Quip:* "a waste good and an vnthrift, . . . born to make the Tauerns rich and himselfe a begger: if he haue forty pound in his purse together, he puts it not to vsury, neither buies land nor marchandise with it, but a moneths commodity of wenches and Capons" (11:291). And yet, as already noted, the claim of social superiority is as strong on one side as on the other. It is again apparent in Greene's address to the *"Gentlemen his Quondam acquaintance"* in the *Groats-worth,* all three of whom he urges to write no more for the actors, "those Puppits . . . that speake from our mouths, those Anticks garnisht in our colours" (12:144). One actor in particular excited anger, with the result of the most famous words in Greene's works: "Yes trust them not: for there is an vpstart Crow, beautified with our feathers, that with his *Tygers heart wrapt in a Players hide,* supposes he is as well able to bumbast out a blanke verse as the best of you: and being an absolute *Iohannes fac totum,* is in his owne conceit the onely Shakescene in a countrie" (12:144). Few scholars doubt that Shakespeare is intended, although they have warmly debated whether plagiarism is Greene's charge or, as most modern opinion holds, only the presumptuousness of writing plays.[76] Either way, the passage, if authentically Greene's, adds Shakespeare's name to the list of Greene's targets—one more indication of close involvement in the London literary world. Moreover, the snobbery of this plea to renounce "rude groomes" (12:144) further evidences Greene's attempt to present himself as a spokesman for the old social hierarchies.[77]

Whether the warning against Shakespeare had specific provocation is unknown. Passing remarks condemning actors, playwrights, or drama itself in Greene's earlier works have led to speculation that his resentments were not new. The Palmer in *Never Too Late* interrupts the tale of Francesco for a discourse on the decline of drama in Rome, ending with the judgment that players deserve "both prayse and profite, as long as they wax neither couetous nor insolent" (8:133), and the author of the *Defence,* perhaps Greene himself, says that Greene justified the sale of *Orlando* to two companies on the grounds that "there was no more faith to be held with Plaiers, then with them that valued faith at the price of a feather: . . . they were vncertaine, variable, time pleasers, men that measured honestie by profite, and that regarded their Authors not by desart, but by necessitie of time" (11:76). The attack on Shakespeare may, then, be a chapter in what C. Elliot Browne a century ago called a "lively feud of some years' standing between Greene and the players."[78] At the same time, such a feud does not clearly account for the singling out of Shakespeare in the *Groats-worth,* and the lines leading into the reference may allude to a particular act of betrayal: "Is it not strange," Greene tells the three writers, "that I, to whom they all haue beene beholding: is it not like that you, to whom they all haue been beholding, shall (were ye in that case that I am now) be both at once of them forsaken? Yes trust them not. . . ." Conjectures as to Shakespeare's possible role in Greene's being "forsaken" by the actors have been many, often involving attempts to show how the two writers' paths crossed in their work for one or another dramatic company.[79] The passage may, of course, have a much narrower meaning. If indeed written by Greene or if a forger's accurate rendition of his attitude in his last days, it may record the fact that old theatrical acquaintances, although as prosperous as the actor Roberto meets in the *Groats-worth* ("my very share in playing apparrell will not be solde for two hundred pounds"), had refused a dying man's call for help—a possibility made the more piquant by the suggestion, several times offered, that the smug and comfortable *Groats-worth* actor represents Shakespeare himself.[80] In any case, full knowledge of the cause of the attack might perhaps help lift from

Greene the burden of having dared assault from mere envy the "quiet unlettered smiler," in Anthony Burgess's phrase, who "had wished Robin Greene no harm" but nonetheless suffered being called "Shake-scene"—"one of those jealous deformations of the great name to which the great name seems to lend itself."[81] As it stands, however, there is no more justification for lifting that burden than there was for generations of bardolaters in assigning it.

"The Manner of the Death and Last End"

Final days. The Shake-scene attack, whatever the conjectures about it, belongs in the context of the last weeks of Greene's life. Two major accounts of his death have survived and, although written for very different purposes, they agree in presenting a picture of illness and poverty. First, for Gabriel Harvey Greene's sorry end fittingly concluded a misspent life. A poem which he gives his own dead brother Richard to speak in *Foure Letters* summarizes the spirit of Harvey's account:

> *COME, fellow* Greene, *come to thy gaping graue:*
> *Bidd Vanity, and Foolery farewell:*
> *Thou ouer-long has plaid the madbrain'd knaue:*
> *And ouer-loud hast rung the bawdy bell.*
> *Vermine to Vermine must repaire at last.*[82]

In the second letter, dated 5 September 1592, Harvey says that he asked about Greene after reading the *Quip* and learned that he lay "dangerously sicke in a shoemakers house near Dow-gate: not of the plague, or the pockes, as a Gentleman saide, but of a surfett of pickle herringe and rennish wine, or as some suppose, of an exceeding fcare."[83] The fear, says Harvey, stemmed from the attack in the *Quip,* to delete which Greene "offered ten, or rather then faile twenty shillinges to the printer"—a "huge som with him at that instant." Hearing soon after that Greene had died, Harvey (he does not say why) called on the shoemaker's wife, Mrs. Isam, and learned the sordid facts of Greene's last days, all of which he reports.[84] Abandoned by his friends, including a "fellow-writer," clearly Nashe, "that was a principall guest at that fatall banquet of picle herring," Greene was visited only by Cutting Ball's prostitute sister and one "Mistris Appleby," who came "as much to expostulate iniuries with her, as to visite him." His nurse was Mrs. Isam, who

"loued him derely." Harvey heard from her of Greene's "lamentable
begging of a penny-pott of Malmesy: and . . . how lowsy he, and
the mother of Infortunatus were." Harvey revels especially in Greene's
poverty: Mrs. Isam told him of Greene's borrowing her husband's
shirt "whiles his owne was a washing" and of his pawning his paltry
belongings. He died in debt to the shoemaker for "the charges of
his windinge sheete, which was foure shillings: and the charges of
hys buriall yesterday . . . which was six shillinges, and four pence";
indeed, says Harvey, "how deeply hee was indebted to her poore
husbande . . . appeered by his owne bonde of tenne poundes: which
the good woman kindly shewed me." Harvey's emphasis on Greene's
debts embodies exactly the bourgeois spirit that Greene had scorned.
It may also reflect Mrs. Isam's dwelling on her own situation in the
hope that this inquirer after the dead Greene might come to her
relief. Harvey gives no evidence of responding, however, but simply
describes her need while also stating that she showed him a last
letter to Greene's abandoned wife, written on the ten-pound bond:
*"Doll, I charge thee by the loue of our youth, & by my soules rest, that
thou wilte see this man paide: for if hee, and his wife had not succoured
me, I had died in the streetes."* Finally, Harvey reports that Greene's
"sweete hostisse, for a tender farewell, crowned him with a Garland
of Bayes: to shew, that a tenth Muse honoured him more being
deade; then all the nine honoured him aliue. . . . it was his owne
request, and his Nurses deuotion." A well-wisher, says Harvey,
wrote a couplet about the garland, but "an other" wrote a mocking
rejoinder: *"Heere Bedlam is: and heere a Poet garish, / Gaily bedeck'd,
like forehorse of the parish."* Near Bedlam, in "the New-churchyard,"
Greene was buried on 4 September 1592, according to Harvey. It
was later the site of a railway station (*PP,* 1:48).[85]

Harvey's account notably lacks any reference to repentance. He
does say that Greene's fear of publishing his attack on the Harveys
showed a revulsion from satire, Greene being "not the first, that
bewrayed, & punished his own guiltines, with blushing for shame,"
but he goes no further, despite pompous generalizations about con-
trition.[86] He refuses to present a Greene redeemed by a last-minute
spiritual awakening, defining him instead as an object-lesson in the
fruits of depravity: "Oh, what a liuelie picture of Vanity? but oh,
what a deadlie Image of miserie? and oh what a terrible Caueat for
such & such?"[87] This portrait of incorrigibility is contradicted by
Cuthbert Burby's epistle to the *Repentance:* "although his loose life

was odious to God and offensiue to men, yet forasmuch as at his last end he found it most grieuous to himselfe . . . I doubt not but he shall for the same deserue fauour both of God and men" (12:155). As printer of one of the works published after Greene's death, Burby of course invites suspicion. The claim of repentance does not end with the epistle, however, for the *Repentance* also includes a purported eyewitness description of "The manner of the death and last end of *Robert Greene* Master of Artes," our second major source.

The anonymous writer of this account (12:184–86) parallels Harvey in several details, including assigning the cause of Greene's illness to "a surfet which hee had taken with drinking." More medical particulars are given than in Harvey: "although continually scowred, yet still his belly sweld, and neuer left swelling vpward, vntill it sweld him at the hart and in his face." Though lying "sore sicke," he could walk "to his chaire & backe againe the night before he departed." At the center of the account lies the picture of Greene's repentance. "Patient and penitent," Greene "did with teares forsake the world, renounced swearing, and desired forgiuenes of God and the worlde for all his offences: so that during all the time of his sicknesse (which was about a moneths space) hee was neuer heard to sweare, raue, or blaspheme the name of God as he was accustomed to do before that time." The final touch was Greene's learning on the night before he died that "his Wife had sent him commendations," leading him to confess "that he had mightily wronged her" and to write her a contrite letter: *"Sweet Wife, as euer there was any good will or friendship betweene thee and mee, see this bearer (my Host) satisfied of his debt: I owe him tenne pound, and but for him I had perished in the streetes. Forget and forgiue my wronges done vnto thee, and Almighty God haue mercie on my soule. Farewell till we meet in heauen, for on earth thou shalt neuer see me more."*

The contrast between this letter and Harvey's version of it epitomizes the contrast between the two accounts. Either Harvey suppresses Greene's repentance in order to blacken his memory, or else the anonymous writer invents it in order to puff the *Repentance*, embellishing the letter itself perhaps as he found it not at Mrs. Isam's but in Harvey's text. We simply do not know. No clearer is the identity of the author of this second account of Greene's death. If not Burby, it may have been Henry Chettle, who, *"about three moneths"* after Greene's death, acknowledged that he had prepared

the *Groats-worth* for the press.[88] The admission brings Chettle into
the events surrounding Greene's death and links him to at least one
of the posthumous works. Moreover, in calling him up to appear
in *Kind-Hartes Dreame,* Chettle presents a repentant Greene, who
claims to have "with humble penitence besought pardon for [his]
infinite sinnes" before dying.[89] Chettle's Greene, however, makes
no direct answer to Harvey but instead demands that Nashe seek
his revenge by attacking Harvey in kind.

Nashe did so in *Strange Newes,* with the comments on Greene's
character noted above. Nashe also responded to Harvey's description
of Greene's dying days, calling him a teller of "palpable lies, damned
lies, lies as big as one of the Guardes chynes of beefe."[90] Certain
elements in Harvey's account he grants, such as the fatal banquet
and the existence of Mrs. Isam, whom he describes as "a bigge fat
lusty wench . . . that hath an arme like an Amazon."[91] He ridi-
cules, however, Harvey's description of Greene's poverty:

I and one of my fellowes, *Will. Monox* . . . were in company with him
a month before he died, at that fatall banquet of Rhenish wine and pickled
herring (if thou wilt needs haue it so), and then the inuentorie of his
apparrell came to more than three shillings (though thou saist the contrarie). I know a Broker . . . shall giue you thirty shillings for the doublet
alone, if you can help him to it. Harke in your eare, hee had a very faire
Cloake with sleeues, of a graue goose-turd greene; it would serue you as
fine as may bee: No more words, if you be wise, play the good husband
and listen after it, you may buy it ten shillings better cheap than it cost
him. . . . If you want a greasy paire of silk stockings also, to shew your
selfe in at the Court, they are there to be had too amongst his moueables.[92]

That Greene's wardrobe would do well for Harvey is perhaps an
amusing insult but hardly a telling defense of Greene or a revealing
comment on his situation. Indeed, Nashe throughout, as seen earlier, manages to attack Harvey more enthusiastically than he defends
Greene, and he makes no comment on Greene's repentance. The
omission may reflect only the fact that Nashe was not with Greene
when he died, however. So Harvey asserts, and Nashe confirms the
point in saying that "the feare of infection detained [him] . . . in
the Countrey" and prevented his restraining the printer of *Pierce
Penilesse,* to which he had intended to add an epistle to Greene,
"telling him, what a coyle there is with pamphleting on him after
his death."[93]

If Nashe's absence explains his lack of comment on Greene's supposed repentance, it also leaves disappointingly little with which to evaluate other accounts of his death. The claim that Greene repented at the end rests on statements by Chettle, Burby, and the author of the description of Greene's death in the *Repentance*,[94] all of whom had reason to assert the authenticity of the posthumous pamphlets by presenting a penitent Greene to the public. For these writers, moreover, Greene offered an object lesson as clearly as he did for Harvey, although on a different basis. No more in them than in Harvey can a line easily be drawn between reporting facts and writing exemplary fiction of the sort echoed in Burby's words: "by his repentance ["the wicked"] may as in a glasse see their owne follie, and thereby in time resolue, that it is better to die repentant, than to liue dishonest" (12:156).

The repentance pamphlets. Within three weeks of Greene's death a new work was entered in the Stationers' Register: *Greens Groats-worth of Wit*. By the end of 1592 this work and two others had appeared, all presented as written during Greene's final illness. The pamphlets are generally consistent with each other and with much that we know about Greene, but no external evidence exists for believing without reservation that all came from his hand. Many of the issues which they raise have been touched on above, but it may be useful to conclude this review of Greene's life with a brief survey of their contents.

The title page of the *Groats-worth* claims that it was *"Written before* [Greene's] *death, and published at his dying request"* (12:97), and a prefatory printer's note says, "this happened into my hands, which I haue published for your pleasures" (12:99). There follows a brief address by Greene himself to gentlemen readers (12:101–2) in which, "though able inough to write," he says that he is "deeplyer searched with sickenesse than euer heretofore." The effects of "sickenesse, riot, incontinence" are manifest, but Greene has repented: "if I recouer," he says, "you shall all see more fresh springs, then euer sprang from me, directing you how to liue, yet not diswading you from loue." Fearing that he may soon die, however, Greene writes this "Swanne-like song" so that "you may as wel be acquainted with my repentant death, as you haue lamented my carelesse course of life." Then begins the tale of Roberto, a prodigal son story suddenly broken off, as noted earlier, with the statement that Roberto parallels Greene. The work concludes with various fruits of repentance: a moralistic poem, ten precepts for virtue, the famous letter to fellow dramatists, a retelling of Aesop's fable of the ant and the grasshopper, and, finally, *"A letter to his wife, found with this booke after his death"* (12:149). This letter bears no resemblance to the letter supposedly given to Isam to carry to Greene's wife beyond its claim of repentance and its admission of suffering: "For my contempt of God, I am contemned of men: for my swearing and forswearing, no man will beleeue me: for my gluttony, I suffer hunger: for my drunkennesse, thirst: for my adulterie, vlcerous sores" (12:150). One puzzling detail in the letter is the statement that Greene has living with him in London the son of his marriage: "Reason would, that after so long waste, I should not send thee a childe to bring thee greater charge; but consider, he is the fruit of thy wombe, in whose face regard not the fathers faults so much, as thy owne perfections" (12:149). If the letter is authentic, Greene's wife did not, as stated in the *Repentance,* take their son away with her. This child, not Ball's sister's child, may be the Fortunatus Greene mentioned by Harvey and perhaps later buried in Shoreditch. We simply do not know, although the letter may gain credibility from the fact that a son seems a gratuitous and even risky invention on the part of a forger.

That rumors of a forger arose immediately after publication is known from the denials of both Chettle and Nashe to have had a hand in the writing. Chettle says that the *Groats-worth "was all* Greenes": it was among *"many papers"* left *"in sundry Booke sellers hands,"* and his own role was limited to making a fair copy, since *"sometimes* Greenes *hand was none of the best."*[95] The claim has been several times challenged, but never disproved. Some have argued that Chettle simply forged it, some that he doctored an unfinished work of Greene's to make it appear autobiographical, and some that he is telling the truth.[96] Even critics who doubt Chettle, however, have tended to consider Roberto's story as based at least loosely on Greene's own life. Moreover, if Chettle wrote the most famous part of the *Groats-worth,* the letter to Greene's fellow playwrights, it was his earliest literary effort and no convincing motive for his using the dead Greene to attack other writers has ever been offered.

The *Groats-worth* was followed by the second posthumous pamphlet, *The Repentance of Robert Greene,* again a work pieced together with various kinds of material. First comes Burby's preface, describing, as noted earlier, a penitent Greene but making no reference to how the manuscript ended up in his hands. Then comes a preface signed by Greene, addressed to "all the wanton youths of England" (12:157) and comprised of a rather impersonal discourse on the vices of youth; perhaps oddly, it makes no reference to Greene's illness. Two substantial sections follow. The first, "The Repentance of Robert Greene, Maister of Arts" (12:161), takes Greene through a traditional conversion: the fear of death in time of illness inspires the admission of sinfulness and leads to despair, but Greene comes to faith in the power of Christ to "purge and cleanse" and waxes "strong in spirite" (12:170). An important step is the reading of Robert Parsons's *A Booke of Christian Exercise, appertaining to Resolution,* a popular work of the time that includes terrifying images of damnation, and the "Repentance" follows Parsons in describing the progress of the soul.[97] The generalized and conventional story that results offers little of biographical interest beyond the conversion itself. Only one scene contains anything approaching vivid detail. "Comming one day into Aldersgate street to a welwillers house," Greene answers the efforts of friends to persuade him from his "bad course of life": "what better is he that dies in his bed than he that endes his life at Tyburne, all owe God a death: if I may haue my desire while I liue, I am satisfied, let me shift after death as I may." Warned of Hell, he answers, "I know if I once came there, I shal haue the company of better men than my selfe, I shal also meete with some madde knaues in that place, & so long as I shall not sit there alone, my care is the lesse" (12:163–64). Whether Greene or a forger wrote the passage, it suggests the public side of Greene's personality, the tendency toward display of self seen earlier. Here is the "vaineglorious and Thrasonicall brauinge" that Harvey describes. Fittingly, Thomas Bowes quotes the passage to epitomize atheism rampant in England.[98]

That Bowes, who may have known Greene at Cambridge, took the passage as Greene's has sometimes been accepted as evidence of authenticity. Many, however, have doubted. One recurrent theory holds that the "Repentance" is based on the "pithy discourse of the Repentance of a Conny-catcher" that Greene promised in the *Blacke Bookes Messenger* (11:5) but did not live to publish. One passage in particular supports this idea: "And though some in this company were Fryers of mine owne fraternitie to whome I spake the wordes: yet were they so amazed at my prophane speeches, that they wisht themselues foorth of my company" (12:164). This passage has to some readers seemed to present more plausibly the voice of a coney-catcher describing his fellow criminals as friars of his own fraternity than the voice of Greene describing his fellow writers or even his fellow blasphemers. Apart from this passage, however, the debate on authenticity has involved little that is concrete, largely because the "Repentance" itself presents generalized images of a sinful Greene, not specific biographical details.[99]

More circumstantial, though equally the subject of doubts, is the second major section of the *Repentance,* "The life and death of Robert Greene Maister of Artes," containing the various pieces of information or misinformation noted earlier, including comments on such matters as Greene's parents, education, and marriage. After the "Life and Death," the *Repentance* ends with three brief sections: a list of twelve precepts *"written with* [Greene's] *owne hand"* (12:182), the anonymous account of Greene's death examined earlier, and a prayer allegedly written *"in the time of his sicknesse"* (12:187). More fruits of repentance, neither the first nor the third of these concluding items contains specific biographical details.

The third of the posthumous pamphlets to be published was *Greenes Vision.* This work begins with two epistles, one signed by the publisher, Thomas Newman, and one signed by Greene himself, both of which support the title-page claim that the work was "Written at the instant of his *death."* Newman goes out of his way to raise the issue of authenticity: "Manie haue published repentaunces vnder his name, but none more vnfeigned than this, being euerie word of his owne: his own phrase, his own method" (12:193). Greene says, or is made to say, that now, in his sickness and sorrow, he regrets his "laciuious Pamphleting." Admitting that "many things I haue wrote to get money, which I could otherwise wish to be supprest," Greene sets his earlier works among the "misdemeanours" for which he now prays mercy (12:195–96). The body of the work that follows describes a dream in which Chaucer and Gower debate the moral function of portrayals of love. All seems plausible enough, and yet an obstacle to accepting the *Vision* as still another deathbed effort arises when Greene promises that a forthcoming work will manifest his reformation: "but for all these follies, that I may with the Niniuites, shew in sackcloth my harty repentaunce: looke as speedily as the presse wil serue for my mourning garment, a weede that I know is of so plaine a cut, that it will please the grauest eie, and the most precize eare" (12:274). Since the work here announced,

Greenes Mourning Garment, had appeared in 1590, the *Vision* could hardly have been "written at the instant of his *death*" in 1592. Yet the promise of the *Mourning Garment* seems an error too naive for a forger to make, and the *Vision* appears to be a work written around 1590 but for some reason never published. That it was among the *"many papers"* Greene left when he died is probable, but that the epistle is trustworthy is highly unlikely: "I write this last, let it be my last will and testament" (12:196).[100]

The authenticity of *Greenes Vision* is an important question, for its debate on portrayals of love bears on an approach to Greene's works. Biographically, moreover, the *Vision* reminds us that the repentance blazoned forth in the posthumous pamphlets had been anticipated two years before in works of undoubted authenticity. Thus, while the late pamphlets raise intriguing questions, they reveal little not otherwise known about the other works or the temperament that produced them. At most they provide further evidence of tendencies evident throughout Greene's career. The problem of repentance clearly absorbed him. Over and over again he presents characters torn by conflicting impulses, characters struggling to gain control of their emotions and overcome temptation. Literary precedents for the portrayal of spiritual struggle are readily found outside Greene, but even the most unsentimental reading can find one source in Greene's own personality. So his contemporaries discussed him—as a moral case in point, as a mixture of qualities to be debated, as a man dealing in full view with "the lust of his owne heart" (12:156). We need not follow them in attempting to decide whether Nashe was right in saying that Greene "inherited more vertues than vices."[101] Nor need we dwell unduly on the paradox voiced by William Winstanley in 1687 and echoed by critics ever since that Greene was, while "writing much against Vicious-ness, . . . too too vicious in his Life."[102] But we should probably recognize that Greene's stylized prose and conventional plots artic-ulate questions of personal importance. Whatever the details of his checkered existence, whatever the truth about his wife and Cutting Ball and Shake-scene, Greene's works must have had peculiar emo-tional resonance for him.

Chapter Two
Greene's Prose Works

To come to *Mamillia,* the first of Greene's works, after considering his life is to be struck first by an air of social pretension. Subtitled *"A Mirrour or looking*-glasse for the Ladies of Englande," *Mamillia* seems to claim a place in Elizabethan society for an author whose back is forever turned on Norwich. Two courtly epistles and a commendatory poem embellish it, and Greene portrays two court-ships carried out with stiff courtesy and accompanied by formal debating on the nature of love. Fittingly, *Mamillia* imitates and borrows from the work of that perpetual seeker after court prefer-ment, John Lyly. In joining the several writers who followed up the success of Lyly's *Euphues,* however, Greene went beyond simple imitation to set up as a kind of rival to Lyly. Lyly's hero realizes his follies by discovering the faithlessness of women; Greene's hero is himself faithless, and *Mamillia* describes his betrayal of two women of surpassing constancy.[1] Authorial digressions make the reversal explicit by attacking "the flitting of mens fancy" (2:103) and de-fending women from the "reproches" of "sundrye large lipt felowes" who "scarcly know what a woman is" (2:106). Whether motivated by true conviction, his own experience, or merely the desire to sound a new note, Greene's adoption of the role of women's cham-pion would continue into his next few works. Indeed, his portrayal of faithful women survived beyond the sense of debate with Lyly. Greene discovered in *Mamillia* a favorite motif, one that many later critics would celebrate as among the most appealing features of his work.

Greene found more in *Euphues* than the portrayal of women, for his rival work absorbs several of the elements on which Lyly's success had rested. Most obviously, Greene imitates Lyly's distinctively ornate style, with its parallel phrases, sound repetitions, long strings of analogies, aphorisms, classical allusions, and bits of quaint lore from natural history. The linguistic display that results from bring-ing together these various devices, none original with Lyly, reflects a larger concern for rhetoric and logic, and *Euphues* and its imitations, including *Mamillia,* contain speeches, debates, letters, and soliloquies based on various persuasive patterns. Both Lyly's mannered style and his interest in the functions of eloquence have inspired a good deal of modern analysis. Less attention has gone to his treatment of moral ideas, although it clearly offered another attraction for his first readers. *Euphues* portrays the growth of youth to wisdom. Euphues himself is a symbolic hero, and the rhetorical setpieces examine moral ideas or illustrate stages of moral awareness. That Lyly's readers reacted to linguistic virtuosity apart from content is thus no more likely than that they suffered through the speeches in order to enjoy the story. Of course the speeches mattered, however alien to the tastes of later audiences, and so did the issues that the speeches explore.

In Greene's reworking of Lyly at the beginning of his own career in prose, then, style is but one element in a larger unity. Greene does imitate Lyly's tricks of language, but he also imitates the exemplary dimension of Lyly's narrative. *Euphues* is an emblematic tale in which the specific stands for the general, and there Greene begins. Early in the twentieth century, when Greene received considerable attention, the exemplary element in his prose fell victim to changing tastes. Elevating pleasure above profit, to use that favorite sixteenth-century pairing, critics saw Greene struggling to free himself from the encumbrance of moral significance; as John Clark Jordan said in 1915, "although he never, even to the end of his career, ceased to shout morality from his title-pages, yet in practice he came to have an almost complete enfranchisement from the traditions of the earlier didactic writers."[2] Jordan's point of view has by no means disappeared, and critics have often echoed it in describing the phases of Greene's career: the euphuistic setpieces of the early works represent Greene's "surrender to the demons of rhetorical or of didactic writing" which "plays havoc with his undeniable gifts"; Greene's romantic tales "reveal the *littérateur* at last allowing his genius for romantic narrative complete freedom"; the coney-catching pamphlets move toward "a presentation of picaresque narrative for its own sake."[3] Several factors help explain such emphasis on the triumph of narrative. The direction of Greene's career, for example—euphuism to romance to coney-catching—encourages the use of him in schemes tracing the evolution of novelistic consciousness. As another factor, Greene's reputation as a popular writer leads easily to the assumption that he addressed his audience on only its lowest level: "Greene is the apostle of entertainment in literature," writes David Bevington, "for whom didacticism is a guise necessitated by the norms of his generation."[4] Works as imitative and repetitive as Greene's can be, moreover, have proved difficult for some critics to take seriously. Even doubts about Greene's character have affected interpretation; as Jordan bluntly says, Greene "lies continually. . . . we wish he were more trustworthy, for it would save us trouble in understanding him."[5]

Sincerity is not at issue, however. Considering the seriousness of Greene's claims of moral purpose is separable from considering the issues inherent in the emblematic situations which he portrays. The exemplary dimension permits critical analysis apart from any question of intention, and it furnishes a starting point for the discussion of Greene's prose in the following pages. The first of two sections will examine some of Greene's characteristic motifs in six works and consider as well the critical issues that arise in approaching him. The second section will review the other works more briefly. Emphasis throughout will fall on seeing Greene's tales as emblematic narratives designed to illustrate, examine, and even challenge attitudes toward life. That is not to say that Greene's statements of moral purpose or his lists of often trite ideas on title pages sufficiently explain his works and their effect. Nor is it to grant allegiance to the tattered concept of an "intended meaning" recoverable by interpretation. It is only to say that, however complex the interplay between Greene's readers and a given text, sympathetic analysis must begin with a sense of the representativeness of situations and characters. Rosemond Tuve has said of the theory of literature that lies behind the use of emblematic motifs, "As sixteenth- and seventeenth-century thinkers conceive of the didactic usefulness of poetry, that ultimate aim does not make of a poem a decorated sermon, or an informative exposition trimmed with metaphors, or a set of lecturer's precepts with examples to match. Least of all does such an aim ask poets to state, and make palatable, orthodox moral codes. . . . But it is basic to Renaissance understanding of the didactic theory that poetry is concerned with truth, as carefully and sensitively seen as may be, and not with the Favorite Truths of the age."[6] Although one would not wish to inflate Greene's merits on the basis of Tuve's eloquent words, his conception of literature is much closer to what she describes than it is to later ones. The exemplary basis of Greene's fiction does not in itself limit complexity; rather it provides the basis, in the tales at their best, for rich and ambiguous treatments of human experience.

Approaching the Prose:
Six Representative Works

Mamillia: Greene's first prose work.   Focused on one topic—love—of the many considered in *Euphues, Mamillia* offers a first example of one of Greene's most characteristic subjects. Indeed, *Mamillia* anatomizes love by embodying contrasting definitions in the title character and her suitor Pharicles. Patently type-figures, they are emblems within an intellectual scheme. Pharicles himself summarizes the scheme midway in the work when he is asked to tell "what thing it is the common people call loue" (2:76). He first describes "the true loue" as "no other thing, but a desire of that which is good; and this good is the influence of the celestiall bountie: so that by the definition it is to be placed in the intellectual part of the mynd, and not in the sensuall" (2:80–81). Pharicles offers this definition only to dismiss it as irrelevant to "common people," however, and proceeds to celebrate passionate love as an irresistible force in human life, concluding, "and therefore, Gentlemen, doe not, as *Hercules* did, who began to be an amorous knight in his age: but loue, when both your bewty is in the bud, and your witte in the flower" (2:84). Pharicles here urges the kind of love that he himself feels. Although he cites Ovid's warning against love as "the losse of a mans selfe" (2:81), passion enslaves him, and Greene's moralizing comments articulate the traditional Christian opposition between concupiscence and rational love. Loving through his senses, not his reason, Pharicles dwells on surfaces, not inner realities; tied to the mutable, any love he feels must be transitory: he "fryed at euery fire, and chaunged his looke at euery leeke, as one that builded vppon bewtie, and not bountie: that did lust, but not loue" (2:77). He thus resembles the "Gentlemen of our time" who "fancy, without affection, that their choyce must needes chaunge, because it is without reason" (2:77). Pharicles realizes this conventional moral framework, admitting to himself that Mamillia's "beautie is the goale . . .: her fayre face, her golden lockes, her coral cheekes: to conclude, her christall corps shadowed ouer with a heauenly glasse." Despite knowing that his love is "fixed vpon her feature," however, he labels the attempt to resist beauty "blasphemy" and vows to

"consent vnto Nature: . . . whatsoeuer the lawes of Philosophy
perswade me, I will at this time giue the raynes of libertie to my
amorous passions" (2:32–34).

Against "amorous passions" Greene poses in Mamillia what Pharicles calls the "desire of that which is good." She comments several
times on the need to penetrate surfaces and move beyond the mutable, knowing that the "fading apples of *Tantalus,* haue a gallant
shew, but if they be toucht, they turne to Ashes: so a faire face may
haue a foule minde" (2:26). Greene establishes Mamillia as a rep-
resentation of rational love even before Pharicles appears by describing her friendship with Florion. Both had served at the Venetian
court, where Florion's love for a woman who betrayed him taught
him the folly of trusting "too much the shape of the body" (2:17).
Now retired from court life, he urges Mamillia to do the same. He
can give such advice because the friendship is "firmely founded on
the rocke of vertue"; symbolic of proper human relationships, it is
"not fleshly fancy" and proves wrong the claim that "loue and lyking
cannot be without lust and lasciuiousnes" (2:15). In the beginning
of the work, then, Mamillia has emulated Florion in forsaking the
court and "the bayte wherein was hidde such a deadly hooke" (2:18).
She has returned to her father's house in Padua, where she becomes
the object of Pharicles's passion. She regards that passion cautiously,
accepting Pharicles's suit, as she eventually does, with a statement
of the kind of love which she represents: "it is not the shape of thy
bewtie, but the hope of thy loyaltie which enticeth me, not thy
fayre face, but thy faythful heart; not thy comely countenaunce, but
thy courteous manners; not thy wordes, but thy vertues; for she
that buyldes her loue vpon bewty meanes to fancy but for a while:
for where the subiect is fading, the cause cannot be lasting" (2:67).

These two type-characters illustrate their contrasting attitudes in
a very simple plot. Mamillia accepts Pharicles after two scenes in
which he vows his love. He falls in love with Publia, however, who,
unaware of his commitment to Mamillia, sends a letter rejecting
him but ending with a note of encouragement. Pharicles misreads
the letter, throws it down in anger, and goes to Mamillia to play
again the first of his "two fishes at the baight" (2:93). Her father
approves Pharicles and sets a marriage date, but Pharicles, returning
home, rereads Publia's letter and discovers that its end contradicts
its beginning; he sends her a passionate letter. When Publia responds
by declaring her love and ironically praising Pharicles's constancy,

the work abruptly ends: "after he knew *Mamillia* heard of his dissē-bling, he cōueid himself closely into *Sicillia,* traueling forth on his journey, pilgrim like: but where his intēt was to remain, no mā knewe. But as soone as I shal either hear, or learn of his aboad, looke for newes by a speedy Post" (2:135).

Whether or not the promise of continuation indicates a plan to complete the story with the reunion that takes place in the sequel Greene later published, *Mamillia* as it stands is self-sufficient: no narrative resolution is necessary to clarify the significance of the simple exemplary action of a work that is less the story of Mamillia and Pharicles than of what they represent. Contrasted emblems of carnal and rational love, hero and heroine are "illustrative characters" as defined by Robert Scholes and Robert Kellogg: "illustrative characters are concepts in anthropoid shape or fragments of the human psyche masquerading as whole human beings. Thus we are not called upon to understand their motivation as if they were whole human beings but to understand the principles they illustrate through their actions in a narrative framework."[7] Greene emphasizes the characters' illustrative quality in a series of generalizations: "by the way, Gentlemen, we see *Pharicles* a perfect patterne of Louers in these our days" (2:94). Indeed, Pharicles himself once seems almost to recognize his own emblematic nature: just after delivering his speech on the nature of love, he tells Publia that *"Ouid,* nor all the maisters of loue could neuer finde out a more perfect definition, then my fancie, fettered in the beames of your bewtie, hath imprinted into my mind" (2:85–86). Just as important as this conception of fiction as "perfect definition," moreover, is the particular content of the formulas of character in *Mamillia.* None of Greene's works about love can be read wholly without reference to the traditional abstractions implicit in the narrative and summarized by Pharicles: "he that loueth only for bewtie, wil eyther loath when age approcheth, or else soone be glutted with plentie: whereas fancy fired vpon vertue, encreaseth euer by continuance" (2:113).

Though *Mamillia* thus looks ahead to Greene's future works, few of them follow an intellectual scheme so rigidly, and even *Mamillia* is not quite so straightforward as its basic outlines suggest. It includes statements antithetical to its declared meaning and never directly controverted within the text, for at several points passionate love is defended on the basis of human nature. Most obviously, Pharicles's several changes reflect his vow to "let not the preceptes of Philosophy subuert the will of nature" since "youth must haue his course" (2:34). Similarly, Mamillia's nurse urges her to love Pharicles on the grounds that "God made not *Adam* and *Eua* single virgins, but ioyned couples: so yᵗ [that] virginitie is profitable to one, but marriage is profitable to many" (2:42–43). Such passages add complexity to *Mamillia* and give it a kind of dramatic life, even though they are themselves conventional statements. Measuring chastity against the claims of the flesh is a familiar argument in Renaissance literature from morality drama onward; Shakespeare's Parolles makes the case, and so does Milton's Comus. In other words, the celebration of natural appetites represents another set of generalizations within the debate at the center of *Mamillia,* producing the conflict of one idea with another. The nature of the generalities inherent in the concrete may thus be confusing and contradictory, but generalities remain in view as the assumed subject of narrative.

A second source of unresolved tension in *Mamillia* is provided by Greene's treatment of rhetoric. Though devoted to the glorification of eloquence, *Mamillia* portrays it as dangerous and misleading.[8] Rhetoric persuades, but does not communicate truth. The master of language is Pharicles, also a master of deceit to "whome both nature and experience had taught the olde prouerbe, as perfect as his *Pater noster,* he that cannot dissemble, cannot lyue" (2:19). Live he does, for "by his crafty cloaking [he] had wonne the hearts of al the Gentlemen of *Padua*" (2:36), and he puts his rhetorical powers to the service of passion as he prepares to approach Mamillia, "framing a sheepes skin for his wooues back, and putting on a smooth hide ouer his Panthers paunch, . . . hoping that . . . he would so reclaime her with his faigned eloquence, as she should sease vpō his lure, & so cunningly cloake her with his counterfeit cal, as she should come to his fist" (2:20–21). Mamillia, of course, is completely deceived. Pharicles's first approach leads her to meditate on the need to proceed slowly, but her love soon overcomes her doubts: "*Medea* knew the best," she says, "and did followe the worst in choosing *Iason:* but I hope not to finde thee so wauering" (2:67). Later, when Pharicles returns from neglecting her to pursue Publia, she at once accepts the lie that he tells to excuse his absence (2:105).

Mamillia's capacity for being deceived is surprising, since the virtuous love she exemplifies includes awareness of the need to see beyond appearance. Knowing that "the bell with the best sound, hath an yron clapper," she generalizes on experience in ways directly applicable to the evaluation of language: "No man knowes the nature of the hearbe by the outward shew, but by the inwarde Juyce, & the operation consistes in the matter, and not in the forme" (2:25–27). Possession of truths about matter and form does not suffice, however.[9] Mamillia ends up no wiser than her father, who suspects Pharicles of deception but believes that "what the heart did think, the tongue would clinck" (2:116). Nor is Mamillia wiser than Publia, who recalls the story of the gods' creating a man "exquisit in forme and feature" except for the lack of "a window in his brest, through which to perceiue his inward thoughtes"; thus, she says, "what a one *Pharicles* is, I may easily gesse, but I know not" (2:89).

Throughout *Mamillia,* then, to the confusion of even the paragon at the center, "in painted speech, deceit is most oftē couered" (2:58). Logic itself can mislead, and characters often comment on each other's use of it, as when Mamillia says to her nurse, "your argumentes haue a spice of the ["shaking palsey"]: for their foundation is but fickle" (2:48). Mamillia asks whether from the "generall" one may "inferre a particular" (2:51), a question at the heart of the analogizing so prominent in euphuistic style. Pharicles, master of the style, rejects analogies when he debates the desertion of Mamillia: "Tush hee that . . . hateth an egge, because *Appeius Sauleius* dyed in eating of one, would be noted for an Asse: so if I should stand to my pennyworth, hauing made my market like a foole, and may chaunge for the better, because other in the like case haue had euill happe, I may eyther be counted for a Cowarde, or a Calfe" (2:91–92). Mamillia finds as many analogies with which to defend virginity as her nurse finds in attacking it (2:40–51), and logic merely expresses attitudes already held. Publia reviews arguments for doubting Pharicles before doing what only emotion justifies, loving him (2:88–90), and the tangles of rhetoric match those of love. Indeed, the two themes are related, for both involve the appraisal of beautiful surfaces; as Mamillia says of Pharicles, "his beauty argues inconstancy; and his filed phrases, deceite" (2:25). Behind both themes lies a larger conflict between the strength of human passion and the awareness of the need for reason.

This conflict is characteristic of Greene. It exists in other works, including the climactic scene of perhaps his finest achievement, *Friar Bacon and Friar Bungay.* Greene's own personality may have led him to portrayals of the conflict; indeed, Pharicles's inner debates over loyalty to Mamillia sometimes resemble the agonies described

in the repentance pamphlets. At the same time, Greene expresses
contradictions of his age, exploring issues treated with ambivalence
in other writers as well. Thus, passages pointing in opposite directions in *Mamillia* have parallels in Shakespeare's plays. On one side
of the debate on human passion, Shakespeare's Theseus warns Her-
mia of the convent:

> Thrice blessed they that master so their blood
> To undergo such maiden pilgrimage;
> But earthlier happy is the rose distill'd,
> Than that which withering on the virgin thorn
> Grows, lives, and dies in single blessedness. [10]

Mamillia's nurse had used the same image: "Whether doest thou
think the ruddy Rose, which withereth in the hand of a man,
delighting both sight and smelling, more happie than that which
fadeth on the stalke without profit?" (2:43). On the other side of
the debate, Greene anticipates at least three times the condemnation
of the flesh symbolized in the caskets of *The Merchant of Venice:* "the
goodliest chest hath not ye most gorgious treasure" (2:25); "a faire
face may haue a foule minde: sweete words, a sower heart, yea rotten
bones out of a paynted Sepulchre: for al is not gold that glysters"
(2:26); "he which maketh choyce of bewty without vertue commits
as much folly as *Critius* did, in choosing a golden boxe filled with
rotten bones" (2:114). In addition to linking the complexities of
Mamillia to Elizabethan attitudes, these parallels suggest the connection to Shakespeare long recognized by critics of Greene. The
first of the works already makes apparent some of what John Churton
Collins had in mind in saying that "we open Greene's Comedies,
and we are in the world of Shakespeare." (*PP* 1:57). [11]

   **Two romantic frame tales: *Perimedes the Blacke-Smith* and
Alcida.** By the end of the 1580s Greene had largely abandoned
fiction modeled directly on Lyly. Although his language did not
change dramatically, his plots grew more complicated as he drew
on the great storehouse of the European romance tradition. Greene
found there, as did Sidney in the *Arcadia,* a source of characters,
situations, and whole stories, ranging as far as to the beginning of
the tradition in Heliodorus, Longus, and Achilles Tatius. [12] The
complex plots, improbable events, and exotic settings which thus
entered Greene's works raise difficult critical questions. If the static

quality of *Mamillia* emphasizes the emblematic basis of the narrative, the case is less clear in a tale of strange adventure, and Greene's romances have often been praised for portraying actions that are moving or exciting on their own terms and which therefore "foreshadow later fiction."[13] Yet the characters and situations of romance again embody generalized thematic archetypes, the pleasures of contemplating which are inseparable from the pleasures of vicarious experience that later generations associated with fiction. Emblematic content is especially clear in *Perimedes the Blacke-Smith,* not among Greene's most satisfying works but one of his most revealing uses of romance conventions. *Perimedes* also provides an interesting example of the many works in which Greene frames stories within a larger narrative: a blacksmith and his wife tell stories to pass their evenings. This favorite device of Greene's raises acutely the question of the independence of narrative from significance. As one critic writes, the frame-story structure attracted Greene "because it is such a very convenient method of offering edification and amusement together—not combined into a single homogeneous whole, but placed so that the canny reader may know where to look for what he wants—the moral in the framework, the fun in the included story."[14]

Any attempt to find links between frame and tales must begin with the idea of Fortune, established as the center of *Perimedes* in Greene's opening description of Perimedes as one whom "Fortune . . . had so thwarted with contrarie constellation, that although hee had but his wyfe and him selfe to releue by his manuell labours, yet want had so wrong him by the finger, that ofte the greatest cheere they had, was hungar, and their sweetest sauce content" (7:11). The last word of the sentence, "content," comes as something of a shock, especially in its euphuistic parallelism to "hungar." The near-oxymoron of Perimedes' "contented pouertie" (7:11) contains the same paradox. As for Shakespeare's exiled Duke in *As You Like It,* the uses of adversity are sweet, not escape from it, and Greene insists on the blacksmith's deprivations. Yet Perimedes feels no pride, envy, or covetousness, but rather "against all spight of Fortune opposed patience, and against necessitie content" (7:12). The language echoes a long tradition of moral thought. Terms like "spight of Fortune," "patience," and "content" reflect condemnations of dependence on Fortune as old as the Stoics' celebration of the mind devoted to virtue, the mind that escapes the power of

Fortune by scorning the transitory and inessential matters that Fortune affects. For Christian writers in the tradition of Boethius's *The
Consolation of Philosophy,* Fortune is merely a word with which to
speak of events that humans do not understand and, since the only
true cause is God's Providence, belief in Fortune's deity reveals lack
of faith in Providence and concupiscent devotion to the world. As
Jack Cade is made to say in *The Mirror for Magistrates,* "Fortune is
the folly and plage of those / Which to the worlde their wretched
willes dispose."[15] Greene calls up these familiar ideas in presenting
Perimedes and his wife Delia as an emblem of Delia's assertion that
"Vertue is not accidentall but sets out her Flag of defiance against
Fortune, opposing himselfe against all the conspyring chances of
this world" (7:61). This focus on states of mind leads directly to
the tales, all of which portray attitudes toward Fortune's gifts. The
tales show characters coming to terms with worldly loss and confirm
the couple in believing that "true richesse consisteth not in the
abondance of wealth, but in the perfect habit of Vertue" (7:61).

Conversation on a moral issue introduces each tale. On the first
night, the couple's simple meal leads to discussion of "the bottom-
lesse sea of gluttonie" (7:15). Physical and moral vocabularies merge
in the description of "diuerse and sondrie passions to torment the
stomack and all the body," and Delia brings out "receipts, com-
pounded of sundrie simples," which are mental, not physiological
prescriptions (such as "twentie ounces of merrie conceiptes, pounded
in the mortar of a quiet resolution") (7:18).[16] In this context, Perimedes tells the tale of Mariana, wife of a governor of Tyre who is
imprisoned with the overthrow of his king. Forced to flee, Mariana
is the victim of Fortune, "who ment to make her a mirrour of hir
inconstancie" (7:23), and she gives the name Infortunio to a son
born during her journey. Mariana's separation from this son and an
older son excites a long soliloquy—without parallel in Greene's
source in the *Decameron*—on "fortune or some contrarie fate aboue
fortune" (7:24–27). She laments the disasters that have befallen her
at the hands of "that fiend and gracelesse monster, the double faced
daughter of *Ianus,* whose pleasure is inconstancie, whose thoughts
are variable." Recognition of Fortune's instability leads to a desperate
welcoming of death: "let fortune see how thou scornest to be in-
fortunate: feare not death which is the ende of sorrowe, and beginning of blisse." Second thoughts prevail, however, and Mariana
overcomes despair in a spiritual process reminiscent of morality

plays: "grace not fortune so much in hir wilfulnesse, bee patient, and so spight hir with content, for hir greatest griefe is to see her crosses borne with an indifferent minde." Accepting adversity as beyond human power, Mariana will henceforth concentrate on the inner life that she can control: "chere vp thy selfe, and leade here a solitarie life in this desert, with such patience, as making a vertue of necessitie, then drowne all dispairing conceipts with content." As she takes up life in a cave, Mariana thus embraces philosophical contentment analogous to the attitude of Perimedes and Delia. For her too the best "sauce was hunger," and, when the local ruler discovers her, she claims to "liue more happie, for that I haue opposed my minde against all mishaps, not caring for fortune, because too lowe for fortune" (7:30).

As the ruler persuades the reluctant Mariana to come to the palace, the narrative turns to a nearby court, where Mariana's elder son, Procidor, has grown up as a slave after being abducted during Mariana's flight from Tyre. The story then moves to its happy conclusion: Mariana and Procidor find each other, he marries a princess, Mariana recovers her younger son, the Tyrian usurper is overthrown, and Mariana's husband regains his position. These events reward Mariana's steadfast virtue. Indeed, they may symbolize, as many critics have said of the endings of Shakespeare's late romances, the operation of Providence, for happy outcome in no way mitigates the commentary on Fortune. When Delia moralizes after her husband concludes the story, she altogether ignores the final joy and comments only on Mariana's losses: "*Delia*, raging against fortune, that was most enuious to them that were most honorable, said that poore men were like little shrubs, that by their basenesse escaped many blastes, when high and tall Ceaders were shaken with euerie tempest, concluding therefore, that *Mediocria* were most *firma*" (7:42). Delia's reaction is consistent with the treatment of the story in the *Decameron*. Boccaccio's narrator also laments "the devious ways of fortune" and explicitly declares the ending irrelevant to the effect: "I warn you it's a sad one, so sad, that although it has a happy ending, the bitterness was so protracted I can hardly believe it could have been sweetened by any happiness that came thereafter."[17]

The next two stories follow the same pattern: moralizing conversation introduces an emblematic narrative focused on attitudes toward Fortune. Discussion of gaming precedes the second tale, narrated by Delia. Forbidden to marry Constance because of his

poverty, Alcimedes takes to sea. Whereas before he had "liued
poorely, and yet contentedly in meane estate," quick success inspires
him with "insatiate couetise" (7:47–48). He puts off his return and
is punished by ending up in prison. Constance hears that his ship
is lost and, falling into despair, resolves to await death in a boat
set adrift; the boat comes to shore, however, and Constance meets
"a poore woman, who made cleane the fishermens nets" (7:49).
Greene reports little conversation, but the example of contented
poverty in a "little cottage" (7:50) serves to educate Constance in
patience. She renounces suicide and becomes a seamstress. Like
Mariana, Constance thus embraces lowly life, and a similar reward
results: she finds Alcimedes, freed to help repel an attack on the
local throne. Imprisonment has apparently cured him of greed, and
both characters learn new attitudes through suffering. Perimedes'
comment on the tale again condemns "the inconstancie of Fortune"
and neglects the possibility that the happy ending might redeem
Fortune. He acknowledges that Fortune can work in two ways,
pointing both to "many rich men . . . driuen to extreame pouertie"
and to "many baze peasants . . . hoisted vp to the top of her
wauering wheele," but his final words take account only of hardship:
"her fauours are such as they include misfortune, and when she
presents the most comicall shewes, then she intends the most balefull
and dismall stratagemes" (7:55–56).

The third tale follows a discussion of wealth: "he onely is riche,
which abandoning all superfluities resteth contented with what Fortune hath fauoured him" (7:58). In the "pleasant Tale tending
somewhat to this effect" (7:62), Melissa loves Bradamant, but her
father, Gradasso, intends her for Rosilius, less worthy but of higher
station. Gradasso is suspicious, hypocritical, and entirely devoted
to the pursuit of Fortune's gifts: "he admitted none into familiaritie,
vnlesse he might sell his courtesie for profit, and they [sic] buie his
fauour with repentance" (7:62). The situation parallels several Elizabethan dramas in that Gradasso's "exacted extortion" so horrifies
the virtuous Melissa that she "sought not onely as farre as she durst,
to pull her Father from such inordinate gaines, but also secretly
made recompence to such as hir father uniustly had almost brought
to ruine" (7:63). In favoring Rosilius's suit Gradasso hopes "to buye
him a sonne in lawe answerable to his owne opinion" (7:64), and
he is unyielding; Melissa and Bradamant must strive to conquer
their love. The unexpected happens, however, when Gradasso is

banished, Rosilius and Melissa with him. Gradasso must face adversity by living "obscurely and in poore estate," Melissa enters service to a merchant, and Rosilius applies himself to "any seruile kind of drudgerie" (7:82). Bradamant, however, follows them into exile and wins favor at the court because of his "excellent wit and rare qualities" (7:83). The reversal of fortune teaches a lesson spelled out to Gradasso by Bradamant himself, who discourses on the "imperfections of *Rosilius,* how his wealth onely respected, whereof now he was depryued, he was a mere peasant and slaue of nature, not able, being exild though noble borne to shew any sparks of honor" (7:84). Consenting to Bradamant's suit, Gradasso must reflect on the independence of human nature from Fortune, and Perimedes summarizes the tale's significance: "Thou seest *Delia* how farre wit is preferred before welth, and in what estimation the qualities of mynde are in respect of worldly Possessions" (7:84–85).

All three stories thus have a clear relationship to the frame, a relationship based on emblematic content, not on style, plot, or character. The disparities between the blacksmith's house and the palaces of the tales do not prevent a basic analogy; indeed, the analogy beneath the disparities itself bears on the theme of Fortune. At the same time, the analogy is partly the result of conventional thematic connotations. Mariana, for example, deprived "of husband, children, coûtrie, friends, yea, and left al alone in a desert," is inevitably the "instance of . . . inconstancie" of Fortune which she calls herself (7:24–25). A recurrent motif in the romances from which Greene borrows, Fortune is both plot convention and thematic convention, for it arouses the moral attitudes that are the real subject of *Perimedes* and other works. Greene describes Fortune not entirely because, as Ernest A. Baker writes, he "fell back upon this easy way of contriving events to fall out . . . from sheer inability to work out the causal nexus in character and motive."[18] Greene's sense of "causal nexus" is a moral sense, and the emblematic narratives that articulate it served Elizabethan readers trained to appreciate symbolic narrative, not the modern novel, which arose, as Ian Watt says, in "a period whose general intellectual orientation was most decisively separated from its classical and mediaeval heritage by its rejection—or at least its attempted rejection—of universals."[19] The relation of particular to general was as much an issue for the bourgeois readers who bought Greene's works as for the nobles and gentry to whom he dedicated them. In fact, *Perimedes* itself provides a model

of the Elizabethan reading public almost too neat in portraying the
blacksmith and his wife responding to literature. As they moralize
on their tales they show an attitude toward romance very different
indeed from that of the father of Dickens's Sissy Jupe three centuries
later: "I used to read to him to cheer his courage, and he was very
fond of that. They were wrong books . . . but we didn't know
there was any harm in them. . . . And often and often of a night,
he used to forget all his troubles in wondering whether the Sultan
would let the lady go on with the story, or would have her head
cut off before it was finished."[20]

Useful as it is in approaching the frame stories, *Perimedes* by no
means indicates the complexity with which Greene sometimes han-
dles the genre. Moreover, a certain patness in the relatedness of
parts diminishes the work—an effect intensified by the happy endings of the tales and the smug contentment of Perimedes and Delia.
A work of greater tension is *Alcida: Greenes Metamorphosis,* published
later the same year, for it contains more serious challenges to assumptions about virtue. *Alcida* is also notable for its tragic perspective. Links to Shakespearean comedy have directed attention to
comic elements in Greene's prose works, but many have tragic
structures and present grim visions of human experience. *Alcida*
both typifies Greene's tragic side and represents one of its most
effective embodiments.

The frame in *Alcida* is a simplified version of those in *Perimedes*
and other works, containing only a shipwrecked traveler and Alcida,
the woman he finds living alone on *"Taprobane,* an Iland situated
far South, vnder the pole *Antarticke"* (9:16). She explains her solitude
by telling the stories of her three daughters, whom the gods changed
into nonhuman form. These metamorphoses show little of Ovid's
elegant playfulness, although something of his cynicism. A sad and
bitter woman, Alcida describes loss and error; her tales portray the
failure of virtue and seem at times like ironic inversions of Greene's
other works. Even the setting contributes to the undercutting of
ideals, for Alcida inhabits a deceptively conventional pastoral landscape. The island, with "wood-land full of thickets" and "meades
full of springs and delightfull fountaines," seems "a sacred Eden,
or Paradise" to the narrator (9:17), and Alcida greets him with
rustic hospitality. The grim stories in her past haunt the island,
however, and in the end her grief enters the landscape when she is

transformed into a fountain, "the gods taking pittie" on "her wonted teares" (9:113).

In the first of Alcida's tales, Nature "had so inricht" her eldest daughter, Fiordespine, "with supernaturall beauty, that shee seemed an immortall creature, shrowded in a mortall carcase" (9:26). She drives men "frantike in affection, fond with fancy, or pained with a thousand perplexed passions" (9:28). In particular, she is worshiped by Telegonus, and his worship is frankly a worship of beauty, the dangers of which he considers only to dismiss: "what of all this prate? thou dost loue: thou honorest beauty as supernatural: thou sayst, *Venus* amongst al the goddesses is most mighty" (9:32). Unfortunately for this adorer of the icon of human perfection, beauty carries with it a curse: Fiordespine is cold, self-involved, and contemptuous of all who surround her. As her mother laments, "liuing thus loued and admired of all: selfe-loue the moth that creepeth into young mindes . . . tickled her with the conceit of her own beauty" (9:26). The perfection of one human quality cuts Fiordespine off from others, as she herself implies in denying Telegonus: "if I knew no other cause to mislike, yet this might suffice, that I cannot loue" (9:39). A letter from Telegonus drives "her into such a furie, that shee in a rage rent it, and flung it into the fire," and she answers with arrogant cruelty: Vulcan and Ixion, she says, "are no conclusions that persons vnworthy should disgrace, by their impudent and worthlesse motions, the honour of excellent personages" (9:45). Her treatment of Telegonus lacks all courtly pretense, all gentility and politeness, as epitomized by the conclusion of her letter: "For thy loyalty, keep it for thy equals: for thy loue, lay it not on me, lest as I disdaine thy person, so I reuenge thy presumption. And so my hand was weary, my eyes sleepie, and my heart full of contempt, and with that I went to bed" (9:46). Beauty appreciated for its own sake breeds cruelty practiced for its own sake, and, as Telegonus languishes in despair, the gods punish Fiordespine by turning her into "a marble piller, fashioned and portraied like a woman" (9:23–24). Forever frozen in inhuman isolation from love, Fiordespine's beauty becomes "immortall" and "supernaturall" indeed. The tale thus offers more than a typical warning against being blinded by beauty, for Fiordespine's vices are the very products of her excellence. Her beauty maddens not only others but her, and it leaves her without function in the world.

Alcida had better hopes for her second daughter, Eriphila, whose peculiar perfections were mental: she "was as wittie, as her sister was beautifull" (9:57). Her courtship by the worthy Meribates follows the path of virtuous love described in several of Greene's works, particularly *Mamillia,* from which he lifts several passages for a second use.[21] Meribates proceeds only after telling himself that his love rests "not vpon . . . a fickle foundation . . . but vpon her wit, which only parteth with death" (9:62). Eriphila in turn proceeds only after weighing the "wise and witty arguments that he vttered" (9:73). When she declares her love, she does so in words identical to those of Mamillia: "it is not the shape of thy beautie, but the hope of thy loyalty which inticeth me . . . for she that builds her loue vpon beauty, meanes to fancie but for a while" (9:77; cf. 2:67). Although all thus seems likely to end well, wit turns out to be as accursed as beauty. Immediately after betrothal to Meribates, Eriphila falls in love with a second man, and soon she loves a third. Thus, while the borrowings from *Mamillia* perhaps show Greene writing *Alcida* in haste, they also show him returning for a darker treatment, giving more emphasis to the power of irrationality only touched on before. Eriphila means what she says in pledging faith to Meribates—she is no hypocritical Pharicles—but she cannot control the restlessness that accompanies her wit. Neither knowledge nor desire of virtue guarantees it. As a result, her quest for novelty forces her down to a level of cruelty as coarse as her sister's: "content you, sir, if you loue me you must haue riuals" (9:84). As Meribates, like Telegonus, pines away, the gods transform Eriphila into a visual image of the identity of wit and fickle fancy: a bird that changes "colours, from gray to white, and then to redde, so to greene: and as many sundry shapes, as euer *Iris* blazed in the Firmament" (9:56–57).

Twice, then, human perfection has destroyed itself in Alcida's daughters. The lesson is heeded by the third daughter, Marpesia, who has no unique excellence but rather vows a general devotion to virtue: she "kept . . . a strict method of her life, and manners, and so foreguarded all her actions with vertue" (9:89). When she falls in love, she picks a youth worthy of her, Eurimachus, and she loves "the qualities of his minde, co-vnited with many rare and precious vertues" (9:91). Her nature is evident, moreover, when she defends her love of the "meanly brought vp" Eurimachus as a choice of merit over wealth: "what hee wanteth in gifts of fortune, hee hath in the minde" (9:90, 93). Thus contrasted to Fiordespine, who could not overlook Telegonus's social inferiority, Marpesia also transcends Eriphila, for her devotion to Eurimachus never flags. Yet this most secure in virtue of the sisters goes on to the longest fall. She turns inexplicably into that familiar figure of vulgar comic tradition, the woman who cannot hold her tongue, becoming a "blabbing" female (9:105), "with childe of . . . newes, laboring with great paines till shee might vtter it to her Gossips" (9:107–8). Greene's colloquialism underlines Marpesia's fall. Twice, despite her love, she reveals secrets of Eurimachus; the first brings his banishment, the second his execution. No more than her sisters, then, can Marpesia adjudge consequences, and her behavior is equally destructive. That her errors plunge her into despair only emphasizes the futility of attempting to regulate human affairs. The gods pity her and turn her into a "Rose tree, which . . . flourished in this barren place so faire and beautifull" (9:88). The conjunction of the "barren" and the "faire" summarizes the treatment of all three daughters and the human ideals which they represent. As the poem on Eurimachus' tomb near the rose tree says,

> *The fairest Iem oft blemisht with a cracke,*
> *Loseth his beauty and his vertue too:*
> *The fairest flowre nipt with the winters frost,*
> *In shew seems worser then the basest weede.*
>
> (9:88)

All three sisters prove lilies that fester, and, in being transformed into allegorical objects explained by poems like the one on Eurimachus' tomb, they become myths of beauty, wit, and virtue. As myths, moreover, they counter the meaning of the emblematic characters in *Perimedes,* showing not only Greene's capacity for portraying tragic conflict but also the fact that the exemplary quality of his fiction does not limit it to the confident restatement of received ideas. Taken together, *Perimedes* and *Alcida* represent opposing poles, between which lie works of sometimes surprising variety and richness.

Menaphon and pastoral romance. Published in the year following *Perimedes* and *Alcida, Menaphon* again draws extensively on romance tradition, given currency by Angel Day's 1587 translation of Longus's *Daphnis and Chloe.*[22] With no interpolated tales, its single sustained narrative is among the longest and most intricate that Greene wrote, and it became one of his most widely read, often reprinted and still highly regarded by critics. In part, its reputation rests on the use of novelistic techniques. Greene portrays a large number of characters and clearly distinguishes them from each other. The plot takes several twists and involves mystification and suspense, with the identity of some of the characters revealed only gradually. Such elements make *Menaphon* more accessible to modern taste than many of Greene's works. Thematically, it has aroused such responses as Walter R. Davis's description of its "highly sophisticated rendering of a rather unsophisticated view of life much like the modern 'absurd.' "[23] Whether or not *Menaphon* thus anticipates later attitudes and techniques, Greene again begins with the identity of abstract and particular in emblematic characters who embody definitions of human experience. Whatever modernity the work has rests on its treatment of those definitions. They are unusually complex in *Menaphon*, for Greene explores, among other concerns, the dimensions of that favorite Elizabethan topic: Nature.

Menaphon combines Greene's treatments of love in *Mamillia* and Fortune in *Perimedes* within the traditional forum for discussing both provided by pastoralism. Love among shepherds is a familiar theme of romance, and fortune is equally conventional, for entrance into a pastoral setting is an emblem for the renunciation of worldliness. In the tales in *Perimedes,* characters enter quasi-pastoral situations in exile from wealth and position, there learning patience in adversity and detachment from fortune's gifts. In *Menaphon,* Sephestia undergoes this transformation. Banished by her father, king of Arcadia, because of her love for Maximus, Sephestia is washed ashore after shipwreck with her infant son and the aged Lamedon. While Menaphon, the king's chief shepherd, secretly watches, a dialogue between Sephestia and Lamedon defines the pastoral environment they have found. Pointing out that her "fal is high, and fortune low," Lamedon offers Sephestia a lesson in attitudes toward suffering and loss: "incurable sores are without *Auicens* Aphorismes, and therefore no salue for them but patience" (6:45). Sephestia at first resists Lamedon's lengthy argument for the attractions of philosophy; "Doues delight not in foule cottages," she says (6:47). At last, however, like Mariana in *Perimedes,* she gives in to her situation and adopts his truisms. Her resignation culminates in an unusually explicit statement of the symbolic element in the narrative: "then, *Lamedon,* will I disguise my self, with my cloathes I will change my thoughts;

for being poorelie attired I will be meanelie minded, and measure my actions by my present estate, not by former fortunes" (6:49). The equation of "cloathes" and "thoughts" defines pastoral dress as a metaphor and, as Sephestia accepts Menaphon's offer of shelter, she goes on to find "such content in the cotage" that she "began to despise the honors of the Court" (6:64). She takes her turn leading out the flocks, and, when asked what animal she would choose if subject to metamorphosis, she names a sheep: "my supposition should be simple, my life quiet, my food the pleasant Plaines of *Arcadie* and the wealthie riches of *Flora,* my drinke the coole streames that flowe from the concaue Promontorie of this Continent, my aire should be cleere, my walkes spacious, my thoughts at ease" (6:75). Idealized landscape and leisurely routine blend into an ordered perspective which counters misfortunes with philosophy. The syntactic parallelism of clean air, spacious walks, and thoughts at ease restates the earlier equation of clothes and thoughts, and Sephestia lives the rational life that is "natural" to humans and possible in the "natural" world of pastoralism. As Walter R. Davis says, "It is no exaggeration to say that in Elizabethan romances the pastoral land is first and foremost a symbol of an explicit ideal as a desirable state of mind, and that the purpose of pastoral is to dramatize a state of mind by showing the correspondence between man's life and his natural context."[24]

At the moral center of *Menaphon,* then, lies Sephestia's ability to find contentment as the shepherdess Samela. From her point of view are perceived the series of unnatural passions of which she is the object, notably on the part of her father and her son. Her father, Democles, sees her some fifteen years after banishing her, and her son, Pleusidippus, sees her some ten years after being kidnapped by pirates; neither realizes her identity and both are immediately infatuated. Their passions may indicate that "Greene was not averse to spicier, hotter fare,"[25] as one critic suggests, but Sephestia's spiritual survival in adversity determines the treatment of the titillating situation. In control of her grief and her ambition, she controls all her emotions. Moreover, her instinctive rejection of Pleusidippus and Democles represents a triumph of Nature. She loves only Melicertus, eventually revealed as Maximus, the husband she had thought lost in the shipwreck following their banishment. Maximus too has taken up pastoral life, in contrast to Pleusidippus, raised at the Thessalian court as heir to the throne, and to Democles, who rules Arcadia. The pastoral imagery thus links love to a larger commentary on Nature and Fortune. Their passions obvious violations of Nature, Democles and Pleusidippus reflect also devotion to Fortune in loving Sephestia as Samela, unable to perceive her true being. Indeed, Pleusidippus first falls in love with Samela's portrait (6:109), and Democles goes into the country to find the woman whose beauty has been rumored—another instance of his addiction to "varietie of vanitie" (6:113). Sephestia's disguise thus serves a doubly symbolic function: Democles and Pleusidippus love her altered form, but Maximus loves Samela for approximating Sephestia.

Links between love and Fortune emerge also from the story of Menaphon, the shepherd who falls in love. First appearing just before Sephestia's dialogue with Lamedon, he helps to define the importance of that dialogue by presenting an image of conventional contentment in a long soliloquy on the serenity of nature (6:36–42). Seeing the "shrubbes as in a dreame with delightfull harmonie, and the birdes that chaunted on their braunches not disturbed with the least breath of a fauourable *Zephirus*," Menaphon finds in nature a system of analogies to human moral concerns: "When thou seest the heauens frowne thou thinkest on thy faults, and a cleere skie putteth thee in mind of grace; the summers glorie tells thee of youths vanitie, the winters parched leaues of declining weaknes. Thus in a myrrour thou measurest thy deedes with equall and considerate motions." Life in a world of sermons in stones gives Menaphon "that which Kings wāt in their royalties." Proud that he does not "gaze so high as ambition," Menaphon also scorns love: "in naming of loue, the shepheard fell into a great laughter." Of "all follies that euer Poets fained, or men euer faulted with," he says, "this foolish imagination of loue is the greatest," for it "makes vertue yeeld as beauties slaue" and "forceth wisdome to be follies thrall."

Sephestia's debate immediately follows Menaphon's soliloquy, and the two set pieces introduce a reversal of the characters: Menaphon abandons the principles which he summarizes as quickly as Sephestia adopts them. Even as she philosophizes with Lamedon, the "glorious obiect of her face" inspires the conversion of this "Atheist to loue" (6:49). Menaphon's passion brings with it ambition, moreover, for the goal of "this follie of the Shephearde" (6:62) is, as he admits to himself, "too high for thy fortunes" (6:56). Sephestia later tells him that "where the parties haue no simpathie of Estates, there can no firme loue be fixed," and, when Menaphon asks whether love "hath . . . respect of circumstance," she answers, "else it is not loue, but lust." Her judgment of his suit echoes the pastoral image of natural order: "discord is reputed the mother of diuision, and in nature this is an vnrefuted principle, that it falteth which faileth in vniformitie" (6:61). The violation of the role of symbolic shepherd established in his soliloquy destroys Menaphon's rapport with the landscape, and he now complains in song, *"Faire fields, proud* Floras *vaunt, why is't you smile / when as I languish?"* (6:105). He joins Democles and Pleusidippus in abandoning a vision of "delightfull harmonie" for a love linked to Fortune, not to Nature. His lament summarizes his situation: *"Loue and Fortune proues my equall foes"* (6:103). Meanwhile, Sephestia's rejection of unnatural suitors reasserts the pastoral ideas ironically denied by Menaphon, the real shepherd, and prepares for the rewarding of herself and Maximus in the happy ending.

While the characters in *Menaphon* thus exist in symbolic relationship to each other within a basic thematic pattern, the symmetries of that pattern do not go unchallenged. Against the control of emotion as a central theme stands an image of human weakness in the face of passion. If we see Sephestia, we also see her suitors; and if they are "wrong," they are also victims of powerful forces. Nature has another sense—as a realm of appetites stronger than the will. Again Menaphon best expresses the issue. Reflecting on his fall from imperviousness to love, he says, "I had thought . . . that he which weareth the bay leafe had been free from lightening, and the Eagles penne a preseruatiue against thunder; that labour had been enemie to loue, and the eschewing of idlenesse an *Antidote* against fancie; but I see by proofe there is no adamant so harde, but the bloode of a Goate will make soft; no fort so wel defenced, but strong batterie will enter; nor anie hart so pliant to restlesse labours, but inchantments of loue will ouercome" (6:55). One set of examples from Nature here retreats before another set in a debate on the lessons that Nature offers. Menaphon had once found moral analogies in the landscape; now he finds altogether different analogies in comparing Samela's "eyes to the grey glister of *Titans* gorgeous mantle, her alabaster necke to the whitenesse of his flockes, her teates to pearle, her face to borders of Lillies interseamed with Roses" (6:49). Menaphon not only abandons old principles, but also adopts new ones, believing that "hee that liues without loue, liues without life" and asking himself, "why shouldest thou not then loue, and thinke there is no life to loue . . . ?" (6:55). The generality of his language moves his story beyond the merely comic reversal of "a contemner of *Venus* . . . nowe by the wylie shaft of *Cupid* . . . intangled" (6:49). He is *"Menaphon,* poore *Menaphon"* (6:53), a victim of love's all too "pliant perswasions" (6:49).

Menaphon's sudden conversion to love, a highly conventionalized and "unnovelistic" episode, allows the juxtaposition of opposing attitudes and dramatizes the difficulties of mediating between them. Greene achieves a similar effect late in *Menaphon* by twice interrupting the action to present contrasting poems on love. Democles, frustrated by rejection, persuades the equally frustrated Pleusidippus to abduct Sephestia to a nearby castle. Democles then (with motives not entirely clear) urges the shepherds to rescue her. Menaphon and Maximus both wish to lead the attempt, and Democles proposes that a singing contest decide the matter—the first interruption. When the attack on the castle begins, Democles ends it by calling out hidden troops to capture Maximus, Pleusidippus, and Sephestia. At this tense moment the story again halts, this time for a comic dialogue between the rustics Doron and Carmela. They sing an eclogue, followed by a poem in which Greene himself intrudes to offer an opinion of love. Only then does the story resume, with a sequence of complicated events, including the explication of an oracle, related so quickly that they take up only two-thirds of the length of the Carmela-Doron section. Both interruptions reveal Greene's essential technique of contrast. The eclogues of Menaphon and Maximus allow a comparison of descriptions of love and a restatement of the opposing attitudes represented by the two characters. The dialogue of Doron and Carmela sets them against all the other lovers in *Menaphon,* and their eclogue in turn is juxtaposed to Greene's own poem. Greene is clearly less interested in dramatic climax than in packing into a small space as many perspectives on love as possible.

The juxtapositions, moreover, again raise conflicts in the definition of Nature, particularly with the movement from Doron and Carmela to Greene's interpolated poem. Illiterate shepherds, Doron and Carmela are pale imitations, indeed parodies, of the other lovers in *Menaphon,* and yet Greene treats them with a certain warmth.

Their translation of love's high terms into their own naive vocabulary indicates kinship in passion with all levels of society: *"Thy lippes resemble two Cowcumbers faire, / Thy teeth like to the tuskes of fattest swine"* (6:138). This final pastoralizing of love asserts the essentialness of passion in Nature. The assertion is immediately matched by another, however, when Greene himself breaks in: "since we haue talkte of Loue so long, you shall giue me leaue to shewe my opinion of that foolish fancie thus" (6:140). He offers a poem that begins with an apparently open question—*"What thing is Loue?"*—but moves at once to describe the dangers of love as *"a discord, and a strange diuorce / Betwixt our sense and reason."* Love in Greene's poem leaves *"behinde nought but repentant thoughts / Of daies ill spent, for that which profits noughts."*[26]

Again, then, Greene moves between conflicting definitions of love, of passion, of Nature. In the process, a view of mankind emerges large enough to include both love and hate, both virtue and vice, both reason and passion. Indeed, beside the images of love in *Menaphon* stand some striking images of brutality. When Sephestia rejects Menaphon he thrusts her back into poverty: "deceitful woman . . . either return loue for loue, or I will turne thee forth of doores to scrape vp thy crummes where thou canst" (6:101). Sephestia's portrait so inflames Pleusidippus that he coarsely insults the princess to whom he is betrothed: "holde, take thy fauors, (and therewith he threw her her gloue) and immortalize whom thou wilt with thy toys." He coldly leaves her with "her eyes red, and her cheekes all to be blubbered with hir iealous teares" (6:110–11). When Democles calls out his troops to end the rescue of Samela, they "slaughtered manie of the shepheards" (6:135); later he sends Sephestia and Maximus to execution on an invented charge. In a work concerned overall with definitions of Nature, such passages raise important questions about human identity. Sephestia faces those questions in regarding her young son: she smiles to see royal blood show up in his instinctive leadership of playfellows, but she worries over "how imperiouslie he behaued himselfe in punishing misorders amongst his equals, in vsing more than iesting iustice" (6:90–91, 98).

Despite evidence of darker human impulses, *Menaphon* ends happily, with what A. C. Hamilton calls the "delighted amazement and wonder of the major characters which the reader fully shares."[27] Although as conventionally "romantic" as Hamilton's words sug-

gest, the ending gives the work the tragicomic structure of Shakespeare's comedies, a structure in which joy after sorrow reflects faith
in human capacity for redemption. Pleusidippus, like Bertram in
All's Well, is a victim of "Natural rebellion, done i' th' blade of
youth, / When oil and fire, too strong for reason's force / O'erbears
it, and burns on."[28] Democles precedes such Shakespearean characters as Angelo, Claudio in *Much Ado,* and Leontes in being over-
taken with guilt: "he leapt from his seate, and imbraced them all
with teares, crauing pardon of *Maximus* and *Sephestia*" (6:145). Such
transformations bring forgiveness and reconciliation, often with social consequences symbolized in multiple marriages; indeed, Greene
anticipates Shakespeare's parades of "couples . . . coming to the
ark"[29] by capping the reunion of Sephestia and Maximus with three
new marriages in the last paragraph of *Menaphon.* No more than
Shakespeare, then, does Greene resolve conflicting definitions of
Nature, but, like Shakespeare, he merges those definitions in a
general image of redemption. As Viola says in *Twelfth Night,* "our
frailty is the cause, not we, / For such as we are made of, such we
be," but Mariana's plea to Isabella in *Measure for Measure* remains:
"They say best men are moulded out of faults, / And for the most,
become much more the better / For being a little bad."[30] Greene's
portrayals of repentance and redemption have often been linked to
his life. That link may be real, but the issues involved are larger
than Greene's own situation. In drawing on the narrative traditions
of romance he worked into new combinations fundamental concerns
of his age.

The claim of new purpose in *Greenes Mourning Garment.*
Turning from "wanton workes to effectual labours" (9:120) in 1590,
Greene offers *Greenes Mourning Garment* as an exemplum in which
"the vanity of youth" is "so perfectly anatomised, that you may see
euery veine, muscle and arterie of her vnbridled follies" (9:123). As
discussed in chapter 1, the claim of reform involves difficulties, but
the *Mourning Garment* itself justifies Greene's description. So thoroughly devoted to the portrayal of youth's errors is it that it seems
rather thin and one-sided beside a work like *Menaphon,* containing
no debate over Nature, no unresolved tension regarding passion, no
tragic sense of human frailty, no troubling assertion of the demands
of the flesh. Greene himself seems aware of single-mindedness: "Thus
. . . haue I made my Mourning Garment of sundry pieces; but yet
of one colour, blacke, as bewraying the sorrow for my sinnes, and

haue ioyned them with such a simpathie of according seames, as they tend altogether to the regard of vnfained repentance" (9:120). Yet this very single-mindedness raises significant questions by giving the work a kind of mythic purity. This quality arises particularly in Greene's borrowing of the parable of the prodigal son, a motif used less systematically in a number of other works. The prodigal figure is Philador, son of Rabbi Bilessi, who rejects his father's advice and sets out to see the world. His travels take him to Saragunta, where he becomes infatuated with one of three predatory courtesans who keep an inn. Their wiles lead Philador to ruin, and, repenting his folly, he wanders in poverty before eventually returning to his forgiving father. Greene acknowledges the basis of the story in the parable—"I haue, onely with humanity, moralized a diuine Historie" (9:125)—and he preserves many details. He also adds new elements, the most interesting being a number of pastoral scenes that redefine the parable and give the *Mourning Garment* an imagistic unity unusual in Elizabethan fiction.

The first of the pastoral scenes comes when Philador meets a shepherd and his wife early in his travels. The encounter serves a narrative function in that the shepherd warns Philador of the three sisters while leading him to Saragunta. In refusing the advice, however, Philador rejects more than a specific warning, for he turns his back as well on values represented emblematically. The warning is a concrete version of the episode as a whole, defining Philador's immanent folly in terms of the traditional opposition between restless passion and pastoral contentment. Greene makes the lesson of the shepherds evident in several ways. First, the setting is an idealized "Champaine, yet full of faire and pleasant springs, and . . . groues" (9:141). As Philador watches the shepherds before addressing them, the narrative suddenly breaks into verse for a poem, *"The Description of the Shepheard and his Wife,"* in which a stylized pastoral vocabulary emphasizes Philador's entrance into a special, and symbolic, realm (9:141–44). The shepherd further underlines the implications of the pastoral image in telling three stories, each prompted by a local landmark and each having obvious relevance to Philador. The first monument commemorates a loyal son, recalling directly Philador's disdain for his father's advice, and the second marks the grave of "a Shepheard, who . . . forswearing his Loue, fell mad, and . . . slew himself" (9:146–47). Erected "as a terrour . . . to beware of the like trechery," the monument holds insufficient terror for Philador, whose own self-destructive course will lead him to comparable despair.

The third tale, related at greater length, is occasioned by the tomb of the shepherdess Rosamond, whose beauty inspired the king and all his courtiers to fall in love. Such disorder resulted that the king commanded Rosamond's admirers to assemble to learn her wishes. They heard her refuse king and nobles, and affirm instead her constant love for the shepherd Alexis. Her choice reflected her sense of social hierarchy and her detachment from the rewards of Fortune: "I am not Eagle-flighted, and therefore feare to flie too nigh the Sunne: such as will soare with *Icarus,* fall with *Phaeton,* and desires aboue Fortunes, are the forepointers of deep falls" (9:157). Rabbi Bilessi, stressing the need to control restless ambition, applies to Philador the same classical allusion that Rosamond uses: "when he saw his sonne beginning to soare too high with *Icarus,* hee cried to him, *Medium tutissimum* [the middle is safest], with a fatherly voice, so reclaiming him from prouing too rauening" (9:132). After repenting, Philador can describe his fall in similar language: "Ah *Philador,* thou wert warned not to be prodigall, and who more riotous? Not for to straine aboue thy reach, and yet thou wouldest needes beyond the Moone" (9:186). In another soliloquy a few pages later, Philador directly echoes Rosamond's statement that "ouer-high desires had often hard fortunes" (9:155): "Ah hunger, hunger, the extremest of all extremes, now doe I see that high desires haue lowe fortunes: that they whose thoughts reach at starres, stumble at stones" (9:188). Rosamond thus has both general relevance to Philador as an example of virtue and more specific relevance as a symbol of the rational control which he abandons. Moreover, Philador also parallels Alexis, who went on to spurn Rosamond. When Alexis, "ouerdoating in his fancies" (9:158), married his new love, Rosamond pined away and died of grief. Alexis repented his desertion and "in a fury hung himselfe vpon a willow tree" (9:162).

The definition of Philador's career supplied by the emblematic shepherd and his tales extends into several other pastoral and rural scenes. By "a brookes side," for example, Philador first laments his condition and reviews his follies (9:184), and when he follows his biblical prototype in swilling pigs he acts out acceptance of humble virtue by adopting a life analogous to that of the shepherds. Later, while lying "in a thicket to shrowde him from the heate of the Sunne" (9:193), Philador overhears a complaining lover; in this symbolic landscape he convinces the lover of the madness of his grief and presents him with a scroll summarizing the dangers of love and of women. The scroll concludes with a pastoral poem describing the growth of the shepherd Tityrus to knowledge of love's follies: "With that he hyed him to the flockes, / And counted loue but *Venus* mockes" (9:204). Pastoral motifs are capped at the end of the *Mourning Garment* when Philador's father proclaims a celebration. The "Shepheards they came in with their Timbrels and Cimballs," and redemption receives symbolic expression in "such melodie, as the Country then required" (9:213). Moreover, one of the shepherds sings of the repentant shepherd Menalcas (9:214–18), who first began to err in growing impatient under pastoral restraint: "I grudg'd and thought my fortune was too low; / A Shepheards life 'twas base and out of kinde." Menalcas' vocabulary echoes Rosamond's, and his journey recapitulates Philador's: "I left the fields, and tooke me to the Towne, / Fould sheepe who list, the hooke was cast away, / *Menalcas* would not be a Country Clowne." Like Philador, Menalcas came to grief and, having learned from "the follies of [his] youth," he returns to where he began: "Fond pride auant, giue me the Shepheards hooke, / A coate of gray, Ile be a country clowne."

The song summarizes the *Mourning Garment* by superimposing the archetypes at its center, the resigned shepherd and the prodigal son. The pastoral motifs thus help unify the tale of Philador and help define its significance by functioning as a kind of imagery of situation. At the same time, verbal echoes in the *Mourning Garment* give pastoralism something of the effect of an imagery of language, an effect quite untypical of Elizabethan fiction. Prose writers constantly use similes, of course, but the similes characteristically appear in lists as parallel definitions of a given situation.[31] They tend thus to arise from the situation itself, not from some larger authorial attitude, and they tend also to be commonplaces drawn from the euphuistic storehouse of striking comparisons. As a result, metaphorical language can rarely be studied in fiction as in Elizabethan drama and poetry; it does not fall into patterns obeying an internal and self-generated logic. To this general rule the *Mourning Garment* is perhaps an exception. Its pastoral elements draw on each other to alter significantly the original parable. By making Philador's journey a rejection of pastoral values Greene makes it something beyond a revolt against simple authority; it becomes a revolt against tradition and convention. A voice of wisdom and experience, Rabbi Bilessi is also a representative of order and form. Greene invents citizen social standing for him ("the chiefe Burgamaster of the whole City" [9:127–28]) and makes a large element in his advice the need for prudence. Rabbi Bilessi outdoes Polonius in praising withdrawal and secrecy, saying to Philador, "hide all thy thoughts in thy hearts bottome" and "euer dissemble thy thoughts to a stranger" (9:138–39).[32] As a result, Philador craves openness and directness. He wants to take the world as he sees it, to trust it apart from the formulations of pastoral literature. In a way, he revolts against pastoral literature itself, with its closed, orderly, and conventional tradition. Rejecting the essential pastoral theme of resignation, he seeks to make a self apart from structure, to create an identity instead of accepting, as Rosamond does, what is presented to him.

The social and psychological dimensions that pastoralism brings to the parable perhaps augment its relevance to Greene's life and, if the *Mourning Garment* does express something of Greene himself in 1590, its most striking feature is pessimism. Philador fails in his attempt to find rewards beyond contentment, and Menalcas' song is a song of disillusionment. He has "noted oft that beauty was a blaze," he has "spy'd the woes that womens loues ensueth," and he has seen "that loue was but a heape of cares" (9:217). Beauty, women, love—all are seen and found wanting by Philador as well. Several characters, even one of the courtesans, describe the mutability of beauty, and nowhere is there, as there is in most of Greene's other works, counterweight to the image of "Beauty . . . that poisoneth worse than the iuyce of the Baaron," "infecteth worse then the Basiliske," and "draweth vnto death" (9:189). Rabbi Bilessi advises Philador "especially against women" (9:178), and only the portrait of Rosamond contradicts him. By the end, Philador can cure the lover he meets by preaching the evils of women and giving him a scroll containing axioms and a poem that "tended to the discouery of womens qualities" (9:201). Greene portrays the wily sisters with "their eyes . . . hookes that draw men in, and their words birdlime that tyes the feathers of euery stranger" (9:163), but no Mamillia, Mariana, or Sephestia plays a redemptive role. Even Rosamond's virtues preserve neither her nor Alexis from disaster. There is, in short, no love, for, as Philador tells his father, "how sweet soeuer . . . desire seemes at the first, it hath a most bitter taste at the last" (9:218). The only warm relationships presented exist between men: the complaining lover responds to Philador's advice by offering to divide his wealth "with a friendly proportion" (9:197); the shepherd tells one tale of a son devoted to his father but two tales of suicide after betrayal in love; in the end Philador rejoins only his father and his brother. The revulsion from love is unrelieved, one element in a vision entirely negative. As a myth, the *Mourning Garment* is a myth of awakening to forbidding realities. If the work conveys Greene's sense of the result of his own attempt to define a self, it is a bitter sense. The world beyond Rabbi Bilessi's ordered existence offers only "experience . . . bought with much sorrow" (9:209).

Coney-catching in *A Notable Discouery of Coosnage*.   Greene's coney-catching pamphlets have attracted interest less for themselves than for the historical and biographical issues that they raise. They have, for example, been seen as a window on sixteenth-century London life, as a healthy corrective to impressions of the era based solely on the Elizabethan masters. The pamphlets can indeed serve this purpose and should be known by more readers, although, as discussed in chapter 1, their claim to firsthand observation of criminals has aroused debate. When commentary has moved beyond such matters, it has focused mainly on the question of realism, with the pamphlets often compared to later fiction. Pruvost entitles his chapter on Greene's last works "Sur le Chemin de la Nouvelle Realiste," and E. A. Baker writes that Greene's "real service was to have . . . initiated a kind of storytelling which, through the rogue-stories and criminal biographies, led to epoch-making developments in the hands of Defoe."[33] Greene draws as much on tradition as he contributes, however, and reading the coney-catching pamphlets as anticipations of the novel can only distract from the appreciation of their own purposes. Yet realism remains an important issue, for the central theme of the pamphlets is exactly their claim of realism: Greene warns the inexperienced of "real" danger and informs the authorities of "real" injustice. He accordingly adopts several strategies designed to persuade to belief in the truth of what he describes. Taken together, these strategies give the pamphlets a claim to authenticity in the portrayal not only of crime but also of social issues and human motives.

A passage from the first of the pamphlets, *A Notable Discovery of Coosnage,* illustrates several of Greene's techniques for establishing authenticity:

> Neere to *S. Edmunds Burie* in *Suffolk,* there dwelt an honest man a
> Shoemaker, that hauing some twenty markes in his purse, long a gathering,
> and neerly kept, came to the market to buy a dicker of hides, and by
> chaunce fel among cony-catchers, whose names I omit, because I hope of
> their amendment. This plain countriman drawn in by these former deuises,
> was made a cony, and so straight stript of all his xx. marke, to his vtter
> vndoing: the knaues scapt, and he went home a sorowful man. (10:31)

The most obvious feature of the passage is its circumstantial detail.
Greene names the shoemaker's home, counts the money in his purse,
describes his errand. Several of the characters in the *Discovery* have
names, and the various episodes nearly always take place on a specific
London street. Often, too, Greene claims, as he does here, to with-
hold the names of coney-catchers in hopes "of their amendment."
He does not name the shoemaker, but he notes his trade and gives
him an identity as "an honest man" and "a plain countriman,"
whose money has been "long a gathering, and neerly kept." The
shoemaker represents trade, thrift, and provincial innocence. In
writing about a shoemaker at all Greene of course appeals to the
"Young Gentlemen, Marchants, Apprentises, Farmers, and plain
Countreymen" to whom he dedicates the pamphlet. His previous
works had been dedicated to the noble but bought by the less than
noble, and Greene now drops the pretense to address his buyers for
what they are.[34] Indeed, he devotes an appendix to that most homely
of issues, the selling of coal, relating two tales of revenge upon
dishonest colliers, one portraying *"a Cookes wife in London"* and one
"a Flaxe wife and her neighbours" (10:57–58). In introducing these
tales by recounting his own meeting with a victimized "pore woman
of *Shorditch,"* Greene describes human priorities far removed from
the world of *Mamillia* and *Menaphon:* "For fewell or firing being a
thing necessary in a commonwealth, and charcoal vsed more than
any other, the poore not able to buy by the load, are fain to get in
their fire by the sacke, & so are greatly coosned by the retaile"
(10:55). Greene identifies himself as a person in touch with daily
realities, in the process perhaps implying that the *Discovery* is honest
merchandise.

Greene's vocabulary—"charcoal," "load" and "sacke," "retaile"—is that of the story of the shoemaker, which includes the
use of the tradesmen's term "a dicker of hides." Throughout the
Discovery Greene uses the language of his readers, speaking informally

in the first person. That he consciously seeks a particular rhetorical effect is clear in his defense of style in the next of the pamphlets: "giue me leaue to answere an obiection, that some inferred against me, which was, that I shewed no eloquent phrases, nor fine figuratiue conueiance in my first booke as I had done in other of my workes: to which I reply that . . . a certaine decorum is to bee kept in euerie thing, and not to applie a high stile in a base subiect" (10:71).[35] Greene counters the linguistic plainness that results from the absence of "eloquent phrases" by using what he claims is criminals' jargon. The shoemaker "was made a cony," being caught by the "three seueral parties" involved: the "Setter, the Verser, and the Barnackle" (10:15), terms which, as Cuthbert says in the *Defence,* Greene "neuer founde in *Tully* nor *Aristotle*" (11:49).[36] Greene reveals the mysteries of a closed society protected by a language that obscures "filthie crafts with . . . faire colours, that the ignorant may not espie what their subtiltie is" (10:39). Greene compares a carpenter, who also "hath many termes familiar inough to his prentices" (10:33), and defines criminal activities as "arts" or "crafts" or "laws." In one passage he lists eight such "laws," spelling out the technical terms used in each (10:37–38).

One more point may be made about the passage on the shoemaker: Greene fits it into the pamphlet with the same illusion of artlessness that marks the language. The anecdote begins abruptly, without declaration of function or transition from a similar tale just concluded, that of a victimized Welshman, which also begins abruptly: coney-catchers' "eares are of adamant, as pitiles as they are trecherous, for be the man neuer so poore, they wil not return him one peny of his los. I remember a merry iest done of late to a welchman . . ." (10:30). At the end of the two anecdotes Greene's only comment actually contradicts what he has just described. That is, the shoemaker manages to help convict the coney-catcher who has cheated him and even to secure for himself the privilege of whipping him, but Greene says, "Thus we see how the generation of these vipers increase, to the confusion of many honest men" (10:33). The structure is thus random and episodic, as bare of "fine figuratiue conueiance" as the language. Partly this structure may result from Greene's piecing together the *Discovery* from various kinds of material; among Greene's shortest works, it may have been written very rapidly. Still, the narrative shapelessness reflects as well the claim to journalism, not art.

The effect of realism secured by Greene's devices is, as suggested above, the essential content of the *Discovery*. At the same time, insisting on the actuality of "consuming moths of the common welth" (10:18) allows Greene to present himself as a commentator on the state of England. Throughout the work runs the sense of national decay described in the dedication: *"I would wish the Iustices appoynted as seuere Censors of such fatall mischiefes, to shew themselues patres patriae, by weeding out such worms as eat away the sappe of the Tree, and rooting this base degree of Cooseners out of so peaceable and prosperous a countrey"* (10:9). "Base minded Caterpillers" infest the realm, preying on all classes, and Greene bewails the "lamentable case in england, when such vipers are suffred to breed and are not cut off with the sword of iustice." The "enormitie is not onely in *London,*" moreover, "but now generally dispersed through all england, in euery shire, city, and town of any receipt" (10:29). Some of the anecdotes reveal the process by which the plague of deceit spreads, for, as country comes to city to be bilked, country learns trickery and cynicism. The coney in the longest tale in the work is a "poor countrie man" (10:20) who is led on by being taught to cheat at cards: "Wel," he says, "Ile carrie this home with me into the cuntrie, and win many a pot of ale with it" (10:23).

As an alarum for England, then, the *Discovery* aspires to social commentary and has a certain ideological content. Perhaps responding to changes of the 1590s, Greene describes social dissolution, with "seruing men . . . , prentises . . . , young gentlemen, merchants, and others" (10:29) jumbled together as victims of coney-catchers who exist outside class structure and apart from restraints of tradition. At the same time, these artists in self-interest are as much a result of breakdown as a cause, for their motives echo those of their victims. The coney seduced by his own willingness to learn to cheat is typical, for beneath the decay of institutions lies moral decay, displayed in each of the two main sections of the work, one on coney-catching and one on cross-biting (*"cosenage by cards"* and *"by whores"* [10:36–37]). The first begins with a description of methods for getting the victim inside a tavern, some of which, such as leaving money for him to find or asking him to carry out a simple errand for a large reward, exploit his desire for gain: "at this the cony stoupes, and for greediness of the mony" (10:20). Once inside, as noted above, the coney eagerly learns a "pretie game," "only for greediness" (10:23). An accomplice enters and the coney helps to cheat him, with quick success allowing for the raising of stakes that will bring ruin when the double-cross is finally worked: that success "flesheth the Conny, the sweetnes of gaine maketh him frolike, and no man is more readie to vie and reuie then he" (10:27).

In the second section, cross-biting depends upon the arousal of lust in "men fondly and wantonly geuen, whom for a penaltie of their lust, [cross-biters] fleece of al that euer they haue" (10:40). Greene describes various tricks, the most subtle being the imper-sonation of an officer who can help hide the behavior of an otherwise respectable man who does "accompany with anie woman familiarly, or else hath gotten some maide with child, as mens natures be prone to sin" (10:45). More common is the use of a prostitute, for "some vnruly mates that place their content in lust . . . feede vpon their vnchast beauties, till their hearts be set on fire" (10:41). Greene describes prostitutes at length, focusing exclusively on their physical appeal and making no effort to turn them into the elegant courtesans of other works. Instead of the polished discourses of the three sisters in the *Mourning Garment,* he describes only the manipulation of appearance, using the same concreteness that marks the *Discovery* as a whole: "these street walkers wil iet in rich garded gowns, queint periwigs, rufs of the largest size, quarter and halfe deep, gloried richly with blew starch, their cheekes died with surfuling water: thus are they trickt vp, and either walke like stales vp and down the streets, or stande like the diuels *Si quis* at a tauern or ale house" (10:42–43). The description locates cross-biting in a world where claims of human nature link victim and criminal together. If cross-biters are "outcasts from God, vipers of the world, and an excre-mental reuersion of sin" (10:39), Greene warns his readers "from lust, that your inordinate desire be not a meane to impouerish your purses, discredit your good names, condemne your soules" (10:44).

Greene speaks, of course, for the exploited in this unholy con-junction, but he lets the exploiters speak for themselves when, between the two halves of the pamphlet, he describes a conversation with "one whom I suspected a cony-catcher" (10:34–35). As Greene attempts to dissuade "him from that base kind of life," the coney-catcher replies with three arguments, all borrowed by Greene from the *Manifest Detection of Dice Play* (1552) but used by him as a kind of commentary on the *Discovery*.[37] In the first argument the coney-catcher boasts of his basic human motives: "Tut sir . . . as my religion is smal, so my deuotion is lesse: I leaue God to be disputed

on by diuines: the two ends I aime at, are gaine and ease." In the
second he surveys the universality of deceit—"fewe men can liue
vprightly"—and identifies himself with lawyers whose "proceed-
inges" are not all "iustice and conscience," officeholders who count
"pilage an honest kind of purchase," and tradesmen who do not
"make all their commodities without falshod." The coney-catcher's
third argument points to the hardships of virtue: "who so hath not
some sinister way to help himself, but foloweth his nose alwaies
straight forward, may wel hold vp the head for a yeare or two, but
ye third he must needs sink, and gather the wind into begers hauen."
The arguments state issues inherent in the anecdotes told on either
side of their central location in the *Discovery.* Moreover, just as
Greene allows the anecdotes to raise those issues, he here allows the
coney-catcher's defense to stand. Convinced that he lives in a world
knit together by base motives, the coney-catcher says, "my resolution is to beat my wits, and spare not to busie my braines to saue
and help me by what meanes soeuer I care not." Greene says nothing,
but simply walks away, "wondering at the basenes of their mindes,
that would spend their time in such detestable sort." Indeed, he
seems naive in reflecting on differences between coney-catchers and
the rest of society, not similarities. Although Greene knows the
coney-catcher that he meets ("he, calling me by my name"), the
arguments that he hears go unanswered and stand as one explanation
for the success of *"pestilent vipers of the commonwealth"* (10:9).

Greene's Career in Prose

The six works discussed in the preceding pages illustrate many
of Greene's techniques in the prose pamphlets and include a wide
range of treatments of some of his characteristic concerns. The works
also represent points in a career that went through a number of
distinct phases; Greene tended to work one vein through several
pamphlets before going on to a new one. The overall shape of
Greene's career can now be examined by reviewing in order the rest
of his more than thirty prose works. Although several are of significant interest and reward a careful reading, only a few can receive
more than brief treatment here. The theoretical questions considered
above must also be neglected. An approach to Greene will be taken
for granted in order to concentrate on characterizing the works,

fitting them into Greene's development as a writer, and suggesting some directions for interpretation.

Early works: 1580–86. Greene followed *Mamillia* with a sequel that continues the reversal of Lyly's treatment of women by demonstrating again that "for inconstancie men are farre more worthie to be condemned than women to be accused" (2:157). Greene intrudes on the story for several digressions on the faithfulness of women, and a debate over whether men or women "be more constant or loyal in loue" is decided in favor of women (2:218–19). Female virtue again finds its embodiment in Mamillia, who remains devoted to Pharicles after his disappearance even though she learns that he has courted Publia. Publia shows equal constancy and, hearing of Mamillia's prior claim, enters a convent rather than "like any other" (2:172); years later she bequeaths her belongings to Pharicles. For his part, Pharicles arrives in Sicily feeling confused and guilty. After living quietly for a time he enters society, but he manages to resist the advances of Clarynda, a beautiful and wealthy courtesan. In revenge, Clarynda accuses him of being a spy, and Pharicles is imprisoned and condemned to death. Mamillia learns of his plight and rushes to Sicily, where she discovers letters that reveal Clarynda's true motives; dramatically entering the courtroom at the last minute, she produces the letters and saves Pharicles. He begs forgiveness, and they are married.

If Greene reverses Lyly in plot, he again imitates him in style. The characters deliver formal speeches on topics ranging from virginity to preparing for death, not all of them bearing clear relation to the story of Mamillia and Pharicles. Modern readers will find some of the speeches tedious enough, but rhetoric is, as in the first part, not simply displayed but also examined. In particular, a letter from Pharicles to Clarynda contains an extremely interesting commentary on her arguments for proving her ability to give up a courtesan's life (2:228–31). Less appealing to modern taste are two long letters from Mamillia that make up an appendix, although they are useful collections of Renaissance truisms on the dangers of eloquence and the blessings of rational love. Mamillia's second letter, moreover, includes the tale of a young woman wooed, like Shakespeare's Portia, by three contrasting suitors.[38]

Also reminiscent of *The Merchant of Venice* is the courtroom appearance of Mamillia, "richly attired and straungely disguised" (2:244), and her forgiveness of Pharicles in this scene may remind us too of Helena in *All's Well* (2:247). Like Shakespeare's Bertram, moreover, Pharicles is an unconvincing object of Mamillia's love. As he says of himself, "all *Padua* despiseth thee as a patterne of leawdnesse: what hope canst thou haue then *Pharicles* to recouer thy credit where euerie man of reputation will refuse thy companie?" (2:206–7). Mamillia's devotion to such a character borders on absurdity, as she comes close to admitting: "although he hath crackt his credit, violated his oath, falsified his faith, and broke his protested promise, yet his inconstancie shall neuer make mee to wauer, nor his fleeting fancie shall not diminish mine affection" (2:155). Any irony in the situation, however, or any tendency for Mamillia to become an object of the reader's judgment, goes undeveloped. Instead, the emblematic Mamillia sees beneath Pharicles' behavior to a presumed true worth, and the equally emblematic Pharicles can and does repent. The plot rewards both Mamillia's constancy and Pharicles' change of heart. The traditional views of human nature inherent in the story are suggested by Pharicles' resemblance to the heroes of morality drama: he escapes not only from destruction but from "languishing in despaire" (2:236), led to happy ending by a figure of almost incomprehensible capacity to forgive. Pharicles recalls another archetype as well, the prodigal son, for his suffering in a strange land brings growth beyond youthful folly. Thus Mamillia, even before she has news of him, hopes "that although *Pharicles* had sowen wilde Oates hee should reape good graine . . . and . . . in time learne to be wise" (2:170). Greene does not render Pharicles' maturation dramatically, the only concrete evidence being his resistance when he "almost yeelded a listening eare to the melodie of this immodest mermaide," Clarynda (2:205). The episode suffices, however, as a temptation scene, epitomizing the growth to moral consciousness implicit in the thematic archetypes which Pharicles, like Bertram, embodies.

The second part of *Mamillia* was the first of several works appearing very rapidly in 1584 and 1585. Next came *Gwydonius,* or *Greenes Carde of Fancie,* notable in containing Greene's earliest extended use of romance motifs. Imitation of Lyly dominates the first half, with moral and social issues considered in letters, debates, and soliloquies of the sort Greene had written for *Mamillia.* Once hero and heroine declare their love, however, they enter into a complicated plot that includes war, revenge, disguise, and a spectacular final scene of recognition, reunion, and marriage. This second half makes use of a number of familiar motifs, and *Gwydonius* is among the most derivative of Greene's works.[39] Its dependence on sources, along with the presence of two halves very different in style, makes the work seem somewhat disjointed. At least one factor unifies it, however: repeated portrayals of conflict between parents and children.[40] The story begins with the quarrel and separation of Gwydonius and his father, both of whom soon regret their anger, and Gwydonius goes on to fall in love with Castania, the daughter of his father's enemy. Since Gwydonius is disguised as a poor courtier, Castania conceals the situation from her father; later, when Gwydonius's identity is revealed, she blames herself for having acted without guidance. Gwydonius's sister and Castania's brother also reject authority by falling in love. These motifs come together symbolically at the end of the tale when the disguised Gwydonius must duel his own father in order both to end the war and to win Castania's hand. Although pieced together and derivative, *Gwydonius* nonetheless shows Greene's tendency to organize narrative around ideas. Both halves dramatize antagonism between desire and duty: in drawing on Lyly Greene portrays Gwydonius as a prodigal son and then as a lover reaching above his (supposed) station; in borrowing motifs of romance he chooses situations that involve forbidden love. The emphasis on youthful rebellion gives *Gwydonius* an interesting psychological dimension and clearly links it to Greene's other works. Moreover, Gwydonius's final triumph is the first of many conclusions presenting the simultaneous resolution of personal and social questions.[41]

More straightforward is *Arbasto, The Anatomie of Fortune,* entered in the Stationers' Register four months after *Gwydonius.* Here a traveler comes upon a priest of Astarte "sitting (as I supposed) at his Orizons," who "leaned his heade vpon his right hand, powring forth streames of watrish teares, . . . and held in his left hand the counterfeit of fortune, with one foote troade on a polype fish, and with the other on a Camelion, as assured badges of his certaine mutabilitie" (2:178–79). This symbolic figure is the former king of Denmark, Arbasto, who has learned that "he only is to be thought happie, whome the inconstant fauour of fortune hath not made happie" (3:184). As an illustration of "what trust there is to be giuen to inconstant fortune" (3:186), Arbasto's life offers Greene's first extended treatment of the theme of Fortune. Interestingly, Arbasto's revulsion from Fortune does not result from his having

been a victim of random and undeserved disaster. Rather, his tale
describes moral weakness and human error; it is a tale of obsessive
love. The euphuistic debates and meditations consider such questions as whether love can be resisted and whether it makes humans
happy, and Arbasto summarizes the dominant image of love in a
soliloquy delivered years before in prison: "in sufferyng reason to
yeelde vnto appetite, wysedome vnto wyll, and wyt vnto affection,
thou haste procured thine owne death and thy Soldiers destruction.
Loue, yea loue it is that hath procured thy losse, beautie that hathe
bred thy bale: fancye that hath giuen thee the foile, and thyne own
witlesse wyll that hath wrought thy woe" (3:219). Such speeches
link love to Fortune in the relationship explored in *Menaphon. Arbasto*
is a simpler and more one-sided treatment, and Arbasto's autobiography has an unrelievedly tragic conclusion. Both of two sisters
with whom Arbasto fell in and out of love die. He recalls with
horror the first on her deathbed: "with staring lookes and wrathful
countenance, seeming by hir ragyng gestures to be in a frensie: but
being kept downe by hir Ladies, she roared out . . . hateful curses"
(3:242). The second met a similar end: "she fell into a frenzie,
hauing nothing in hir mouth but *Arbasto, Arbasto,* euer doubling
this word with such pitiful cries and scriches, as would haue moued
any one but me to remorse" (3:252). Passion destroyed both sisters,
and, filled with contempt for his "loathsome life" (3:252), Arbasto
has withdrawn to contemplate in solitude the "polype fish" and
"Camelion," emblems—"badges" Greene calls them—of the power
of Fortune over human irrationality.

Happier in conclusion is *The Myrrour of Modestie,* which also
appeared in 1584. A retelling of the story of Susanna and the elders,
written *"more largelie then . . . in the Apopcripha"* (3:5), the *Myrrour*
is the only work of its kind which Greene published. He defines it
as a "perfect Glasse" to show "howe the Lorde deliuereth the innocent
from all imminent perils, and plagueth the bloudthirstie hypocrites
with deserued punishments," but perhaps a greater point of interest
is the parallel between Susanna and Greene's other heroines. He
again comes forward as the champion of women, writing, he says,
because *"requested . . . of a certaine Gentlewoman"* (3:5). In ampli-
fying the story Greene adds no new incidents or characters. Instead,
he adds lengthy speeches, especially when the elders attempt to
seduce Susanna in the garden and when Daniel lectures on divine
justice before proving that the elders have lied. Notable in such

passages is the ease with which Greene fits the language of works like *Mamillia* to the original story.[42] With Susanna described as peerless for both "the pure complexion of hir bodie" and "the perfect constitution of hir minde" (3:10), Greene is on familiar ground and uses many of his favorite phrases, allusions, and similes. The verbal continuity with other works perhaps reveals not only the power of language to define situation, but also the moralizing and rhetorical interests of Greene and his readers.

Those interests dominate *Morando: The Tritameron of Love,* unique among Greene's works in the slightness of its plot. A widow and her three daughters spend three nights visiting a gentleman and three young friends, each night devoted to formal debate of an issue: whether more for men or for women "Loue doth much, but money doth all" (3:61), whether "it be good to loue or no" (3:84), and whether "by natural constitution women are more subject vnto loue then men" (3:99). Some lively teasing arises, and one of the men falls in love with one of the women, but no narrative structure emerges; at the end the widow simply takes her daughters back home. A rather unfocused work results, one in which the various speeches never cohere as more than a kind of anthology. Moreover, only the second night's topic—whether "it be good to loue or no"— involves issues important in Greene's other works; that debate ends when the widow points out that the two sides are based on conflicting definitions of love—love for "the vertue of the minde" and love for "the beautie of the bodie" (2:98–99). Passages so useful in approaching Greene are few in *Morando,* however, and Greene seems content to offer eloquent discourse as its own reward. Part 2, apparently published somewhat later, is much the same sort of work. The three gentlemen follow the widow and her daughters home for further conversation. The debaters of love in part 1 end up betrothed, giving the work a certain roundness, but their story has no twists and turns to invest it with significance. Greene draws on several sources for long speeches on Fortune and on friendship, and part 2 is as unfocused and disjointed as part 1.

The lack of energy in these two works perhaps indicates that Greene's dependence on Lyly had run its course, ending with the imitation of Lyly's most obvious characteristics only. Henceforth Greene's fiction would make greater use of complicated plots, often derived from the romance literature drawn on in *Gwydonius.* A transitional work published between the two parts of *Morando* marks

out that path, *Planetomachia,* in which Greene sets three very lively
and dramatic tales within a frame—his first use of this device.
Planetomachia is at the same time perhaps the most impressive of
Greene's earlier works. The frame portrays "a ciuill conflict between
the seuen Planets: . . . shewing their nature and essence, and what
proper qualities their celestiall configuration and influence doth
infuse into humaine bodies" (5:7). After two prefaces, one a defense
of astronomy and the other a Latin dialogue on the planets (both
lifted from other writers),[43] the work proper begins with a dispute
between Saturn and Venus. Each tells a tale to illustrate the baneful
influence of the other, and Jupiter then tells a third tale. The title
page calls *Planetomachia* "the first parte of the generall opposition
of the seuen Planets," indicating that Greene planned a sequel, but
a second part never appeared.

   If the debate in the frame suggests *Morando,* the three tales are
far removed from courtly conversation. Influenced by Italian novellas—Greene's first use of this important source[44]—they portray
passion and bloody revenge, and are as melodramatic, and perhaps
as repellant, as anything Greene wrote. In one, a widowed king
falls insanely in love with a courtesan when an eagle drops her
golden shoe into his presence. The situation has its comic side when
the king, shoe in hand, takes to his bed: "a shoe of golde is the
only thing that bewitcheth my mind: such a straunge fancie, as
time hath neuer made report of the like" (5:109). Matters turn
tragic, however, after the king marries the courtesan. He finds her
in bed with his son, slays them both, and poisons himself. In the
equally grim third tale a woman explains the meaning of a nightly
ritual in which she stabs a heart over and over and drinks from two
skulls (they are the skulls of her murdered brothers, and the heart
is the heart of their murderer). In the first and perhaps most interesting of the tales, the cruel and melancholy Duke Valdracko of
Ferrara, called by Jordan "Greene's supreme achievement" in characterization,[45] illustrates for Venus the evils of a saturnine temperament. Valdracko's daughter Pasylla falls in love with Rodento, son
of his oldest enemy. The lovers hide their feelings, but Valdracko
discovers the situation and decides to use it to destroy his enemy.
Claiming amity and offering his daughter in marriage, he hires an
assassin to murder Rodento's father, and, after the marriage, has
Rodento himself poisoned. Pasylla learns the truth and steals into
her father's bedchamber, where, "pulling off hir garters," she "boūd

him hād and foot" (5:94). She curses him and stabs him, and then she stabs herself. This grotesque bedchamber scene underlines the horror of the destruction of natural love, and all three stories describe hatred, rivalry, and murder within families and between friends. Particularly effective is this first tale because of Valdracko's pretending that the young people's love will end the feud between families. Instead it leads to four deaths, confirming the claims for human need of her influence that Venus makes in debating Saturn: "those natiuities which are fauoured wyth my happye aspecte, dispose the minde to a continuall pronenesse and forwardnesse: vnto pitie, friendshippe, amity, and loue" (5:41).

Venus' defense of herself is part of a larger structure in which this compelling work portrays the ambiguity of the forces operating on human beings. Beside her defense Greene sets Saturn's attack: "loue sotteth the senses, infecteth youth, destroyeth age, and is the very plague both to the minde and body" (5:101). Indeed, when Venus concludes her tale, the planets debate its meaning, and Saturn and Jupiter offer an interpretation altogether different from hers: "it was the wilfull forwardnesse of *Pasylla* in her doting fancies, and her lasciuious loue in liking her fathers enimy, that procured these haplesse euents" (5:97). Like modern critics disputing *Romeo and Juliet,* the planets offer conflicting perspectives. A general sense of human helplessness throughout all three stories results, summarized in Valdracko's inability to turn back from villainy despite the knowledge of its nature he reveals in a soliloquy: "What doest thou mean, *Valdracko,* to trouble thy mind with such balefull passions, or so much as in thought to intend such desperate attempts, the performance whereof is so vnnatural, as such bloudy actions, if there be any Gods, cannot escāpe without some deadly & direful reuēge?" (5:89). Valdracko's reference to universal justice only emphasizes the sense of powerlessness, for he and the other characters in the stories end up prisoners of uncontrollable emotions. All stand like the king in the second tale facing the sight of his wife in his son's arms: "a quaking cold possessing his limmes, hee stoode trembling for the horror of such a brutish fact, till his chilling feare turning into a flaming choler, hee fell almost into a raging frenzie" (5:134–35). The recurrent image of the failure of human control, presented in the context of unresolved debate over external forces, shows that the turning toward more complex narratives in *Planetomachia* represents also a turning toward more complex treatments of issues.

Even a work like *Mamillia* contains areas of depth, but *Planetomachia* looks ahead to the richness of *Menaphon* and Greene's other mature works.

Romance and frame stories: 1587–89. *Planetomachia* was one of only two works Greene published in 1585, the other being *An Oration or Funerall Sermon uttered at Roome.* This curious and neglected pamphlet translates a sermon delivered at the funeral of Pope Gregory XIII. Greene's motives are not entirely clear. On the one hand, his translation makes available a celebration of the papacy, perhaps a sign of the conservative temperament seen in some of his other works and perhaps evidence for a recent conjecture that Greene had links to a circle of Catholic recusants.[46] On the other hand, Greene claims on the title page to present the sermon as an instance of "papistical adulation," an assertion developed in his preface and in a series of mocking marginal glosses. Perhaps, as virtually the only recent commentator on the translation suggests, Greene aimed to appeal to Catholic and Protestant alike.[47] In any case, the *Oration* did not lead Greene in new directions. He completed the second part of *Morando* in 1586, and then in 1587 returned to the structure of *Planetomachia* in *Penelopes Web,* the first of a series of romances and frame stories published in quick succession.

Instead of the planets of *Planetomachia,* Homer's Penelope and her maids converse in *Penelopes Web.* They discuss female virtue, as Greene again takes on the role of women's champion, dedicating the work to two countesses and calling it a "Christall Myrrour of faeminine perfection" on the title page. Three stories told by Penelope support the claim by illustrating the "speciall poynts that are requisite in euery woman, Obedience, Chastitie, and Silence" (5:162). In the first, a king exiles his wife in order to marry a concubine but reforms when he sees his wife's Griselda-like loyalty in the face of his cruelty. In the second, the devotion to chastity of a farmer's wife inspires a nobleman to renounce his obsessive pursuit of her. In the third, a king settles his throne on the one of his three sons who has the most virtuous wife (shown by her ability to keep silent). The tales are straightforward exempla, and *Penelopes Web* is not among Greene's more substantial works. Perhaps its most interesting point is Penelope's opinion that she "cannot thinke . . . that there is any husband so bad which the honest gouernment of his wife may not in time refourme" (5:162). The statement focuses the stories on the motif of male reformation important throughout

Greene's works. The second tale in particular treats this theme directly, portraying an archetypal confrontation between the misguided male aggressiveness of the nobleman and the patient female virtue of the farmer's wife. Her poverty subjects her to male manipulation (the nobleman strips her and her husband of their tenant-farm and imprisons her in his castle), while also allowing her opportunities to express the disdain for wealth and honor felt by Greene's pastoral heroines. The conclusion brings a victory for the heroine over male domination and a conversion for the hero from destructive fantasies. Brevity and clarity give the story an abstract, formulaic quality, and it translates into myth the male and female conflict underlying such more elaborate stories as that of Prince Edward and Margaret in *Friar Bacon and Friar Bungay*. Indeed, the nobleman's first sight of the farmer's wife is quite reminiscent of the opening scenes of the play: "he espied a woman homely attired, of modest coūtenance, her face importing both loue and grauitie: who seeing the Noble man approch, dying her christall cheekes with a vermillyon hue, after humble salutations brought him in a countrie Cruse such drinke as their Cottage did afford" (5:204). As the farmer's wife, like Margaret of Fressingfield, performs her hostess's duties for the intruding stranger, the confict between male and female begins, to be resolved only when the nobleman feels "a remorce in his conscience for offering vyolence to so vertuous and chast a mynd" (5:216).

Greene apparently intended his next work as a companion to *Penelopes Web,* for he moves from Penelope to her husband and the other Greek warriors in Troy for *Euphues His Censure to Philautus.* Moreover, just as *Penelopes Web* displays "faeminine perfection," the title page of *Euphues His Censure* promises examination of "the vertues necessary . . . in euery gentleman . . . especially debated to discouer the perfection of a souldier." In taking up this new theme, Greene resurrects Lyly in his title and preface: "by chance some of Euphues loose papers came to my hand, wherein hee writ to his friend Philautus from Silexedra" (6:154). The playful ruse serves no function other than to introduce the discussion of the qualities of a gentleman, and the body of the work includes no reference to *Euphues.* Instead, Greene portrays the conversation of Trojans and Greeks during a truce in the war. This framing action has some interesting elements and may have influenced Shakespeare in *Troilus and Cressida.*[48] Greene calls up Homer's main characters, clearly individualizes them, and allows the conversation to have some rather tense moments, as when Hector says that Paris "hath brought a trull from Greece" (6:167). Moreover, the four stories told within the frame all have a certain relevance to the war and its causes: one centers on the punishment of adultery, one involves an invasion, and two describe a city under siege. The narrators do not call attention to parallels to their own situation, however, but instead offer the tales to illustrate the generalizations they defend in the framing debate: Helenus' tale shows the importance of wisdom, Hector's of fortitude, and so on. The tales serve this purpose well enough, although in atmosphere they resemble the grim tales of *Planetomachia*—enough so to invite speculation that Greene first intended one or more of them for the sequel to *Planetomachia* which he never published. As in the earlier work, all four conclusions portray the dissolution of natural bonds: in the first, suicide follows adultery, the second ends in mass murder at a marriage feast, a youth slays his two brothers in the third, and soldiers rise up to massacre the senators of Athens in the fourth. Such images of people at the mercy of destructive emotions reflect conflicts among the planets in *Planetomachia,* but here a connection to the frame is less clear. It may be, however, that Greene, like Shakespeare, saw the siege of Troy as a story of moral confusion and human error, and that the opening words of *Euphues His Censure* establish a context that makes the tales of disaster a comment on the goals of the tellers on both sides: *"Helena* the haplesse wyfe of vnhappy *Menelaus,* beawtified frõ aboue, to inflict a mortall punishment vpon men beneath: honored in Greece more for her beawty then hir honesty (a fault which fondlings account for a fauour) . . . through her lawlesse consent to *Paris,* so troubled the quietnesse of Asia, that *Priamus* flowrishing as prince of that parte of the worlde, was with his sonnes and daughters brought to ruine: (the ende of voluptuos appetites) which they mayntained with the sworde" (6:155–56).

The question of the relevance of stories to a frame exists also in Greene's next work, *Perimedes,* as seen earlier, but not in the one after that, *Pandosto,* comprised of one long story. As in *Menaphon,* published the following year, Greene abandons the structure of *Planetomachia* and its immediate successors, framing *Pandosto* only with his own brief definitions of significance on the title page, in the epistles, and in the opening sentences. This apparent "decision to abandon ornate pronouncements and concentrate upon plain storytelling" has attracted many critics; "here at last," writes C. S. Lewis, "the story is the thing."[49] Paradoxically, such praise of Greene's eschewal of significance has often preceded the greater praise of Shakespeare for adding significance in borrowing the story for *The Winter's Tale;* as J. J. Jusserand said a century ago, "Greene had, in truth, only modelled the clay; Shakespeare used it, adding the soul."[50] A study of critical expectations for the two works might prove very interesting indeed. Ample material for such a study exists in the many comparisons between Shakespeare's version and Greene's original, for the accident of being a Shakespearean source has made *Pandosto* the most often analyzed of Greene's romances. Because commentary is thus readily available, *Pandosto* may be summarized with only a brief noting of its place in the context of Greene's career. Its emblematic situations have parallels in many of his works, and they involve such characteristic issues as pastoral contentment, conflict between male and female attitudes, the power of emotion over humans, repentance and forgiveness, Fortune, and the meanings of Nature. *Pandosto* is a rich and suggestive work. Indeed, its simultaneously tragic and comic ending, combining the spirit of *Planetomachia* with the spirit of *Perimedes,* indicates its complexity. The tendency to compare *Pandosto* both to modern fiction and *The Winter's Tale* limits appreciation, however. Seen from the perspective of Greene's own works, it can perhaps still prove as appealing as it apparently was to Shakespeare.

About the time of *Pandosto* Greene wrote the intense and troubling *Alcida,* and shortly afterward came *The Spanish Masquerado;* no better indication of the difficulties of reading Greene's works biographically could be asked. The *Masquerado* is joyful, patriotic, and without moral tension. A celebration of the defeat of the Spanish Armada the previous year, it gleefully mocks Spain and the Catholic church, drawing on a generation of English propagandists. Of Philip of Spain, for example, Greene writes, "nousled from his infancie in the darke and obscure dungeon of Papistry, . . . drunke with the dregges of that poyson which the whore powreth out to the Kinges of the earth . . . he sleepeth securely in ye Popes lap" (5:253). Greene claims in the epistle that the work reflects his "conscience in Religion" (5:241). Little of conscience seems involved, however, in a work so clearly designed to appeal to the audience of common readers suggested by the dedication not to a nobleman but to the sheriff of London. Indeed, Greene's sense of audience in the *Mas-*

querado is one of its most important features. It offers, as one of its
few recent commentators writes, "a fairly accurate image of the
Elizabethan mood the year after the Armada,"[51] and students of
Shakespeare's chronicle plays might well profit from reading Greene's
account of "this our little Iland, which defended by God, and
gouerned by so vertuous a Princesse as GOD hath chosen after his
owne heart, standeth and withstandeth their forces, without aide
of speare or horse, hauing the wind and sea Captains sent from aboue
to quell the pride of such hereticall enemies of the Gospell" (5:252).
Also of interest is Greene's method. The work consists of twelve
emblems, each bearing a Latin motto and followed by a "glossa."
The technique shows Greene's interest in the allegorical pictorial-
izing of his age and can perhaps be linked to the use of exemplary
characters and situations in his fiction.

Greene returned to more typical concerns in another work of 1589,
Ciceronis Amor. This tale of Cicero in love became his most often
reprinted work (at least nine editions by 1640),[52] despite having
one of his least eventful plots. He abandons the complex action of
Greek romance and Italian novellas prominent in his last several
works and focuses exclusively on the intricacies of love. Cicero,
Lentulus, and Fabius all love Terentia, but Terentia loves only
Cicero; meanwhile Flavia loves Lentulus and Cornelia loves Fabius.
The story moves to the straightening out of these relationships so
that at the end, as in *A Midsummer Night's Dream,* all love is properly
returned. So tangled are matters of love that war breaks out—as
Cicero says, "Beauty is like to bring *Roome* to confusion" (7:214)—
but a meeting of the Senate secures a peaceable conclusion.

That love becomes a political issue requiring public debate indicates its power and importance, perhaps the dominant note of
Ciceronis Amor. Cicero, most fabled of orators, in the end delivers
to the "Conscript Fathers and graue Senators of *Room*" not a speech
on Catiline but such maxims as "the platforme of loue is able to
receiue but one impression" (7:213–14). Earlier, the power of love
is demonstrated in the interpolated tale (based on *Decameron, 5.*1)
of a young man "of clownish capacitie" who comes upon the sleeping
Terentia and gapes in awe. The experience transforms him. Whereas
he had before used "fashions and woordes from a harshe and grose
voyce, resembling rather a bruite beast than a reasonable creature,"
after seeing Terentia he "became verie studious, grew to haue deepe
insight into philosophie, to be skilfull in musicke, to ride a horse

and to be expert in all gentle and manlike actiuitie" (7:185–88). Love fittingly has quasi-religious status among the shepherds, who call a beautiful valley "the vale of Loue" in "perpetuall memorie" of the happy love between Phillis and Coridon (7:177–80).

Love's power also shows itself in the ease with which it overtakes the three main characters. The wisdom reaped by Cicero from his studies pales before love. Lentulus, a brave soldier, willingly re-nounces war (7:115). Love's greatest triumph is Terentia, a vestal virgin for whom "Loues poyson was preuented with an antidote" (7:138). Cupid aims his arrow, but her heart is "of such proofe as the boult rebounded and brake into a thousand shiuers" (7:109). She is an "enemie to his amorous Philosophie" (7:106), her heart, as Venus says, "framed of the purest Diamond, which as it is hard to entertein loue, so it is cleane, fit for the receit of vertue" (7:108). Later, however, when Terentia contemplates what she has heard about Cicero, Cupid shoots a second arrow, "headed with desire, and fethered with conceite," and this time he succeeds (7:157). The celebrant of "the sweete life of virgins" (7:139) joins the others; "yet," she says, "must I loue" (7:158).

Curiously, moral commentary by Greene or the characters them-selves does not accompany these conversions. If love's confusions reflect blinding by passion, if war reveals a destructive element in desire, Greene does not make such dangers explicit. Indeed, he emphasizes the virtuousness of all of the characters. The strength of Cicero's mind allows him to control the expression of his love for Terentia, stoically repelling her advances out of friendship for Lentulus. Lentulus in turn has perfectly honorable intentions, and, when Terentia requests that he drop his suit, he withdraws to private suffering without bitterness toward her. Terentia's virtue is manifest not only in Cupid's difficulties in wounding her but also in her ability to love Cicero even though Lentulus is the better match. Lentulus is blessed with Fortune's gifts, including military glory and great wealth, while Cicero has risen from lowly birth to win honor solely through merit. Thus, when Terentia "yeelds her selfe captiue to the sonne of a poore country villager" (7:190), even her companion vestal virgins "smilde that in forsaking a flower shee light vpon a weede" (7:177). Neither taunts nor advice shake her, however; the "more his fortune," she says, "if it be hee whose vertues hath made . . . master of his owne desires" (7:211). Greene portrays the dilemma facing Terentia in other works, including the story of

Marpesia in *Alcida,* where the right choice is made but the outcome
is disastrous. No comparable irony arises in *Ciceronis Amor.* Terentia's
goodness supports a larger structure in which no character suffers
serious reproach. One of Greene's least ambiguous works results,
apparently secure and unquestioning in its portrayal of human success. As an invincible force, love can lead to strife and sorrow in
even the best of humans, but it also ends strife and brings joy in a
conclusion that knits Rome together in new community; when
Terentia announces before the Senate that "she cannot leaue to loue
and onely to loue *Cicero,*" "the people shouted, none but *Cicero.*
Whereupon before the Senate *Tully* and *Terentia* were betrothed,
Lentulus and *Fabius* made friends, . . . *Lentulus* . . . maried to
Flauia, and *Fabius* wedded to the worthy *Cornelia*" (7:216). As
Lentulus had said, "Ladies beleeue me, Loue is of more force then
warres" (7:127)

Farewell to folly: 1590.   Greene wrote one other work in the
period of frame stories and romances, *Orpharion,* although just when
he wrote it is unclear. He had promised it in "the next tearme" in
the epistle to *Perimedes* (7:9), registered on 29 March 1588, but it
was not registered until 9 February 1590—a delay that Greene
blamed on the printer (12:7). When it appeared Greene had em-
barked on the series of works bidding farewell to treatments of love.
Thus bridging two periods, *Orpharion* looks backward in form, with
two tales set within a framing story. The narrator in the frame
suffers from the "continuall perturbations Fancy affoordes to such
as account beauty the principal end of their affects" (12:9) and
searches for Venus in hope of a cure. Falling asleep when a shepherd
whom he meets plays his pipe, he dreams that he is on Olympus
and hears the gods discussing "what they thinke, or what they haue
heard of womens Loues" (12:21). Orpheus tells the story of Lidia,
a princess so proud that she scorns a man of incredible bravery and
devotion, Acestes, who defeats her father's enemies and lays crowns
at her feet. When he conquers her father in revenge, Lidia pretends
a change of heart in order to trick Acestes into being imprisoned.
She then orders that he be starved to death, a process Greene describes in grotesque detail: "he greedely fed on the flesh on his
armes, spilling the bloode with his own teeth, which before he had
so prisde in many battailes: which when he had done, readie to giue
vp the ghost, seeing the bare bones of his armes, he fell into this
last complaint . . ." (12:61). The scene fits into a series of violent

notes in Orpheus' tale, and torments in the underworld now punish Lidia's pride: she hangs by her hair "in so thicke a smoake and stinking a fog, as no tongue can expresse, nor imagination conceiue it" (12:26). The gods discuss the meaning of the tale when Orpheus concludes, Venus claiming that, "sith [Lidia] was enemy to my loue . . . it rather toucheth *Iuno* or *Diana*" than Venus herself (12:63). A tale told by Arion answers to the point by reversing Orpheus' image of women in the character of Argentina, the devoted wife of the king of Corinth. When Marcion conquers and exiles her husband, he takes her prisoner and courts her "with many faire promises and amorous conceits, but all in vaine" (12:86). Finally she consents, on condition that Marcion fast for three days. He emerges from the fast maddened by hunger, shouting, "thinkst thou . . . that famisht men haue minde on beauty? or is hunger to be satisfied with loue?" (12:91). The experience cures him of lust, and he restores Corinth to Argentina's husband and returns to his own kingdom.

As comments on the nature of women, the two tales point in opposite directions; "these extremes," says Mercury, "infer no certain cōclusions" (12:93). The tales share more than Mercury grants, however, and more than the motif of hunger, for both portray the renunciation of passionate love. Acestes and Marcion, although infatuated with very different women, come to the same insight. In that insight *Orpharion* looks ahead to the works proclaiming Greene's own reformation, works foreshadowed in the frame as well when the narrator, waking from his dream, wakes cured: "I found that either I had lost loue, or loue lost me: for my passions were eased" (12:94). Moreover, Greene coyly signs the end of *Orpharion,* perhaps to suggest that the narrator can be taken as a mask for Greene himself: "I left *Erecinus* and hasted away as fast as I could, glad that one dreame had rid me of fancy, which so long had fettred me, yet could I not hie so fast, but ere I could get home, I was ouertaken with repentance. Robert Greene" (12:94).

One other work of this period has been seen as "a kind of prologue to [Greene's] subsequent ethical pamphlets":[53] *The Royal Exchange,* a translation of Orazio Rinaldi's *Dottrina delle virtù, et fuga de' vittii* (1585). Greene aims at the audience of *The Spanish Masquerado,* addressing the lord mayor, the sheriffs, and the citizens of London in two prefaces celebrating English virtues. Rinaldi's work contains 239 aphorisms, arranged alphabetically in 154 categories; each maxim is a statement fulfilled in four entities or qualities (e.g., "Four things

procure sloth . . ." [7:239]). Although some of the aphorisms are
simply factual, most are moral and many are mildly ironic. Greene
cuts the number of aphorisms overall but adds two of his own, both
of interest. The first, in listing "foure sorts of men [who] must not
be shamefast," includes actors along with "cosoners," flatterers, and
beggars (7:323), a judgment bearing on Greene's attitude toward
the drama; the second lists the four punishments that "follow the
adulterers vice" (7:324), a topic treated several times in works to
come.[54] Greene also adds a paragraph of commentary to most of the
aphorisms, composed mainly of proverbs and classical allusions.
Taken from various sources, these passages are no more original than
other parts of the *Exchange*, and the work as a whole reveals little
about Greene or his interests. It does show him, however, presenting
himself to the public in entirely didactic terms, taking up the role
he would play in the next two years: "heere you may buy obedience
to God, . . . reuerence to Magistrates, fayth to freendes, loue to
our neyghbours, and charitie to the poore" (7:227).

The changed purpose perhaps thus anticipated in *Orpharion* and
the *Exchange* is announced in *Never Too Late* and continued into its
second part, *Francescos Fortunes.* Bound together in the earliest surviving edition of either, the two parts were apparently conceived
together, for the first leaves the main story incomplete. In that
story, Francesco and Isabel fall in love, but Isabel's father objects
to Francesco's lack of wealth and locks her away. She escapes and
elopes with Francesco. Their happy and respectable life in time
induces reconciliation with Isabel's father and all seems well. When
Francesco visits Troynovant on business, however, he falls in love
with the courtesan Infida, who gradually empties his purse. Im-
poverished and thrust out by Infida, Francesco repents of his follies
and resolves to return to Isabel. Here the first part ends. In the
second, Francesco restores his fortunes by writing plays and dem-
onstrates his virtue by rejecting Infida's renewed interest. News of
Isabel's successful defense of her virtue inspires Francesco once again
to remorse, and he finally returns home, where Isabel forgives him.

As discussed in chapter 1, details in Francesco's story may reflect
Greene's own life, and perhaps an autobiographical element explains
the problems of *Never Too Late*. Greene carries the slender story
through two volumes in one of his most obviously pieced together
works, adding bulk with such devices as poems, a list of precepts,
a zodiac of love, a discourse on drama, and the story of an attempted

seduction of Isabel echoing the *Myrrour of Modestie.*[55] *Never Too Late* lacks the consistency of vision found in the *Mourning Garment,* probably the best work of this period. Nothing in it matches the pastoral imagery of the *Mourning Garment,* and the portrayal of the dangers of the world is less coherent. The pilgrim who tells the story of Francesco says, for example, that "women are vniuersally *mala necessaria,* wheresoeuer they be eyther bred or brought vp" (8:27), and that "their generall essence bee all one as comming from *Eua*" (8:24), and yet he describes the peerlessly virtuous Isabel. It is difficult to agree with Collins, in short, that the struggle between "pure love" and "frenzied passion" in *Never Too Late* is "depicted with terrible intensity and vividness" (*PP,* 1:4).

If not among Greene's most impressive works, this "adieu to all amorous Pamphlets" (8:109) does contain one new element: Francesco's story takes place in England (although "for that the Gentleman is yet liuing I will shadowe his name" [8:33]) and has a decidedly unaristocratic flavor.[56] Francesco is "so generally loued of the Citizens, that the richest Marchant or grauest Burghmaster would not refuse to graunt him his daughter" (8:34). Isabel's father reacts as a solid citizen to her failure to find a worthy suitor, speaking more bluntly than Greene's kings and noblemen ever do: "all are but little worth, if they be not welthie" (8:36). Language, too, has changed, with more similes from everyday life, as when Infida, discovering Francesco's poverty, "found that all his corne was on the floore, that his sheepe were clipt, and the Wooll solde" (8:102). Greene uses more graphic detail than in earlier works, some of it quite homely and familiar, as in the description of Isabel's elopement "without hose, onely in her smocke and her peticoate with her fathers hat and an old cloake" (8:53). Such passages occur with a comic effect unusual in Greene when he portrays the love of the boorish and ugly Mullidor for a beautiful shepherdess. Thus does Mullidor's mother misinterpret the symptoms of love, for example: "*Mullidor* fetcht a great sigh, and with that (being after supper) he brake winde; which *Callena* hearing, oh sonne (quoth she) tis the Collick that troubles thee; to bed man, to bed, and wee will haue a warme potled" (8:187). Greene's attempt to adapt style to content, to embody the bourgeois and English orientation of *Never Too Late* in appropriate language, may reflect his sense of audience. He may have recognized an appeal to a new set of readers in his reformation, a possibility that might also explain the greater use of explicitly

Christian language than in previous works (8:144ff., for example).
He had already spoken to citizen readers of moralistic, perhaps
Puritan, bent in *The Spanish Masquerado* and *The Royal Exchange,*
and would certainly attempt to attract them in the coney-catching
pamphlets of the following year. Whether or not with such conscious
intentions, the style in *Never Too Late* represents new departures.
Unenergetic and somewhat shoddily assembled, this "true English
historie" (title page) nevertheless has an innovative and exploratory
dimension.

Between the two parts of *Neuer Too Late* Greene may have written
the work published after his death as *Greenes Vision* (see chapter 1),
devoted entirely to the proclamation of literary reform. After claiming that rumors of his authorship of the scurrilous *Cobbler of Can-
terbury* has induced a crisis of conscience, Greene describes a dream
of Gower and Chaucer debating literary morality, each telling a tale
to illustrate ways of instructing an audience in virtue. Perhaps the
most interesting element is Chaucer's defense of Greene's earlier
works: he does not celebrate the pleasures of romance but asserts
didactic content in Greene's tales of love. "Hath he not discouered
in his workes," Chaucer asks, "the follies of loue, the sleights of
fancy, and lightnesse of youth . . . ?" (12:219). He quotes twenty
sentences from Greene that are "worthie graue ears, and necessarye
for young mindes" (12:221–23). Gower's contrary argument anticipates many later critics in charging that profit is a mere excuse for
pleasure in Greene, since "the lightnesse of the conceit cracks halfe
the credite, and the vanitie of the pen breeds the lesse beleefe"
(12:220). How accurately either view reflects Greene's real sense of
his own earlier purposes cannot be gauged, nor, perhaps, need be,
since explicit didactic intention may determine aspects of Greene's
works but hardly their whole content. Nor does Greene's seriousness
in giving the victory to Gower and declaring revulsion from his
"sundrie bookes in print of loue" (12:212) matter for approaching
the earlier works. Perhaps the best commentary on the *Vision* as a
review of Greene's career is the fact that the *Farewell to Folly,* soon
published as further evidence of reformation, had probably been
written several years before.

Although the epistles to the *Farewell,* as noted in chapter 1 (where
its date is discussed), go further than others of this period in re-
gretting Greene's "forepassed youth" (9:229), the *Farewell* itself
resembles such earlier works as *Planetomachia* and *Penelopes Web* in

form and content. Greene tells three stories, framed by discussion at the farm of Farneze, a nobleman who flees Florence to avoid "the mutinous factions of the Guelphes and Ghibellines" (9:235–36). Florence lies in moral and social collapse. Schism infects the church, the "trafficke of merchants" has given way to war, and the senators have exchanged robes for armor. Farneze and his wife, their three daughters, and four young men escape to create a miniature society set against a world in which "the nobilitie with ambition and the commons with enuie, so dissented in their seuerall thoughts, that the particular ruine of the Citie, and the generall subuersion of the weale publique was daily expected." The Florentine strife thus does more than get a noble company into leisured isolation for the telling of stories, for it provides an image of society dominated by the vices illustrated in the stories. The company has come to the country as an act of renunciation. Although beautiful, the farm is "by scituation melancholie, . . . fitter for one giuen to metaphusical contemplation than for such yong Gentlemen, as desired sooner to daunce with *Venus,* than to dreame with *Saturne*" (9:237), and Farnese defines it as a place where his guests may "refine . . . senses dulled with the tast of sundrie vaine obiects" (9:238). Indeed, the conversation begins with a discussion of the value of a memento mori occasioned by "a ring with a deaths head ingrauen" (9:239).

The tone of the conversation, devoted to pride, lust, and gluttony as kinds of folly, follows from this beginning.[57] All three discussions emphasize the universality of sin. Pride, for example, is "naturally inserted into the minde of man" (9:245) and infects "souldiours, schollers and courtiers" and "all other estates whatsoeuer" (9:254). The stories illustrate such statements, and they share a somber element consistent with the contemplative spirit of the frame. In the first a tyrannical king cannot renounce pride after his overthrow; in the second Semiramis avenges her husband's death by having the lustful Ninus executed after she becomes queen; in the third a duke hangs himself after being dragged while drunk onto a scaffold, "all besmeared in his owne vomite" (9:346). The stories are among Greene's most effective, and all deserve a closer reading than space here permits. In particular, the first of the three is significant in its portrayal of Maesia's adoption of humble life; one of the most interesting of Greene's emblematic pastoral heroines, Maesia, like Sephestia in *Menaphon,* transforms "hir thoughtes with hir apparell" (9:265). Her song—*"Sweet are the thoughts that sauour of content"*—

is among Greene's best-known poems, and it ends with a summary of pastoral symbolism: *"Obscured life sets downe a type of blis, / a minde content both crowne and kingdome is"* (9:279–80). Beneath such motifs, however, remains the melancholy element of the three stories. Maesia's song, for example, is overheard by an exiled king who entirely rejects its implications and stalks off "in a melancholy furie" to nurse his "peruerse stomacke" (9:284). All the stories culminate in punishment, not repentance, and show a certain coldness in their view of human affairs. Whether seen in terms of Greene's claimed new purpose of 1590 or set back with the earlier works, the stories of the *Farewell* are like the "image of death figured" in the ring in the framing narrative, which "should be a glasse whereby to direct . . . actions"; even "the pagans . . . vsed the picture of death as a restraint to all forward follies" (9:240).

    Coney-catching and repentance: 1591–92. When Greene promised to write only for moral edification in the works of 1590, he may or may not have had in mind the coney-catching pamphlets to which he next turned. The pamphlets proclaim moral purpose, of course, but they hardly fulfill Solomon's charge at the end of the *Vision* that Greene "abiure all other studies" and "onely giue [himself] to Theologie" (12:279). Indeed, *The Defence of Conny Catching* mocks Greene for trifling with the exposure of crime when he could instead write of high matters —"either Philosophically to haue shewen how you were proficient in *Cambridge,* or diuinely to haue manifested your religion to the world" (11:49). If *A Notable Discovery of Coosnage* was not intended by Greene as the fruit of literary reform but simply another idea to develop before going forward, its several sequels may represent his response to a demand which he had not anticipated but was willing to satisfy. Such a sequence of events would explain the fact that *The Second Part of Conny-catching* bears signs of hasty assembly and is generally a less interesting work than its predecessor. Greene gives a shortened version of the card game that occupies half of the first pamphlet and brief descriptions of six new crimes, including horse-stealing, shoplifting, and lock-picking. The several illustrative stories are rather mechanical accounts of particular tricks. Greene uses again the various devices for establishing authenticity, referring to himself even more often in claiming knowledge of criminals and victims (e.g., 10:114, 129) and in describing the effects of the first work on its readers (e.g., 10:70, 95). Such passages enliven the *Second Part,* a brisk and appealing work that effectively gives the impression of direct observation, but from it emerges no coherent attitude toward society or the relation between those who revolt against authority and those who do not.

The Thirde and Last Part of Conny-catching moves still farther away from the original inspiration of the *Discovery,* for a framing device entirely removes Greene from the body of the work. That is, he claims to have met an officer of the law whose "notes of notorious matters" have ended up in his hands and "are in our booke compiled together" (10:144–45). The device relieves Greene of the need to account for his sources, to claim acquaintance with coney-catchers, or to keep up the pretense, if pretense it had been, of threats against him. Moreover, since the Gentleman "in seuerall papers sent the notes" (10:145), no need for unity in topic or approach exists. The *Thirde Part* is simply an anthology of ten tales of deceit. Each has its own title, and Greene includes no transitions and adds no conclusion, defining the nature of the work in the opening sentences of the first tale: "What lawes are vsed among this hellish crew, what words and termes they giue themselues and their copesmates, are at large set downe in the former two bookes: let it suffise yee then in this, to read the simple true discourses of suche as haue by extraordinarie cunning and trecherie been deceiued" (10:146). Something like picaresque fiction results, the more so in that Greene's rogues go unpunished in all but one of the ten tales. Deprived of the perspective provided by Greene's voice in the first two pamphlets, the tales suggest also the moral ambiguity of Jonson's *The Alchemist.* Jonson knew the pamphlets, drawing on them in *Bartholomew Faire,*[58] and Greene shows something of Jonson's love of circumstantial detail. He describes the strollers in St. Paul's and the crowd at the Red Bull theater; children are taken for a walk in Finsbury Fields and a ballad-monger attracts an audience in Gracious Street; drinking customs are strictly observed and linens are treasured among the costly commodities of the age. Such details make the *Thirde Part* a readable portrayal, if not a compelling analysis, of Elizabethan life. The least complex of the three parts as a literary work, it is perhaps the most accessible to modern readers.

The next work in the series is considerably more impressive, as Greene returns to the concerns of the *Discovery* in *A Disputation between a Hee Conny-catcher, and a Shee Conny-catcher.* The role of prostitutes in the art of cross-biting moves to the center as Nan and Lawrence, a prostitute and a cut-purse, wager a dinner on "whether

whores or theeues are most preiuditiall to the Commonwealth"
(10:230). Lawrence ends up buying the dinner: "thou hast tolde
mee such wonderous villanies, as I thought neuer could haue been
in women" (10:235). The second half of the *Disputation* presents
"The conuersion of an English Courtizan," a first-person tale of sin and
repentance. The two halves exist in direct and obvious contrast to
each other, but both are devoted to the portrayal of human weakness.

Nan wins the debate in the first half for two reasons. She dem-
onstrates that women cut purses as resourcefully as men, and she
shows that women have a power for evil that men lack: sexual
attraction. Her winning the admiration of the hardened, cynical
Lawrence is grimly humorous, as is her contempt for the world that
she dupes.[59] Despite her good-natured banter with Lawrence, Nan
is at heart cold and passionless. She can play any role, takes more
pride in wit than in beauty, and is frankly above faithfulness to her
husband ("hee knowes it, and is content lyke an honest simple
suffragen" [10:232]). Hers is, in short, the ideal mentality for
exploiting the weaknesses of others; if, she says, a merchant's son
"fall into the companie of a whoore, shee flatters him, shee inueagles
him, shee bewitcheth him, that hee spareth neither goods nor landes
to content her, that is onely in loue with his coyne" (10:231).
Greene has told the tale before, but he tells it this time from the
opposite point of view, as though recasting the *Mourning Garment*
and *Never Too Late:* "if he be married, hee forsakes his wife, leaues
his children, despiseth his friendes, onely to satisfie his lust with
the loue of a base whoore, who when he hath spent all vpon her
and bee brought to beggerie, beateth him out lyke the Prodigall
childe" (10:231). Trading with zest in human frailty, Nan boasts
of how "you men theeues touch the bodie and wealth, but we ruine
the soule" (10:235). She glorifies herself as a Shoreditch temptress
whose sexual power is both irresistible and fatal: *"Lawrence, Lawrence,*
if Concubines could inueagle *Salomon,* if *Dalilah* could betraie *Samp-
son,* then wonder not if we more nice in our wickednes then a
thousand such *Delilahs,* can seduce poore young Nouices to their
vtter destructions" (10:233).

The image of frailty is reversed in the second half of the *Disputation*
in the autobiography of the English courtesan, who, before her
reformation, fell victim to the sexual energies that Nan exploits.
Spoiled as a child, the courtesan at "thirteene yeere old," she says,
"feeling the rayne of liberty loose on myne owne necke, began with

the wanton Heyfer, to ayme at mine own wil" (10:240). The comparison suggests the growth of natural instincts, and the girl was also "an vnbridled Colte" (10:240) and a blossom "ready to fall from the Tree" (10:241). Eventually, she says, a "shifting companion" "cropt the flower of my virginity," satisfying "the sweet of mine owne wanton desires" (10:247); afterwards "he could not desire so much as I did grant" (10:250). Appetite thus unleashed, she left her lover for a second and then a third, placing her "delight, in nothing more then the desire of new choyce" (10:253). Eventually she came to a "Trugging house" in London, where, she says, "I gaue my selfe to entertaine al companions, sitting or standing at the doore like a staule" (10:268).

It is a sordid tale, and not without a prurient side, but it broadens to include both sexes in the image of human frailty in Nan's debate with Lawrence. It also broadens the grounds for human sympathy. The courtesan has reformed, inspired by a young man "modest and honest" who "greeued that . . . such rare wit and excellent bewtie, was blemisht with whoredomes base deformitie" (10:271). The young man, however sentimental his portrait, embodies a capacity to accept human nature and to forgive, also illustrated in an interpolated tale in which a man who discovers his wife's infidelity with his most trusted friend resolves not to seek revenge but to "reclaime his wife, and keep his friend" (10:260).[60] Significantly, the English courtesan's redeemer, now her husband, is a clothier, to be balanced against the many tradesmen whose blindness Nan and Lawrence mock. The contrast forms but one element in the larger interplay between halves. The sympathy given to the courtesan, and, more broadly, to women's sexual appetite—rare enough in Elizabethan literature—alters the effect of Nan's flippant certainties, setting the Disputation among Greene's more complex and substantial works.

Coney-catching pamphlets received most, but not all, of Greene's attention in late 1591 and early 1592. In February he wrote two brief prefaces for Lodge's *Euphues Shadowe* while Lodge was on a voyage. Two months before, *A Maidens Dreame* had been registered, the only poem that Greene published outside the confines of one of the prose works. An elegy for the death of Sir Christopher Hatton, *A Maidens Dreame* is an undistinguished dream-vision in which such allegorical abstractions as Justice, Prudence, and Fortitude appear as mourners. The poem ends with the flight of Hatton's soul from his "liuelesse bodie" and a plea by Astraea to rejoice, since "soules in heauen are placed by their deeds" (14:316–17). The pictorial quality of the poem, with the various abstractions presented as emblems, shows again Greene's interest in visual symbolism. Otherwise, *A Maidens Dreame* bears little relation to Greene's other works. An obvious attempt to win the favor of the dedicatee, whose family, like Greene's, came from Norfolk,[61] the poem reveals nothing of Greene's attitude toward the political and social issues at which it glances, although the fact that he wrote about Hatton at all is perhaps further evidence, along with works like *The Spanish Masquerado,* that Greene was not untouched by such issues.

Another diversion from coney-catching pamphlets was *Philomela*. Greene claims to have written this work "long since" and resurrected it to present to the wife of the man who had accepted the dedication to *Euphues Shadowe,* subtitling it *The Lady Fitzwaters Nightingale* in her honor (11:109–10). The claim may be genuine, for *Philomela* resembles several of Greene's earlier works: it uses motifs from Greek romance and it celebrates feminine virtue, portraying a heroine who, like Susanna and Pandosto's queen, is unjustly accused of adultery. Greene's treatment of the invincibly high-minded Philomela, divorced and exiled by her deluded husband, made *Philomela* one of Greene's most admired works in the nineteenth century. For John Colin Dunlop in 1816, for example, "the character of Philomela is so exquisitely drawn, with so many attractions of saint-like purity, that the fancy which portrayed it, must have been at times illuminated by the most tender and sublime conceptions."[62] Twentieth-century readers will perhaps be more taken with Greene's portrayal of Philippo, Philomela's husband, an emblematic figure of obsessive jealousy presented with great force and consistency.

Throughout the first half of the work Philippo urges his closest friend, Lutesio, to test Philomela by attempting to seduce her. When Lutesio fails, Philippo remains unsatisfied. He begins to doubt Lutesio himself, and suspicion grows to full-scale delusion. Spying on Lutesio and his wife, Philippo looks through a keyhole to see them "standing at a bay windowe, hand in hand, talking verye familiarlye: which sight strooke such a suspitious furye into his head, that he was halfe frantick" (10:156–57). Philippo is reminiscent here of Leontes in Shakespeare's *Winter's Tale,* based on Greene's own Pandosto, and, in misinterpreting what he sees, he also resembles Othello. Other similarities to *Othello* exist. Like the play, *Philomela* is set in Venice, and Greene's hero is as subject to fits of savage brutality as is Shakespeare's: "But *Philippo,* as if he had participated his nature with the bloudthirstie Caniball, or eaten of the seathin root, that maketh a man to be as cruell in heart as it is hard in the rynde, stept to her, & casting her backward, bad her arise strumpet" (10:163). When he knows the truth, Philippo, like Othello recalling his punishment of the malignant and turbaned traducer of the state, pleads, "I craue my selfe iustice against my selfe" (10:190), and Philomela eventually forgives him because he loved her not wisely, but too well: *"Philippo* did not woorke thee this wrong because he loued some other," she tells herself, "but because he ouerloued thee" (10:198).

The parallels to *Othello* by themselves make no case that Shake-speare knew *Philomela,* but they help suggest the power of Greene's portrayal. Philippo's character is perhaps best revealed when his suspicions finally come to dominate his mind and he reveals them to Philomela. The two are in bed, and Philomela "started, being new quickned with childe, & feeling the vnperfect infant stirre." Philippo asks the cause, and Philomela, "ready to weepe for Ioy," explains:

shee taking his hand laying it on her side, said: feele my Lorde, you may perceiue it mooue: with that it leapt against his hand. When she creeping into his bosome, began amorouslye to kisse him and commend him: that though for the space of fower yeeres that they had been married she had had no childe, yet at last hee had plaied the mans parte, and gotten her a boy. This toucht *Philippo* at the quicke, and doubled the flame of his Ielousie, that as a man halfe lunaticke he lept out of the bed, and drawing his rapier, began thus to mannace poore *Philomela.* (10:157–58)

This remarkable scene enlarges the emblematic content of Philippo's character by defining his madness as a horrifying revulsion from normal life. Moreover, the psychological element epitomizes much of *Philomela* as a whole. Philippo's madness destroys institutions by assaulting the human feelings on which they rest. Thus, after bribing two slaves to testify falsely, he divorces his wife and exiles his friend. And when he knows the truth he cannot escape his obsessive temperament, paying for gnawing jealousy with "the knawing worme of a guiltye conscience" (10:193). At the mercy of successive waves of passion, Philippo claims to have killed a prince in order that execution may end his despair, the nature of his pretended crime symbolizing the destruction of institutions which he has caused.

Philomela, having learned that he has repented, tries to save him by stepping forward to claim that she killed the prince. As it turns out, both are proved innocent, but no reconciliation takes place, for Philippo faints immediately, the victim of one last passion: *"Philippo* in a sound betweene greefe and ioy was carried away halfe dead to his lodging: where he had not lyen two houres, but in an extasie he ended his life" (10:203). Philomela returns to Venice, where she lives a "desolate widdow" (10:204), and Lutesio does not reappear. There is no recovery from the scene in the bedroom.

With *A Quip for an Upstart Courtier,* registered three weeks after *Philomela,* Greene again wrote directly of the world around him, turning into prose and augmenting a satirical poem of the 1540s by one F. T., *The Debate between Pride and Lowliness.*[63] The narrator dreams of a pair of cloth breeches and a pair of velvet breeches, walking and talking by their own power and symbolizing, respectively, old values and new fashions. They debate which is "most antient and most worthy" (11:228), and a jury to decide the issue is selected from passersby on the road. Each of the dozens of prospective jurors who are interviewed represents some particular status, occupation, or guild. In the end the verdict goes to Cloth Breeches as "most worthy to bee rightly resident, & haue seison in Frank tenement heere in England" (11:294). Greene apparently did not find the old poem out of date; as quotations from the *Quip* in chapter 1 above indicate, it allowed him to comment on prodigality, social pretensions, and other current issues. The attack on the Harveys contained in the first printing is quite consistent with the *Quip* as a whole. Its contemporary flavor, moreover, links the work to the coney-catching pamphlets. Like them, the *Quip* is partly an exposé, subjecting sharp practice and shoddy workmanship to satirical scrutiny. Cloth Breeches says to the skinner, to take one of innumerable examples, "if you haue some fantastike skin brought you not worth two pence, with some strange spottes, though it bee of a libbet, you will sweare tis a most pretious skin, and came from *Musco* or the farthest parts of *Calabria*" (11:269–70).

Much of the *Quip* is given over to such homely concerns, although attention also goes to lawyers and clergy and the like, and the language is appropriately slangy and direct, with a liveliness and bluntness reminiscent of Nashe.[64] The language helps make the *Quip* an authentically humorous work. Beyond its sprightly attack on particular abuses, the *Quip* is a debate over values, posing old against new in a struggle given large implications in statements such as Cloth Breeches's claim to "belong to the old and auncient yeomanry, yea and Gentility, the fathers," while Velvet Breeches belongs "to a company of proud and vnmannerly vpstarts the sonnes" (11:223). The class reference summarizes the national focus of the *Quip* as a portrait of traditions dying under a spreading blight of selfishness and deceit. The psychological overtone of Cloth Breeches's image of fathers and sons is also striking, especially in view of Greene's life and his other works. Interesting in its own right, the condemnation of excess and self-indulgence in the *Quip* thus also brings together a number of motifs important in the works of this period.

Either the *Quip* or the *Disputation* was the last work that Greene certainly completed. One other was published before his death, but as he says in its preface, he had intended it as part of a larger project. Illness preventing the completion of the *"Blacke Booke"* (11:6), Greene published *The Blacke Bookes Messenger,* entered in the Stationers' Register less than two weeks before he died. In it he returns to coney-catching, telling the story of Ned Browne, "a man infamous for his bad course of life and well knowne about *London"* (11:6). Browne speaks in the first person; "imagine you now see him," says Greene, "standing in a great bay windowe with a halter about his necke ready to be hanged, desperately pronouncing this his whole course of life" (11:6). The autobiography thus delivered had been intended for pairing with "a pithy discourse of the Repentance of a Conny-catcher lately executed out of Newgate" (11:5) in a structure apparently modeled after the *Disputation,* and Browne begins with the boasting and defiance of the debate between Nan and Lawrence: "as I haue euer liued lewdly, so I meane to end my life as resolutely" (11:9). His tone would have been balanced by a second part showing, like the story of the English courtesan, how "through the woonderfull working of Gods spirite," a coney-catcher "repented him from the bottome of his hart" (11:6).

The balancing of halves as originally conceived would presumably have produced the moral tension of the *Disputation.* Standing by itself, Browne's story conveys something of that tension on a lesser scale, for Browne does not in fact maintain his pose of defiance until the end. He begins by offering "the manner and methode" of his "knaueries" as a subject fit for laughter (11:9), and humor indeed arises from the exploits that he relates: one, for example, is built around a chamberpot and involves more graphic detail than is usual in Greene (11:32–33). In boasting of his friends' cleverness Browne describes a Jonsonian gallery of quacks who sell love powders, poisons, and shares in the finding of the philosophers' stone; one offers a "Letter full of Needles, which shall bee laide after such a Mathematicall order, that when hee opens it to whome it is sent, they shall all springe vp and flye into his body" (11:28). Browne trades wives with a fellow rogue and devises new words to *"Crosbite the old Phrases vsed in the manner of Conny-catching"* (11:7). The exuberance of Browne's career is heightened, moreover, by the sober stupidity of his victims, including a pompous maltman ("This Senex Fornicator, this olde Letcher" [11:21]) and "a fat Priest that had hanging at his saddle bow a capcase well stuft with Crowns" (11:18).

Browne's promotion of himself as appealing antihero, however, finally crumbles. "Better is it," he says in the end, "to be a poore honest man, than a rich & wealthy theefe," and his last words include such precepts as "trust not in your owne wits," "Beware of whores," and "scorne not labor" (11:35). Greene sets conflicting elements side by side in this final scene. On the one hand, Browne begs mercy for his "manifolde offences": "and so Lord into thy hands I commit my spirit" (11:36). On the other, Greene says, "thus this *Ned Brown* died miserably, that all his life had been full of mischiefe and villainy, sleightly at his death regarding the state of his soule" (11:36). The work ends with the grim image, countering the earlier humor, of "rauenous Wolues" that dig up Browne's grave and devour his corpse (11:36).

It is tempting to relate the ambiguity at the end of the *Messenger* to the debate over Greene that followed his death. Even in view of the posthumous repentance pamphlets, however, such a link is needlessly melodramatic. It is enough that this last of the works published before his death ends with the tension and complexity that mark Greene's best prose works. The emblematic method first used in *Mamillia,* the dependence on type-figures and conventional situations, did not lead Greene to the reduction of life to inherited formulas. Rather it led to the dramatization of the interplay of conflicting attitudes and the difficulties of describing human experience. Moreover, that the conflict at the end of the *Messenger* poses repentance against defiance makes it doubly appropriate, for Greene thus ended his career with a version of the split in human nature between reason and emotion that many of his works explore.

For all the differences in language and subject, the struggle in Ned Browne is not so far removed from Pharicles' description of two kinds of love in *Mamillia* a decade before.

Chapter Three
Greene's Plays

As discussed in chapter 1, Greene's dramatic career involves a number of unanswered questions, and his plays cannot be set in order with his prose works and surveyed for evidence of literary development. The dates of the plays are uncertain, and, indeed, the canon itself remains a matter of debate. Nevertheless, Greene's achievement in drama can be described on the basis of the plays universally recognized as his. Such a description is the purpose of this chapter, and the many plays doubtfully assigned to Greene will be ignored (see the bibliography for commentary on the authorship of some of them). Five plays make up the accepted canon: *Alphonsus, Orlando Furioso, A Looking Glasse for London and England, Friar Bacon and Friar Bungay,* and *James IV.*

The last two of these works, *Friar Bacon* and *James IV,* are Greene's best plays, and on them his reputation as a dramatist largely rests. Their connection to Shakespeare's comedies has heightened interest in them, moreover, with a great deal of attention going to Greene's use of such "Shakespearean" elements as pastoral atmosphere and idealized heroines; Greene "wrote two plays," says Thomas Marc Parrott, "each of which plants something new and fragrant in the pleasant garden of Elizabethan comedy."[1] The attention is by no means misdirected, for numerous parallels in plot and character certainly exist. At the same time, deeper and more subtle parallels in structure and meaning also exist. Greene shares with Shakespeare what Norman Sanders calls "a fundamental kinship or sympathy in comic view,"[2] and estimating both Greene's influence and his own achievement requires a broader analysis than his plays have generally received. Indeed, focus on motifs of romantic comedy has perhaps distracted attention from some of Greene's contributions to the drama. He has traditionally been placed among the "University Wits," young men in London writing the plays that set Elizabethan drama on its course.[3] Because the concept of the University Wits assumes that a native dramatic tradition somehow needed the inspirations of classical education in order to become a genuinely

Renaissance phenomenon, it has proved less useful to dramatic criticism in recent years than in the past, when less emphasis was placed
on the medieval inheritance of Elizabethan playwrights. Still, the
innovations of the writers of Greene's generation undeniably mark
a beginning. What Lyly, Marlowe, and the others wrote for the
stage had lasting effects, and Greene must be granted his place
among these writers. He too shows a greater complexity of structure,
a wider range of characters, and a larger capacity for tension and
ambiguity than can be found in earlier English drama.

In *James IV* and *Friar Bacon,* moreover, Greene did more than
help establish a polished and appealing comic form, for he also
helped make that form a vehicle for expressing ideas and attitudes.
His plays tend to be unified by the implications of the situations
that they portray. Perhaps paradoxically, the use of motifs of older
drama partly explains this quality: Greene's plays often recall mor-
alities in juxtaposing images of vice and virtue and in portraying a
central character's moral growth. As Werner Habicht has said, "there
would be more justification in describing Greene's plays . . . as a
climax in the development of the interlude than as prototypes of a
'new' kind of drama."[4] Greene's experience in prose fiction led in
much the same direction, for the plays, like the prose works, have
emblematic elements.[5] The relation of concrete to abstract can lead
to comparable complexity, and many of the same questions about
the nature of experience arise. Greene's plays, in short, offer more
than motifs which Shakespeare would treat with mastery. They repay
attention whether considered for their own sake or as stages in the
development of Elizabethan drama.

Alphonsus, King of Aragon

Alphonsus, King of Aragon is often regarded as Greene's first play,
with the case for an early date resting mainly on two factors: general
awkwardness and heavy-handed imitation of Marlowe's *Tamburlaine.*
The first point has aroused little opposition (nor will it here), and
the second is obvious enough. Like "mightie *Tamberlaine,*" as he is
referred to in the play itself (l. 1444), Alphonsus rises "from the
pit of pilgrimes pouertie / . . . / Vnto the toppe of friendly Fortunes
wheel" (ll. 352–54), fulfilling the potentialities of his heroic self,
not his station. In the process he borrows many of Tamburlaine's
characteristic mannerisms.[6] His courtship of Iphigina, for example,

echoes Tamburlaine's hyperbolical celebrations of Zenocrate's beauty
(ll. 1609–20), and, like Tamburlaine refusing to spare the virgins
of Damascus, Alphonsus refuses to recall a vow and relent to Iphigina's pleas for her father (ll. 1727–32). He shows Tamburlaine's
generosity toward subordinates, dramatically crowning them kings
of the realms he has won (ll. 719ff.), and he shows his brutal
symbolism in treating conquered enemies: *"Enter Alphonsus, with
a Canapie carried over him by three Lords, having over each corner a Kings
head, crowned"* (l. 1453). Behind such actions lies a defiance of the
gods as bold as Tamburlaine's, if not always as eloquently expressed:

> And as for *Mars* whom you do say will change,
> He moping sits behind the kitchen doore,
> Prest at command of euery Skullians mouth,
> Who dare not stir, nor once to moue a whit,
> For fear *Alphonsus* then should stomack it.
>
> (ll. 1483–87)

Imitation of Marlowe makes *Alphonsus* Greene's least characteristic
play, and criticism has tended to stress the disparity between Marlowe's style and Greene's temperament. Yet the play overall is less
"Marlovian" than the parallels to *Tamburlaine* suggest. Only in
specific instances does Greene attempt Marlowe's rhetorical effects,
and *Alphonsus* is less sensational, less exciting, less awe-inspiring.
Partly the scaling down simply reflects Greene's limitations as an
imitator of Marlowe, but it may also result from his seeing in
Tamburlaine not only a new kind of play but a reworking of an old
kind: the chivalric romance.[7] Venus strikes a chivalric note in her
lament in the prologue for a time when

> . . . euery coward that durst crack a speare,
> And Tilt and Turney for his Ladies sake,
> Was painted out in colours of such price
> As might become the proudest Potentate.
>
> (ll. 7–10)

Venus' promise of "doughtie deeds and valiant victories" (l. 40)
recalls plays like *Clyomon and Clamydes,* not *Tamburlaine,* as do the
sing-song cadence, stock phrases, and archaic diction of her description of Alphonsus going off to battle:

> He is transformed into a souldier's life,
> And marcheth in the Ensigne of the King
> Of worthy *Naples,* which *Belinus* hight;
> Not for because that he doth loue him so,
> But that he may reuenge him on his foe.
> Now on the toppe of lustie barbed steed
> He mounted is, in glittering Armour clad.
>   (ll. 356–62)

The characters often address each other in the high-flown terms of
knightly adventure: "Presume not, villaine, further for to go," says
Albinius, "Vnles you do at length the same repent" (ll. 176–77).
The old-fashioned chivalric element in language is matched by summarizing prologues to each act, a descent of Venus (resembling that
of Providence in *Clyomon and Clamydes*),[8] a brazen head through
which Mohamet speaks, and assorted dreams, spirits, and prophecies. Such devices contribute to a sense of high heroics and magical
events that seem to bear only dim relation to the daring Marlovi-
anism of other features of the play.

   More than a matter of influences to be traced, this contrast between chivalric and Marlovian notes reflects a fundamental division
in Greene's conception of his hero, a division with ethical implications. Chivalry dominates the opening of the play and serves to
define Alphonsus in purely sympathetic terms as an avenger of
wrongs done to his father, Carinus, whose throne has been usurped
years before. Alphonsus sets out to regain his birthright, pledging
his sword to his "iust attempt" (l. 152). Learning that Belinus,
king of Naples, is gathering troops to repel an invasion by Flaminius,
the usurper he has sworn to defeat, Alphonsus conceals his identity
in order to enlist—on condition that he can keep anything he wins,
"although it be the Crowne of *Aragon*" (l. 345). He slays Flaminius
in hand-to-hand combat and claims his right. It is "the iust reuenge
of mighty *Ioue*" (l. 389), and Alphonsus thus appears as an unknown
knight-at-arms who defeats the wicked. Set on the side of right by
his archetypal role, Alphonsus presents an image permitting no
serious ethical examination.

   Just at this point, however, the mood of the play shifts, with
the imitation of Marlowe overtaking the echoing of chivalric romance. When Belinus grants Alphonsus's request for Flaminius's
crown, Alphonsus exacts a pledge of honors due and then suddenly

demands submission: "come yeeld thy Crowne to me, / And do me homage, or by heauens I sweare / Ile force thee to it maugre all thy traine" (ll. 487–89). It is the first truly Marlovian note in the play, and the action from this point on follows *Tamburlaine* more closely: Alphonsus defeats Belinus, who flees to the Great Turk for help, and he then defeats the Turk and his allies, becoming the greatest ruler of the world and winning the hand of the Turkish princess. Here too begin the borrowings from Marlowe's language, particularly in Alphonsus's boasting speeches of lyrical self-display; as he says to Belinus, for example, "My deeds shall make my glory for to shine / As cleare as *Luna* in a winters night" (ll. 497–98). The emergence of Alphonsus's rebellious individualism complicates the response of the audience, making impossible the simple certainties of chivalric romance. Once Flaminius is killed, Alphonsus's claim to admiration rests not on the justness of his cause but on his self-defined fitness for glory.

The doubleness of Greene's definition of his hero is reflected as well in Greene's treatment of Fortune. On the one hand, Alphonsus defies Fortune, claiming to "clap vp *Fortune* in a cage of golde, / To make her turne her wheele as I thinke best" (ll. 1481–82). On the other hand, the defeated duke of Milan, dressed as a pilgrim, delivers a conventional speech on "the chance of fickle Fortunes wheele":

> I, which erewhile did daine for to possesse
> The proudest pallace of the westerne world,
> Would now be glad a cottage for to finde
> To hide my head; so Fortune hath assignde.
> (ll. 1270–75)

Moments later he meets Carinus, himself reduced by Fortune years before and able, in the opening scene of the play, to lecture his son Alphonsus on patience in adversity with a speech echoing many of Greene's prose works: "Bridle these thoughts, and learne the same of me,— / A quiet life doth passe an Emperie" (ll. 145–46). These competing attitudes toward Fortune are not reconciled in the play. Indeed, in the first scene, when Alphonsus answers the plea for resignation with insistence on revenge, Carinus blandly approves, hoping that Alphonsus will return "with such a traine as *Iulius*

Caesar came / To noble *Rome,* when as he had atchieu'd / The mightie
Monarch of the triple world" (ll. 164–66). Even more confusing is
the outcome of the meeting between Carinus and the duke of Milan.
Given the sentiments that both have expressed and the rural setting
in which they find themselves, a reconciliation of these two exiles
might be expected. Instead, the duke expresses continuing hatred,
and Carinus reveals his identity and stabs him. He then leaves his
exile for Naples "to see if *Fortune* will so fauour me / To view
Alphonsus in his happie state" (ll. 1349–50).

Both of these scenes involving Carinus contain a shocking element
that resembles the effect Marlowe achieves in having Tamburlaine
dramatically cast aside his shepherd's gown. They suggest that Greene
recognized the audacity of Tamburlaine's assault on convention.
Still, Greene's hero, unlike Marlowe's, is royal by birth, a fact that
contains and qualifies the excitement of his winning crowns. At
least one critic has accordingly suggested that *Alphonsus* is an attack
on *Tamburlaine,* designed to counter Marlovian rebelliousness with
an affirmation of traditional values.[9] Certainly the case can be made,
for at the center of the play lie competing definitions of what its
hero represents. The tension that results links *Alphonsus,* however
crude its dramaturgy and its verse, to Greene's prose works and
their concern for the implications of events. Its capacity for emblematic action is perhaps summarized when Carinus slays the duke
of Milan, violating not only his earlier speech to Alphonsus but also
the attitudes inherent in the emblem that he presents as an exiled
king.

Also characteristic of Greene is the attempt to unify the plot of
Alphonsus. Tamburlaine is held together by the dynamic personality
of its hero, revealed in successively grander episodes of conquest.
Greene appears to strive for a more complex dramatic pattern, as
seen in his use of Venus and the Muses as prologue, chorus, and
epilogue. The presence of Venus in a tale of war is of course incon-
gruous at the start, as she herself admits in a passage that has
sometimes been seen in relation to Greene's own movement from
fiction to drama:

> I, which was wont to follow *Cupids* games
> Will put in vre *Mineruaes* sacred Art;
> And this my hand, which vsed for to pen

> The praise of loue and *Cupids* peerles power,
> Will now begin to treat of bloudie *Mars*.
>
> (ll. 35–39)

Why Venus should want to present a tale of war is a mystery to which an answer gradually emerges: by the end of the play she has replaced Mars as the guiding force in Alphonsus's life. Her elevation begins in act 3, when Amurack, the Great Turk, considers battle on the side of Alphonsus's enemies, and his wife, Fausta, seeks to learn the future from a sorceress. The sorceress arranges for Amurack to have a prophetic dream and, as he babbles out his vision while sleeping, Fausta and her daughter, Iphigina, learn among other matters that Iphigina will marry Alphonsus. They object violently, and Amurack banishes them. Fausta gathers "all the armie of *Amazones*" and enters the war (l. 948). Obstacles to the fulfillment of the prophecy increase when Alphonsus and Iphigina meet on the battlefield. Alphonsus refuses to fight, informing Iphigina (and, for the first time, the audience) that he loves her: "loue, sweete mouse, hath so benumbed my wit, / That though I would, I must refraine" (ll. 1598–99). The scorn with which Iphigina answers raises explicitly the role of Venus in the play: "Your noble acts were fitter to be writ / Within the Tables of dame *Venus* son, / Then in God *Mars* his warlike registers" (ll. 1601–3). Alphonsus offers kingdoms and riches, Iphigina rebuffs him again, and he vows in anger that he will defeat her in battle and that, if she will not be a bride, she will "serue high *Alphonsus* as a concubine" (l. 1631).

So matters stand until, in the last scene, Alphonsus leads in the captured Amurack with Fausta and Iphigina. Contemptuously refused when he hints of marriage in return for freedom, Alphonsus orders the imprisonment of the Turk and his family. At this point, however, Alphonsus's father enters for a reunion with his son and, appraising the situation, persuades all parties to agree to marriage. In offering to approach Iphigina on Alphonsus's behalf, Carinus summarizes the two halves of Alphonsus's career: "you fitter are / To enter Lists and combat with your foes / Then court faire Ladyes in God *Cupids* tents" (ll. 1818–20). The reconciled Iphigina again states the split in explaining her earlier rejection of Alphonsus:

> But *Cupid* cannot enter in the brest
> Where *Mars* before had tooke possession:

> That was no time to talke of *Venus* games
> When all our fellowes were pressed in the warres.
>
> (ll. 1853–56)

In both Alphonsus and Iphigina, then, love triumphs, and the fact that Carinus arranges the marriage while dressed *"in his Pilgrimes clothes"* (l. 1750) perhaps adds a symbolic element to the transcendence of war; as Norman Sanders suggests, Carinus "speaks on behalf of love itself."[10] Greene develops such transcendence at length in *James IV*. Here, Carinus's final words give the story a formulaic comic conclusion which justifies Venus' promise that Alphonsus's career will unfold "in the maner of a Comedie" (l. 102):

> Now, worthy Princes, since, by helpe of *Ioue*,
> On either side the wedding is decreed,
> Come let vs wend to *Naples* speedily,
> For to solemnize it with mirth and glee.
>
> (ll. 1911–14)

When Venus reappears in the epilogue her presence is at last fully appropriate. Calliope's earlier assertion that Venus "rules the earth, and guides the heauens too" (l. 97) is confirmed by the changes of heart in the characters. The revelation of the grounds of Venus' interest in Alphonsus echoes the action within the story that her comments frame. That the structure which Greene thus brings to Marlowe's episodic pattern is tragicomic, involving individual transformation and ending in reconciliation, clearly reveals his own interests as a dramatist. The structure is one of several features which link *Alphonsus,* despite its imperfections, to Greene's more successful plays.

Orlando Furioso

Orlando Furioso carries further the split between Alphonsus as chivalric hero and Alphonsus as Marlovian superman, for separate and antagonistic figures, hero and villain of the play, represent the two character-types. Orlando is the central character in a romantic tale inspired by Ariosto, while Sacrepant shares Tamburlaine's rebellious spirit and devotion to self. Emphasizing the contrast is the fact that each briefly takes on the role of the other: Sacrepant tries his hand at love, although he scorns it when rejected, and Orlando rants of war and glory during his madness. Orlando's raving has

led a number of critics to see the play as a parody of *Tamburlaine*. [11]
This view may be in part a response, however, to a general awkwardness in language and to the prominence of such crudely humorous actions as Orlando's mistaking a fiddle for a sword, and for
neither of these elements can Greene be held wholly responsible.
That is, the text as we have it is obviously corrupt, and it may
contain, as W. W. Greg has argued, revisions made by a touring
company over some period of time. [12] Although a surviving actor's
copy of Orlando's part includes versions of many speeches that are
probably closer to what Greene actually wrote, the tone and spirit
of the play are difficult to assess, and the overall structure is a safer
guide to Greene's intentions than details of language.

In its larger design the play portrays the victory of Orlando over
Sacrepant, and the victory of love over war and madness. Like
Alphonsus, Orlando Furioso ends with a comic vision of social
integration:

> Thus, Lordings, when our bankettings be done,
> And Orlando epowsed [sic] to Angelica,
> Weele furrow through the mouing Ocean,
> And cherely frolicke with great Charlemaine.
>
> (ll. 1454–57)

In giving the play this shape Greene alters entirely the meaning
and effect of the story as he found it in Ariosto's *Orlando Furioso*. [13]
In Ariosto, the capricious Angelica is loved by many, including
Orlando, but falls in love with Medoro when she finds him wounded
in a shepherd's hut. She leaves behind a gold bracelet that Orlando
had given her, and, through it and inscriptions carved on trees,
Orlando discovers her love and goes mad. Angelica marries Medoro,
and there is no reconciliation with Orlando, eventually cured of his
madness. Greene's Orlando again goes mad when he discovers evidence of Angelica's love for Medor, but it is Sacrepant, rebuffed by
Angelica and eager for her father's throne, who carves the inscriptions and sets in trees the poems that Orlando reads. Angelica
remains constant to Orlando throughout. When Orlando is restored
to sanity and learns the truth, he kills Sacrepant and returns to
Angelica, who generously forgives him.

The change in Angelica's nature brings a change in moral focus,
evident particularly in the treatment of Orlando's madness. In Ariosto

the meaning of madness is tied to Angelica's inconstancy. Like Fortune, she is fickle, and, like those who devote themselves to Fortune's gifts, those who love her invite an inevitable fall. Orlando's madness is thus simply the extension of a love that is itself a kind of madness; it is a metaphor for loving Angelica in the first place. By creating a faithful Angelica, Greene reverses her symbolic value. She becomes a wronged heroine, suffering passively from the males who betray her. It is a favorite situation with Greene, of course, linking the play to his prose works. Angelica's similarity to Greene's fictional heroines is especially clear when she becomes a shepherdess. The pastoral interlude arises when her father, Marsilius, learns of Orlando's madness and orders Angelica's exile, believing (as do the other males in the play) that she loves Medor (ll. 739–40). She later appears *"like a poore woman"* (l. 863), disguised as a "faire shepherdesse" who claims to be the "daughter . . . vnto a bordering swaine, / That tend my flocks within these shady groues" (ll. 869–73). The interlude was probably longer in the original text,[14] and probably more effective, but even here Angelica's soliloquy identifies her as an image of suffering virtue: "causeles banisht from thy natiue home, / Here sit, Angelica, and rest a while, / For to bewaile the fortunes of thy loue" (ll. 863–65).

Angelica's moral identity had been established even before Orlando's betrayal in another scene recalling Greene's prose works, the confrontation of suitors for her hand which opens the play. In a scene without parallel in Ariosto, the soldan of Egypt and the kings of Cuba, Mexico, and "the bordring Ilands" (l. 74) state their claims to "this happy prize" (l. 12), all offering the material splendor most eloquently described by Rodamant, king of Cuba, where

> The earth within her bowels hath inwrapt
> As in the massie storehowse of the world,
> Millions of Gold, as bright as was the Showre
> That wanton Ioue sent downe to Danae.
> (ll. 41–44)

All four royal suitors end by declaring, "But leauing these such glories as they be, / I loue, my Lord; let that suffize for me" (ll. 34–35), but each is careful to read his glories into the record. In contrast to these proclamations of magnificence, Orlando's case, although equally hyperbolic, is based on his veneration of beauty

and on the bravery which "the fame of faire Angelica" has inspired
in him: "neither Country, King, or Seas, or Cannibals, / Could by
dispairing keep Orlando backe" (ll. 115–18). He concludes by
varying the tag-line of the other suitors: "But leauing these such
glories as they bee, / I loue, my lorde; / Angelica her selfe shall
speak for me" (ll. 126–28). Angelica thus faces a choice roughly
comparable to that faced by Terentia in *Ciceronis Amor* or Rosamond
in *Greenes Mourning Garment,* and she makes it by refusing glory for
love; Fortune, Fate, Venus, or Cupid, she says, "Hath sent proud
loue to enter such a plea, / As nonsutes all your princely euidence"
(ll. 158–59). In selecting Orlando, the man called by his angry
rivals a "stragling mate" (l. 170) and an "vntaught companion" (l.
183), Angelica makes the moral choice required by this obviously
emblematic situation, first used by Greene in his prose works as
early as the second part of *Mamillia.*

Angelica's devotion to "the bands which louely Venus ties" (l.
460) embodies a conventional, indeed sentimental, sort of morality,
but its effect on the definition of Orlando's madness is less than
straightforward. Transformed by Greene from betrayed to betrayer,
Orlando must confront weakness not in Angelica but in himself.
Sacrepant's manipulations are an immediate cause of jealousy, but
a prior cause is Orlando's disposition to be led astray. Sacrepant
merely externalizes what already exists within Orlando. This symbolic relationship between hero and villain is suggested when the
mad Orlando parodies Sacrepant's devotion to military heroism,
tearing off a man's leg and using it for a club, knighting the
unrecognized Angelica for supposed deeds in battle, and marching
in *"with a Drum, and* Souldiers *with spits and dripping pans"* (l. 882).
Moreover, just as Orlando's delirium reveals a buried similarity to
Sacrepant, Sacrepant's brief courtship of Angelica ends with a rejection of love that anticipates Orlando's reaction to the discovery
of inconstancy. "Thinkst thou my thoghts are lunacies of loue?"
asks Sacrepant:

> No, they are brands fierd in Plutoes forge,
> Where sits Tisiphone tempring in flames
> Those torches that doo set on fire Reuenge.
> I loud the Dame; but braud by her repulse,
> Hate calls me on to quittance all my ills.
>
> (ll. 494–99)

These parallels between the two characters establish Orlando's madness as the result of destructive emotions that must be purged before union with Angelica. The madness makes explicit the madness of jealousy itself—"infecting iealousie" it is called by the enchantress who cures Orlando (l. 1203)—and he displays in exaggerated form the intense passions felt by such Shakespearean characters as Leontes and Claudio *(Much Ado)* and by Greene's own Pandosto and Philippo.

While objectifying inner obstacles to love, Orlando's madness reflects also the nature of his love. He fails to perceive Angelica clearly because he is blinded by irrational passion, as he himself suggests when he describes his progress in excess at the moment of reconcilement: "Pardon thy lord, faire saint Angelica, / Whose loue, stealing by steps into extreames, / Grew by suspition to a causeles lunacie" (ll. 1399–1401). In allowing his love to steal "into extreames," Orlando resembles his prototype in Ariosto, and Greene thus retains elements of Ariosto's attack on love, the dangers of which Orlando still illustrates. That Greene's Angelica is worthy of rational love does not determine the nature of the emotions that can be felt toward her. The series of admonitory references in the play to such exemplary figures as Cressida, the Sirens, and Medusa point less to the evil of offering temptation than to the folly of succumbing to it, as when the soldan of Egypt cites Helen of Troy in explaining his refusal to join the other disappointed suitors in battle against Marsilius:

> . . . when Prince Menelaus with all his mates
> Had ten yeres held their siege in Asia,
> Folding their wrothes in cinders of faire Troy,
> Yet, for their armes grew by conceit of loue,
> Their Trophees was but conquest of a girle:
> Then trust me, Lords, Ile neuere manage armes
> For womens loues that are so quickly lost.
>   (ll. 227–33)

As in the story of Helen, frustrated love leads to war when Angelica's suitors attack her father; as Sacrepant tells her, "Thy lawless loue vnto this stragling mate / Hath fild our Affrick Regions full of bloud" (ll. 453–54). When Angelica nonetheless defends her choice of Orlando, Sacrepant responds in a speech which summarizes the condemnations of love throughout the play:

> Shall such a syren offer me more wrong
> Than they did to the Prince of Ithaca?
> No; as he his eares, so, Countie, stop thine eye.
> Goe to your needle, Ladie, and your clouts;
> Goe to such milk sops as are fit for loue:
> I will employ my busie braines for warre.
>
> (ll. 470–75)

Sacrepant's scorn for the debilitating and demeaning "lunacies of loue" (l. 494) is uttered in anger and reflects as well his arrogant militarism, but the same point is made less directly in Orlando's madness. That is, just as Orlando parodies Sacrepant as a soldier, he parodies himself as a lover. In his first appearance after discovering Angelica's faithlessness he enters *"attired like a madman"* and raves of "Woods, trees, leaues; leaues, trees, woods" (l. 788), not only raising up for burlesque the pastoral associations of love but also recalling his own earlier habits as a lover: "Hard by, for solace, in a secret Groue, / The Countie once a day failes not to walke. / There solemnly he ruminates his loue" (ll. 511–13). In his next appearance he mistakes Angelica for a man and then reverses the error by accepting as Angelica a clown who is dressed like her. His address to the clown caricatures the Petrarchan lyricism of his earlier worship of the "matchles beautie of Angelica" (l. 98):

> Are not these the beauteous cheekes,
> Wherein the Lillie and the natiue Rose
> Sits equall suted with a blushing red? . . .
> Are not, my dere, those radient eyes,
> Whereout proud Phoebus flasheth out his beames?
>
> (ll. 971–76)

The play offers ample support, then, for the judgment that the "heauen of loue is but a pleasant helle, / Where none but foolish wise imprisned dwell" (ll. 570–71). Symbolized by Orlando's madness, the dangers and follies of passion are also described in comments on the nature of women, who are, says Orlando's servant, "vnconstant, mutable, hauing their loues hanging in their ey-lids" (ll. 629–30). Orlando himself makes the case against "Discurteous women" as the "woe of man" most forcefully, bursting into bitter invective when he first discovers Angelica's supposed treachery:

O could my furie paint their furies forth!
For hel's no hell, compared to their harts,
Too simple diuels to conceale their arts;
Borne to be plagues vnto the thoughts of men,
Brought for eternall pestilence to the world.

(ll. 672–84)

Antifeminist passages seem out of place in a play with the virtuous Angelica at its center,[15] but they point not toward her but toward Orlando, defining a realm of false devotion and broken commitment that he must transcend.

That Orlando in the end comes to his senses grounds the play in a movement from order to disorder and back to order, one of the most basic of comic rhythms. Like the confusion of *A Midsummer Night's Dream,* Orlando's madness is an irrational interlude out of which new resolution grows. The surrounding action of the war for Marsilius's throne underlines the pattern, since Marsilius's enemies are Angelica's former suitors, and the end of war contributes to the final harmony, as in *Alphonsus, James IV,* and such prose works as *Gwydonius.* Moreover, Orlando is not the only character in the play to undergo change. Mandricard vows to join the other rejected suitors in attacking Marsilius and goes to Mexico to gather troops; when he returns he is converted from his designs by the sheer worthiness of Marsilius's character and henceforth will "meditate on nought but to be frends" (l. 787). More dramatic is the repentance of Sacrepant, who begins as antagonist both in love and in war, craving both Angelica and a crown: "By hooke or crooke," he says, "I must and will haue both" (l. 242). As noted above, Sacrepant is a Tamburlaine, but he lacks Tamburlaine's compelling force and sometimes seems closer to such self-proclaimed villains as Shakespeare's Edmund and Richard III:

Sweet are the thoughts that smother from conceit:
For when I come and set me downe to rest,
My chaire presents a throne of Maiestie:
And when I set my bonnet on my head,
Me thinkes I fit my forhead for a Crowne;
And when I take my trunchion in my fist,
A Scepter then comes tumbling in my thoughts;

My dreames are princely, all of Diademes.
Honor,—me thinkes the title is too base.
(ll. 246–54)

By the end of the play, however, Sacrepant's lies about Angelica
have become "the sting that pricks [his] conscience" (l. 1255).
Wounded by Orlando, he confesses all and, when Orlando exits,
breathes his last in a vision of despair:

Heauen turne to brasse, and earth to wedge of steel;
The worlde to cinders. Mars, come thundering downe,
And neuer sheath thy swift reuenging swoorde,
Till like the deluge in Dewcalions daies,
The highest mountaines swimme in streames of bloud.
Heauen, earth, men, beasts, and euerie liuing thing,
Consume and end with Countie Sacrepant.
(ll. 1285–91)[16]

Sacrepant and Orlando, set against each other throughout, thus
achieve analogous forms of enlightenment in a play built around
moral transformation as a means of comic resolution. How effective
this design was in Greene's original script cannot be determined,
but enough remains to indicate the ambitiousness of *Orlando Furioso*.
Greene draws on a number of sources and traditions—Ariosto, Marlowe, his own prose, and morality drama among them—making
the play, to an unsympathetic critic, "less a gallimaufrey than a
farrago."[17] He seems clearly to attempt, however, to bring to such
disparate material a unified structure and thematic coherence. The
process took him toward what would become some of the most
characteristic elements of Elizabethan comedy.

A Looking Glasse for London and England

Greene collaborated with Thomas Lodge on *A Looking Glasse for
London and England*, one of several Elizabethan plays with scriptural
sources.[18] Dramatizing God's threatened destruction of Nineveh and
bringing to the stage Hosea (Oseas) and Jonah (Jonas), the *Looking
Glasse* recalls morality drama both in specific features and a general
homiletic character: Nineveh is a mirror in which London should
see its own sins. As Jonas tells the audience in the epilogue: "In
thee more Sinnes then Niniuie containes" (l. 2267). A series of

distinct plots illustrates the extension of corruption to all levels of society: we see the depraved king of Nineveh and his court, a usurer and his victims, and a smith's apprentice and his roistering companions. The scenes are separated by sermons to the audience by Oseas, brought to sit *"ouer the Stage in a Throne"* by an angel (1. 152) so that he may ponder the "mightinesse of these fond peoples sinnes" in preparation for preaching in Jerusalem (1. 180). Jonas provides still another plot, his attempt to flee God's will presented in three scenes, in one of which he appears *"cast out of the Whales belly vpon the Stage"* (1. 1398) before he enters Nineveh to announce its impending destruction. Jonas's dramatic appearance is but one of many spectacular theatrical effects, for a notable feature of the play is its symbolic use of costume and stage machinery.

Several efforts to divide the parts between the two authors have been made, and there is widespread agreement that Greene wrote the story of the king and that Lodge wrote the usurer scenes, with other sections assigned less confidently.[19] The movement of several characters back and forth, however, ties the plots together, and a number of analogies emerge as the characters move in parallel steps toward repentance. The play thus seems to reflect a single inspiration, and its guiding force is more likely to have been Greene than Lodge, partly because the theme of repentance suggests many of Greene's other works. Indeed, Greene refers to Nineveh in two of the pamphlets of 1590 proclaiming his reformation, and the Puritan tone of the *Looking Glasse* is consistent with those works and the repentance pamphlets. Moreover, the constructive power required to weave together the parts of the play suggests the hand of Greene, "his crafts master," said Thomas Nashe, in "plotting Plaies."[20] To go beyond this general sense of the importance of Greene's role is impossible, however, and the *Looking Glasse* will not here be analyzed in detail. It must suffice to say that the mass repentance at the end renders in stylized terms some of Greene's most characteristic motifs. If he indeed had a major hand in the play, it is hardly his most moving or ambivalent portrayal of the struggle for reason, but the use of the theme itself, grounded in the play's structural complexity and theatrical symbolism, shows a command of dramatic possibilities put to subtler use in *Friar Bacon* and *James IV*.

Friar Bacon and Friar Bungay

Friar Bacon and Friar Bungay is Greene's best-known work and one of the most familiar of non-Shakespearean Elizabethan plays. Its reputation rests both on its own merits and on its widely acknowledged historical significance in the development of comic form: it is among the earliest comedies routinely included in anthologies of Elizabethan drama. In *Friar Bacon,* runs traditional commentary, Greene assembled the elements of a new genre, one which provided a model for Shakespeare's comedies and, through Shakespeare, became a central literary tradition. The name that this new genre eventually acquired summarizes its characteristics: romantic comedy.[21] Readings of *Friar Bacon* have accordingly focused for over a century on such matters as the portrayal of love, the pastoral elements, the idealized heroine, the setting in the past, and the improbabilities of the plot. More generally, critics have found a positive and optimistic note in the play which is consistent with a definition of romantic comedy as devoted to the triumph of human nature, expressing itself in love and achieving fulfillment and reward despite social barriers, impeding circumstances, and moral errors.

If many of the most important features of *Friar Bacon* have thus been carefully examined and warmly appreciated, concentration on genre has perhaps involved the neglect of other aspects of Greene's achievement. The issues are suggested in the opening scene, which begins with a description of hunting in the fields of Suffolk:

> Alate we ran the deere, and through the Lawndes
> Stript with our nagges the loftie frolicke bucks,
> That scudded fore the teisers like the wind:
> Nere was the Deere of merry *Fresingfield*
> So lustily puld down by iolly mates,
> Nor sharde the Farmers such fat venison,
> So franckly dealt, this hundred years before.
>
> (ll. 3–9)

The pastoral image of peace, plenty, and community embodies the familiar Elizabethan vision of an ordered natural world and a stable social world. Out of sympathy with this vision, however, is the Prince of the Realm himself, young Edward. Although he had been "frolicke in the chace," Edward has been "changde to a melancholie

dumpe" (ll. 10–11) by the sight of Margaret, daughter of the Keeper
of Fressingfield, and Lord Lacy contrasts his infatuation to pastoral
order in a simile: "Why lookes my lord like to a troubled skie /
When heauens bright shine is shadowed with a fogge?" (ll. 1–2).
Edward's love is thus presented as a violation of natural and social
harmony. In one sense it disrupts pastoral "atmosphere," and Edward must be purged of desire for Margaret before the gratifications
of romance can prevail; he must, as the story develops, resign her
to the man she loves. At the same time, the destructiveness of
Edward's passion defines the rural setting as a perspective on moral
and social issues, standing not only for emotion's wish but also for
attitudes and values that triumph by the end of the play. It is the
emblematic dimension suggested by the moral resonance of these
opening lines which is easily slighted in approaching *Friar Bacon*
through definitions of its genre. Emphasis on warmth and charm
and on the realization of comic form tends to strip away some of
the content of the play. [22] To examine instead the embodiment of
ideas in the action is to discover that the ideas, although Renaissance
commonplaces, provide the basis for a complex dramatic unity.
Indeed, the particular form of the play as determined by content is
at least as interesting and important as its approximation to any
formal archetype. Moreover, the construction of *Friar Bacon* emphasizes conficts that give the play more roundness in its view of
human nature than at first appears.

The clearest sign of the limitations of concentrating on genre is
the presence of Friar Bacon himself, whose magical powers are presented as both good and evil. On the one hand, Bacon is a "braue
scholler" (l. 95), a dedicated man of art who labors at nature's secrets
for the benefit of mankind. The sight of far-off scenes in his "glasse
prospectiue" is "free for euery honest man" (l. 1774). His greatest
achievement is the Brazen Head, almost perfected after seven years
and designed not to enrich Bacon but to "read Philosophie" (l. 228)
and "tell out strange and vncoth Aphorismes" (l. 1549). Bacon's
powers serve the nation, moreover, for the Brazen Head will "com-
passe *England* with a wall of brasse" (l. 201) so strong "that if ten
Caesars livd and raignd in *Rome,* / With all the legions *Europe* doth
containe, / They should not touch a grasse of *English* ground" (ll.
230–32). His besting of the German Vandermast in conjuring is a
triumph for England which earns the praise of the king himself:
"*Bacon*, thou has honoured *England* with thy skill, / And made faire

Oxford famous by thine art" (ll. 1255–56). Finally, the feats of
"*Englands* only flower" (l. 491) beg approval with their humor. He
is the "frolicke Frier" (l. 322) and the "iollie frier" (l. 490), in his
first appearance embarrassing a skeptical fellow scholar by conjuring
up the hostess of his favorite tavern. There is ample evidence, then,
of Bacon's status as a benevolent Merlin-figure,[23] a student of nature
whose hunger for knowledge involves neither malice nor greed.

Yet Bacon remains a magician, a necromancer who has "diued
into hell, / And sought the darkest pallaces of fiendes" (ll. 1537–
38). The secrets of the Brazen Head reward "seuen yeares tossing
nigromanticke charmes, / Poring vpon darke *Hecats* principles" (ll.
1545–46). Whether Bacon's powers embody "black magic" or "white
magic" has aroused lively debate,[24] but Greene clearly includes
diabolic elements in the portrayal. As the defeated Vandermast
admits, "Neuer before was knowne to *Vandermast* / That men held
deuils in such obedient awe, / *Bacon* doth more than art" (ll. 1235–
37). His career is a spiritual adventure resembling that of Marlowe's
Faustus, except for the formal compact in blood, and the two plays
are indeed related, although which came first and influenced the
other is unknown.[25] Like Faustus, Bacon reaches beyond what is
appropriate for mortals; his magic expresses intellectual presumption. Both of the setbacks that Bacon suffers in the play thus force
him to confront his human limitations. First the Brazen Head fails
because of a servant's stupidity—itself a reminder of weakness and
a parody of Bacon's larger failure. Bacon reacts with a recognition
of what he has dared:

> But proud *Asmenoth* ruler of the North,
> And *Demogorgon* maister of the fates,
> Grudge that a mortall man should worke so much.
> Hell trembled at my deepe commanding spels,
> Fiendes frownd to see a man their ouermatch;
> *Bacon* might bost more than a man might boast.
>
> (ll. 1635–40)

The forces opposing Bacon's success here are demonic, but the
lack of Christian perspective is more than made up for in Bacon's
reaction to his second and final setback. When two Oxford students
come to view their fathers in Bacon's magic glass, they watch them
kill each other and then repeat the action in Bacon's chambers. The
four deaths lead Bacon to break the glass and renounce magic forever:

> The houres I haue spent in piromanticke spels,
> The fearefull tossing in the latest night
> Of papers full of Nigromanticke charmes,
> Coniuring and adiuring diuels and fiends,
> With stole and albe and strange Pentageron;
> The wresting of the holy name of God,
> As *Sother, Elaim,* and *Adonaie,*
> *Alpha, Manoth,* and Tetragramiton,
> With praying to the fiue-fould powers of heauen,
> Are instances that *Bacon* must be damde,
> For vsing diuels to counteruaile his God.
>
> (ll. 1831–41)

Bacon's recognition of magic's dark side condemns the impatience with human limitation which necromancy represents. In the background lies the scorn for worldly wisdom in Greene's source, *The Famous Historie of Friar Bacon:* "the knowledge of these things, as I have truly found, serveth not to better a man in goodness, but only to make him proud, and think too well of himself. What hath all my knowledge of Natures Secrets gained me? Only this, the loss of a better knowledge, the loss of divine Studies, which makes the immortal part of man, (his soul) blessed" (*PP*, 2:13).[26] Bacon overcomes the despair that recognition of his devotion to the world has brought, however, and accepts the possibility of mercy:

> Yet, *Bacon,* cheere thee, drowne not in despaire:
> Sinnes haue their salues, repentance can do much,
> Thinke mercie sits where Iustice holds her seate,
> And from those wounds those bloudie *Iews* did pierce,
> Which by thy magicke oft did bleed a fresh,
> From thence for thee the dew of mercy drops,
> To wash the wrath of hie *Iehouahs* ire,
> And make thee as a new borne babe from sinne.
>
> (ll. 1842–49)

Greene thus sets two images of Bacon's magic against each other, and neither quite cancels out the other; instead, the terms for evaluating magic shift.[27] The potential for good is genuine, but Bacon must renounce the destructive power of forces that he cannot fully control. "This glasse prospectiue," he says, "worketh manie woes" (l. 1820). Watching the deaths in his chamber as helplessly as his servant watches the Brazen Head, the man of apparently limitless power accepts his weakness. Bacon is saved in the end not because his magic is white but because his renunciation of it is also a renunciation of pride. He undergoes a full Christian repentance and submits to God's mercy: "Ile spend the remnant of my life / In pure deuotion, praying to my God, / That he would saue what *Bacon* vainly lost" (ll. 1850–52).

The issues raised by Bacon's story are difficult to reconcile with much of the criticism of the play, especially as it was written early in this century. Little room exists for Bacon's description of his deeds as fresh wounds in the side of Christ, for example, in C. F. Tucker Brooke's comment on Greene's moving from prose to drama: "By dressing his essentially fictional themes in rough dramatic guise, he instituted a new species of comedy, which from first to last comprised stories of love and sylvan adventure rather than plays dealing with human character and conflict."[28] Even more damaging to a narrow view of romantic comedy is the fact that Greene's treatment of magic complicates considerably his treatment of the "love and sylvan adventure" on which Brooke's notion of genre rests. That is, magic and the beauty that inspires love are analogous in the play, as pointed out by William Empson in a well-known comment and discussed by all subsequent critics.[29] The analogy functions to define love's limits and its dangers. Prince Edward's infatuation is thus linked to magic in the first scene, when Ralph Simnell, the Prince's fool, suggests Bacon's aid in obtaining Margaret: "they say he is a braue Nigromancer, that he can make women of deuils, and hee can iuggle cats into Costermongers" (ll. 95–97). When Edward adopts the suggestion, he also makes his own motives clear:

> *Lacie,* the foole hath laid a perfect plot;
> For why our countrie *Margret* is so coy,
> And standes so much vpon her honest pointes,
> That marriage or no market with the mayd:
> *Ermsbie,* it must be nigromaticke spels
> And charmes of art that must inchaine her loue,
> Or else shall *Edward* neuer win the girle.
>   (ll. 121–27)

A few scenes later, when Bacon does help Edward, magic operates destructively. The magic glass reveals that Lacy, in disguise to woo

Margaret on Edward's behalf, has fallen in love himself and that Friar Bungay is about to marry him to Margaret. Bacon strikes Bungay dumb to prevent the marriage, and his magic and Edward's love thus cooperate to frustrate legitimate desire. To bring about the scene Greene alters the source, where it is Bacon who acts benevolently on behalf of virtuous love and Bungay who counters him.[30]

Enchanted by Margaret's beauty, Edward resembles Pharicles and the other irrational lovers of Greene's prose in his devotion to what Pharicles had called Mamillia's "chrystall corps" (2:32):

> . . . her sparkling eyes
> Doe lighten forth sweet Loues alluring fire:
> And in her tresses she doth fold the lookes
> Of such as gaze vpon her golden haire.
>
> (ll. 52–55)

Edward's "lure is but for lust," says Margaret (l. 640), and he illustrates not delightful subjection to Cupid but arrogance and selfishness. A classical comparison in the first scene summarizes his feelings well enough:

> *Ermsbie,* if thou hadst seene as I did note it well,
> How bewtie plaid the huswife, how this girle
> Like *Lucrece* laid her fingers to the worke,
> Thou wouldest with *Tarquine* hazard *Roome* and all
> To win the louely mayd of *Fresingfield.*
>
> (ll. 84–88)

The linking in the figure of Tarquin of sexual passion and royal irresponsibility (hazarding *"Roome* and all") is reflected in Edward's florid application to the "bonny damsell" in "stammell red" (ll. 16–17) of the clichéd phrases of the alien language of the court:

> Her bashfull white mixt with the mornings red
> *Luna* doth boast vpon her louely cheekes:
> Her front is beauties table where she paints
> The glories of her gorgious excellence:
> Her teeth are shelues of pretious Margarites,
> Richly enclosed with ruddie curroll cleues.

> Tush, *Lacie,* she is beauties ouermatch,
> If thou suruaist her curious imagerie.
>
> (ll. 56–63)

The effect of Margaret's "curious imagerie" is symbolized when Edward allows Ralph Simnell to wear his clothes. Significantly, Ralph himself first proposes a change (ll. 31–34), just as he first proposes seeking Bacon's aid, and he makes its meaning clear in a variation of the motif at the end of the first scene: "Mary, euery time that *Ned* sighs for the Keepers daughter, Ile tie a bell about him: and so within three or foure daies I will send word to his father *Harry,* that his sonne and my maister *Ned* is become Loues morris dance" (ll. 163–66). The results of the change of costume are seen in three scenes (ll. 499ff.). The sight of the fool in Edward's clothes in the first and third of these scenes frames Edward's use of Bacon's magic glass and the prevention of the marriage of Margaret and Lacy in the middle scene. Moreover, the fool's failure to deceive the Oxford scholars in the third of the scenes prepares for Edward's moral awakening in the scene that follows.[31] A scholar says to Ralph and Edward's friends,

> Why, harebraind courtiers, are you drunke or mad,
> To taunt vs vp with such scurilitie?
> Deeme you vs men of base and light esteeme,
> To bring vs such a fop for Henries sonne?
>
> (ll. 890–93)

In the next scene Edward asks himself, *"Edward,* art thou that famous prince of *Wales,* / Who at *Damasco* beat the *Sarasens,* / And broughtst home triumphe on thy launces point . . . ?" (ll. 1035–37).

Edward's realization of love's effect on him parallels Bacon's coming to an understanding of magic.[32] Moved by the dedication of Margaret and Lacy to each other in the face of his threats against Lacy's life, he renounces passion for higher ideals. Asking himself whether it is "princely to disseuer louers leagues" (l. 1039), he uses a metaphor from battle, his own proper realm: "in subduing fancies passion, / Conquering thy selfe, thou getst the richest spoile" (ll. 1043–44). The metaphor identifies personal with public honor, defining Edward's reform as a choice both of public responsibility and of duty to his own nature. At the same time, Edward's failure to force Margaret to love him exposes the limitations of his power. His "plumes" have been "puld by *Venus* downe" (l. 1038), and, in "subduing" and "conquering" "all his thoughts" (l. 1046), he has, like Bacon, defeated pride.

Edward's renunciation requires, of course, the assumption that Lacy's love possesses the moral superiority that Lacy claims in defending himself against Edward's wrath: "the louely maid of *Fresingfield* / Was fitter to be *Lacies* wedded wife, / Then concubine vnto the prince of *Wales*" (ll. 944–46). Yet the love between Margaret and Lacy is not quite so unambiguously presented as Lacy's sermonizing suggests. Margaret knows that her "looks" of love have "bewicht" Lacy (l. 965), and Friar Bungay pledges his magic to aid her in attracting him: "Feare not, the Frier will not be behind / To shew his cunning to intangle loue" (ll. 657–58). Bungay's help is not needed, as it turns out, for the power of Margaret's beauty suffices. As Lacy describes falling in love, "when mine eies suruaied your beautious lookes, / Loue, like a wagge, straight diued into my heart, / And there did shrine the Idea of your selfe" (ll. 693–95). Lacy inspires comparable idolatry in Margaret, who calls herself one "whome fancy made but ouer fond" (l. 962). She compares Lacy to Paris in appearance (ll. 646–47) and admits, "I fed myne eye with gazing on his face" (l. 964). The feelings of Margaret and Lacy are expressed, in short, in the language of Edward and seem equally based on the beauty that is tainted by analogy to magic. Greene's treatment of the triangle does not clearly separate lawful and lawless passion. Lacy and Margaret again show the inability of human nature to resist emotion, for, as Margaret says in defending disobedience to the Prince,

> Then, worthy *Edward,* measure with thy minde,
> If womens fauours will not force men fall,
> If bewtie, and if darts of persing loue,
> Is not of force to bury thoughts of friendes.
>   (ll. 970–73)

If language does not reveal the superiority of Margaret and Lacy's love, its merits emerge more clearly from the fact that Edward's opposition provides a test of love. That the threat to kill Lacy only increases the lovers' dedication and their willingness to declare it affirms the grounds of Margaret's indignation: "Why, thinks King *Henries* sonne that *Margrets* loue / Hangs in the vncertaine ballance of proud time?" (ll. 1016–17). For Lacy, moreover, the survival of love under trial is the final step in a moral progress that parallels and anticipates Edward's progress. Lacy begins the play as one of Edward's "frolicke Courtiers" (l. 134). He has no lines as coarse as Warren's approval of the plan to direct Bacon's magic toward Margaret's chastity—"thats a speedy way / To weane these head-strong puppies from the teat" (ll. 131–32)—but Lacy agrees, of course, to act on the Prince's behalf, doing so, moreover, with full commitment: "I will, my lord, so execute this charge, / As if that *Lacie* were in loue with her" (ll. 157–58). Indeed, he prays for the success of Edward's designs: "God send your honour your harts desire" (l. 171). As Edward's surrogate, Lacy expresses a symbolic identity with him, and he frees himself both from Edward and from Edward's attitudes when he decides to love Margaret on his own: "Honour bids thee controll him in his lust; / His wooing is not for to wed the girle, / But to intrap her and beguile the lasse." Love gives Lacy strength to "abide [his] Princes frowne," for "better die, then see her liue disgracde" (ll. 675–80). Here Lacy, alone in Suffolk when the other courtiers go to Oxford with the Prince, steps outside the courtly and the masculine and sees in new perspective. Like Benedick in *Much Ado about Nothing,* he moves to the other side of a male-female dichotomy and, separated from the jesting fellowship of "frolicke Courtiers," he transcends them. Lacy's experience embodies a stylized conversion equivalent to those of Edward and Bacon. Although generally neglected by commentators on the play, Lacy is another repentant figure, triumphing over himself and, in the process, elevating his love for Margaret above Edward's selfish passion.

Edward's acquiescence to Lacy, discussed above, prepares for the celebration in Oxford that completes the first half of a play divided into two parts. Edward joins his father and accepts a match with Elinor of Castile, who turns out to be entirely worthy of his new state of mind. The match knits together two realms, translating love's triumph into national terms. Edward assumes his public role, like Shakespeare's Prince Hal, and his renewed amity with Lacy restores harmonious relations among social classes. The image of an ordered world in the description of hunting which opens the play is recalled at the beginning of this climactic scene in the German Emperor's pastoral portrait of Oxford, "richly seated neere the riuer side: / The mountaines full of fat and fallow deere, / The batling pastures laid with kine and flocks" (ll. 1089–91). The same scene includes the exuberant demonstration of English supremacy in Bacon's triumph over Vandermast, and Bacon brings the first half of the play to stirring conclusion in describing the feast of celebration which will follow (ll. 1337–58).

The resolution proves false, however, for a series of disappointments at once begin. Bacon's troubles we have seen: his plans for the Brazen Head fail and his magic glass leads to death. Margaret's story turns equally grim, and it too leads to renunciation, at least temporarily. First, Lambert and Serlsby become unwelcome rivals for her hand. Then comes Lacy's letter to announce that he no longer loves her. Margaret's reaction is spontaneous and apparently irreversible: "I will straight to stately *Fremingham,* / And in the abby there be shorne a Nun, / And yeld my loues and libertie to God" (ll. 1517–19). Margaret's next appearance makes the parallel between her decision and Bacon's renunciation of magic explicit. Bacon ends his repentance scene vowing to "spend the remnant of [his] life / In pure deuotion," and Margaret immediately enters *"in Nuns apparrell"* accompanied by her pleading father: *"Margret,* be not so headstrong in these vows: / Oh, burie not such beautie in a cell" (ll. 1853–54). The analogy works a last variation on the links between love and magic. Bacon had come to realize human vanity and the limitations of worldly wisdom, and Margaret exchanges "aspiring sinnes" (l. 1868) for a "humble minde" (l. 1883), turning away from "the vaine Illusions of this flattering world" (l. 1860) to pursue "the hermonie of heauen" (l. 1863). She defines love as the idolatrous passion implicit in some of the language of love earlier in the play: "I loued once, Lord *Lacie* was my loue; / And now I hate my self for that I lovd, / And doated more on him than on my God" (ll. 1864–66). Like Bacon, Margaret will submit to higher love, "to him that is true loue" (l. 1914), and her view of the world is, if anything, even more fervently ascetic: "To shun the pricks of death, I leaue the world, / And vow to meditate on heauenly blisse" (ll. 1873–74). Here, then, is a fourth conversion in the play and, though Margaret's single-minded zeal seems excessive to some critics,[33] it is the most generalized and all-encompassing of the four. Lacy's desertion has undermined the concept and possibility of love, and disillusionment renders Margaret incapable of life in the world: "The world shal be . . . as vanitie, / Wealth, trash; loue, hate; pleasure, dispaire" (ll. 1515–16).

If Margaret's renunciation is a fourth conversion in the play, one more remains: the reversal of her decision when she learns that Lacy intended his letter "but to try sweete *Peggies* constancie" (l. 1924). Lacy's motives in sending the letter bear no very close scrutiny. As an editor of the play says, "no realistic motivation would have been necessary" for this conventional testing of a Griselda figure, "for Greene's audiences would have found the logical emphasis where in fact it occurs, in Margaret's response."[34] Yet Greene seems almost to go out of his way to raise questions about Lacy's character. The letter comes with no warning and appears as authentic to the audience as it does to Margaret. It links Lacy again to the world of shallow prodigals, and Margaret appropriately compares it to "the scrowles that *Ioue* sent *Danae*" even before reading it (l. 1475). In the letter, moreover, Lacy shows himself master of an elaborate euphuistic style epitomizing the court values that encroach on rustic virtue: "The bloomes of the Almond tree grow in a night, and vanish in a morne; the flies *Haemerae* . . . take life with the Sun, and die with the dew; fancie that slippeth in with a gase, goeth out with a winke; and too timely loues haue euer the shortest length. I write this as thy grefe, and my folly . . ." (ll. 1481–86). In both style and substance Lacy appears to step away from Margaret's moral realm, as he has from her rural setting in joining the court at Oxford.

Although the letter expresses only the persona of inconstant courtier which Lacy adopts in order to test Margaret, the impression it gives can be linked to other elements in Greene's portrayal of Lacy. There is, for example, the very cruelty of the test, its callous disregard for the feelings of a woman whose virtues Lacy boasts of at court after sending the letter but before learning its effect: "he discourseth," says the king of Castile, "of the constancie / Of one surnam'd, for beauties excellence, / The faire maid of *Fresingfield*" (ll. 1703–5). At the same time, Lacy's test suggests an ignorance of Margaret's real nature that parallels the superficial affections of Greene's Orlando and other misguided Elizabethan heroes. Equally troubling is Greene's handling of Lacy's arrival in Fressingfield to tell Margaret the truth and take her back to court for marriage (ll. 1890–1943). He comes accompanied by Warren and Ermsby, his apparent reimmersion in male camaraderie symbolized in a noisy, colorful entrance *"booted and spurd,"* according to the stage direction. The entrance interrupts Margaret's dialogue with her father as she stands *"in Nuns apparrell"* describing her contempt for the world; indeed, the men appear just as she addresses the absent Lacy in a passage of teary sentimentality: "Farewell, oh Loue, and with fond Loue farewell, / Sweet Lacie, whom I loued once so deere! / Euer be well, but neuer in my thoughts." As the three men stride in, Lacy's first words strike a jarring and intrusive note: "Come on, my wags, weere neere the Keepers lodge." Seeing the Keeper and his daughter, Ermsby makes a coarse joke—"The old lecher hath gotton holy mutton to him"—and Lacy greets him with loud heartiness: "Keeper, how farest thou? holla man, what cheere?" When the Keeper points to Margaret, explaining that "she leaues the world because she left your loue," Lacy turns to her with no change in tone: "Why, how now, *Margret?* what, a malecontent? / A Nunne? what holy father taught you this . . . ?" Even less attractive is Lacy's focus on his own feelings as he urges Margaret to revoke her decision: "twere iniurie to me," he says, "To smother vp such bewtie in a cell," adding, "What, shorne a Nun, and I haue from the Court / Posted with coursers to conuaie thee hence . . . ?" He makes no reference to his letter, as though having forgotten it, and, when Margaret mentions it, he dismisses it in a single sentence.

The details of the scene thus make Lacy appear as unfeeling and arrogant as the unnumerable faithless lovers and mistreaters of women in Greene's prose works. Both his maleness and his social superiority ring offensive—"will faire *Margret* leaue her loue and Lord?"—and he feels no need of explanation or apology. It is not simply his decision to test Margaret that might disturb an audience, then; that can be accepted as a traditional device. It is rather his behavior as Greene presents it. Greene in fact makes matters as difficult as possible as the debate between Margaret and Lacy approaches its climax. Warren and Ermsby grow impatient, and so does Lacy himself. Warren presses Lacy, "we cannot stay, my Lord; and if she be so strict, / Our leisure grants vs not to woo a fresh," and Ermsby turns to Margaret:

> Choose you, faire damsell, yet the choise is yours,
> Either a solemn Nunnerie, or the Court,
> God, or Lord *Lacie:* which contents you best,
> To be a Nun, or els Lord *Lacies* wife?

As Lacy adds his own voice—*"Peggie,* your answere must be short"—
Margaret faces what is perhaps the most remarkable question in all
of Elizabethan drama: "God, or Lord *Lacie."* She chooses Lord Lacy.

Margaret's choice does not resolve the tension between the constant love that Lacy stands for and the impression which he gives
when he enters with his flippant court friends and prods Margaret
to do his will. We can interpret that tension in various ways. We
can argue, for example, that Greene's tendency to sympathize with
female characters so gets the better of him that he loses control of
the scene. Or we can argue that objections to Lacy do not arise if
he is seen as a mere device for the revelation of Margaret as an
exemplary character. Or we can argue that, because Margaret's renunciation of the world is inherently misguided, Lacy strikes just
the right tone for educating her in the realities of experience. Whatever we do with the tension, however, it is undeniably present and
a sign of the complexity with which Greene treats characters whose
actions embody significant human issues. Indeed, the tension of
this climactic scene lies finally between issues and not merely between conceptions of Lacy. The generality of Margaret's answers to
Lacy's arguments enlarges the confrontation beyond the characters:
"Is not heauens ioy before earths fading blisse, / And life aboue
sweeter than life in loue?"

Margaret's question also links her decision to the issues raised by
the renunciation of Friar Bacon and the moral growth of Edward
and Lacy. All the plots provide foundation for her realization that
love is a "fond conceite, / Whose hap and essence hangeth in the
eye," and her acceptance of Lacy thus reverses not only her own
story but also the direction toward otherworldliness in the play as
a whole: "The flesh is frayle; my Lord doth know it well, / That
when he comes with his inchanting face, / What so ere betyde I
cannot say him nay." This last conversion seems almost to parody
the others, even reasserting links between magic and love in recognizing Lacy's "inchanting face." Beneath parody, however, lies a
common recognition of frailty. Lacy's *"booted and spurd"* boister-
ousness embodies human claims that cannot be denied, and Lacy's
pleas are less concerned with asserting his love than with pointing
out the waste and unhappiness of Margaret's decision to "smother
vp such bewtie in a cell." To "die a maid" is a "tedious life" in a
"solemne Nunnerie," and a series of expressions of horror at the
thought of the cutting of Margaret's hair finally ends when she

decides not to be "shorne" and bids farewell to "all the shew of holy Nuns."

In choosing Lacy, Margaret answers a question posed years before in *Mamillia:* "Whether doest thou think the ruddy Rose, which withereth in the hand of a man, delighting both sight and smelling, more happie than that which fadeth on the stalke without profit?" (2:43). Her answer sets her closer to Friar Bacon than at first appears. That is, if she reverses the ascetic direction of the play set by Bacon's conversion, she matches him in recognizing human weakness.[35] For both, moreover, there are two stages. Bacon moves first to despair and then to repentance, while Margaret moves from despair to reconciliation. Bacon must retreat from the world to humble himself, while Margaret must see the world from his perspective and then return to it. Bacon thus responds to his insight in one way and Margaret in another, but the alternatives are not undermined by the contrast. Both characters are included in the celebration that ends the play.

James IV

Often seen as Greene's last play, *James IV* resembles *Friar Bacon* in presenting pure fiction as historical fact: Greene transfers to Scotland and the court of James IV a tale he had found among Cinthio's novellas.[36] If thus not the chronicle play its title suggests, *James IV* shares with chronicle plays a concern for the peace and prosperity of kingdoms. Commentary on national corruption, especially flattery and parasitism, occurs throughout the play: "Sooner may the Moore bee washed white / Then these corruptions bannisht from this Realme," says a lawyer (ll. 2021–22), and even a comic servant says, "Was neuer such a world, I thinke, before, / When sinners seeme to daunce within a net" (ll. 1797–98). A series of illustrative scenes dramatize such judgments: the king accepts the service of a flatterer who then, in a parallel scene, hires three servants of his own (1.2); an Englishman and a Scot discuss national affairs (1.3); the king's advisers lament conditions and then one by one abandon the court (2.2); a servant quarrels with a royal purveyor over the king's authority (3.2); a lawyer, a merchant, and a divine debate the causes of corruption (5.4).[37] The public focus of such scenes is misleading, however, for they involve no coherent social analysis.[38] National disorder in *James IV* does not result from class tensions, new conditions, or some other social cause. Instead, disorder reflects the moral weakness of the Scottish king. The course of the nation follows the course of James IV's behavior, and his enlightenment at the end of the play restores national health. For his part, James is another in the long list of Greene's heroes who fall to folly and then triumph over it. Indeed, he acts out once again Greene's old tale of rational and irrational love.

James IV thus has a kind of double structure. A satiric portrayal of the disastrous effects of corruption at court, it is also a tragicomic romance in which happy ending follows repentance. These two perspectives are established in a prologue in which Oberon, king of the Fairies, confronts Bohan, a disillusioned courtier who has retired from the world to live in a tomb. Bohan resembles the several hermits and contemplatives in Greene's prose works (*Never Too Late* and *Arbasto,* for example), and his comments on his former life show the bitterness of the satirizing malcontents found in a number of Elizabethan plays[39]: "my pride was vanitie, my expence losse, my reward faire words and large promises, and my hopes spilt, for that after many yeares seruice one outran me; and what the deele should I do there? No, no; flattering knaues, that can cog and prate fastest, speede best in the Court" (ll. 48–52). Against this figure of cynical disillusionment Greene poses Oberon, whose tiny subjects—"Puppits," Bohan calls them (l. 13)—rouse Bohan by dancing about his tomb. When Oberon approaches as Bohan's "friend," Bohan reacts in anger: "I reck no friend nor ay reck no foe; als ene to me" (ll. 2–4). When Oberon claims to visit "for loue," Bohan is scornful: "The deele awhit reck I thy loue" (ll. 7–9). Oberon's overtures establish him as an image of reconciliation contrasting to Bohan's cynicism, and the two characters embody the tension between satire and tragicomedy in the play which follows. By the end, Oberon's perspective prevails, and the victory is a victory for an optimistic view of human nature. "I tell thee, *Bohan,*" he says, *"Oberon* is King / Of quiet, pleasure, profit, and content, / Of wealth, of honor, and of all the world" (ll. 608–10). At the beginning, however, Bohan dominates; indeed, he himself has written the story of James IV in order, he says, to "shew . . . whay I hate the world by demonstration" (ll. 101–2).[40]

The issues defined by Oberon and Bohan are developed in the opening scene, a long scene rich in emblematic elements setting the main characters in symbolic relationships with one another.

James has married Dorothea, and her father, king of England, joins him in celebrating a union both of individuals and of kingdoms. As James says to the English king, "First, lawes of friendship did confirme our peace, / Now both the seale of faith and marriage bed, / The name of father, and the style of friend" (ll. 115–17). Dorothea thus represents "bands of loue that death cannot dissolue" (l. 132) on multiple levels, and, in granting her the Scottish crown "in signe of loue" (l. 136), James gives the scene a ritualistic, ceremonial element which heightens her symbolic function: "Nobles and Ladies, stoupe vnto your Queene, / And Trumpets sound, that Heralds may proclaime / Faire *Dorithea* peerlesse Queene of Scots" (ll. 138–40). Harmony evaporates, however, when James, dispatching Dorothea and the court to escort her father to his ship, reveals to the audience an overpowering passion for Ida, daughter of the countess of Arran. The first lines of his soliloquy describe both personal and national disruption: "So let them tryumph that haue cause to ioy: / But, wretched King, thy nuptiall knot is death, / Thy Bride the breeder of thy Countries ill" (ll. 184–86). James knows that Dorothea is "Englands choysest pride" (l. 190) and that he has been "misled by loue" (l. 188), but he cannot resist the "Scottish *Idaes* bewtie" (l. 194). Greene thus presents him as a conventional idolatrous lover at the mercy of desire, as clearly emblematic in his way as Dorothea is in hers. It was, he says, "in the Chappell" (l. 192) that he first fell in love with Ida, a traditional setting for the birth of passion, and he describes the course of his love in the familiar terminology of Christian psychology: he is "bewitcht" (l. 191) by an image "that lodgeth" in his heart, having "entred" there, he says, "through mine eyes" (l. 200).

When James turns to Ida and hints at his feelings, her answers establish her as another of Greene's favorite thematic archetypes, the virtuous pastoral heroine. Her eagerness to return to the country borrows the vocabulary of the many emblematic figures portrayed in Greene's fiction:

> I count of Court, my Lord, as wise men do,
> Tis fit for those that knowes what longs thereto:
> Each person to his place; the wise to Art,
> The Cobler to his clout, the swaine to Cart.
>
> (ll. 211–14)

Ida's virtues rest on a sense of social place, a refusal to aspire beyond her rural station, and her distrust of court values as threatening to her identity echoes Bohan in the prologue:

> . . . the Court is counted *Venus* net,
> Where gifts & vowes for stales are often set:
> None, be she chaste as *Vesta*, but shall meete
> A curious toong to charme her eares with sweet.
>   (ll. 222–25)

Ida thus associates love not with pastoral freedom, but with the court; the country is a place where shepherds can sing of love's dangers: "And weele I wot, I heard a shepheard sing, / That, like a Bee, Loue hath a little sting" (ll. 231–32).

James reluctantly grants Ida permission to return to the country when Dorothea returns from seeing off her father, and, after dismissing the court, he returns to meditation on his passion. Again he confesses guilt and confusion—"fond King, thy honor doth engraue / Vpon thy browes the drift of thy disgrace" (ll. 274–75)— but again he cannot resist: "Nor earth nor heauen shall part my loue and I" (l. 292). His only worry is how to pursue Ida, a problem solved when Ateukin comes forward to volunteer his services. Ateukin is still another emblematic character, combining a number of traditions into a single image of dedicated villainy. Vice-figure, Machiavel, parasite, and astrologer, Ateukin flatters James with an almost comic transparency. The flattery points up the depth of the king's folly and also rounds off this first scene by confirming Bohan's disillusionment. Built around such symbolic contrasts as that between Ida and James and that between Dorothea and Ateukin, the scene has moved in a highly stylized way from the ritual installation of Dorothea as queen to the installation of the corrupt Ateukin as chief counsellor: "Winne my loue," says James, "and I will make thee great" (l. 385). At the center of the scene lie contrasts within James himself, monarch and lover, torn between Dorothea and Ida. In the stylized soliloquy that Ateukin overhears, he resembles a morality hero in posing alternatives and defining the significance of his choice:[41]

> Thy new vowd loue, in sight of God and men,
> Linkes thee to *Dorithea* during life;

> For who more faire and vertuous then thy wife?
> Deceitfull murtherer of a quiet minde,
> Fond loue, vile lust, that thus misleads vs men,
> To vowe our faithes, and fall to sin againe!
> (ll. 276–81)

James's choosing to pursue Ida focuses the scene on his weakness and on the general human weakness that has disillusioned Bohan. Disaster must follow from mankind's tendency to "vowe our faithes, and fall to sin againe."

After the long opening scene, Greene separates the characters, minimizing interplay between them until all come together in the end. Ida, for example, next appears in the country in a scene in which a series of encounters illustrates her character and the values that she represents. She begins by discussing with her mother the merits of humble life, restating her attitude toward "delights, or pompe, or maiestie" as "meanes to draw the minde / From perfect good, and make true iudgement blind" (ll. 678–81). She declares instead that to be "honest poore" is "the greatest good":

> For she that sits at fortunes feete alowe
> Is sure she shall not taste a further woe,
> But those that prancke on top of fortunes ball
> Still feare a change, and fearing, catch a fall.
> (ll. 683–87)

Ida's comments on Fortune recall Greene's prose works, and her comparison of human life to her needlework gives the pastoral image the explicitly Christian elements of some of those works:

> I with my needle, if I please, may blot
> The fairest rose within my cambricke plot;
> God with a becke can change each worldly thing,
> The poore to earth, the begger to the King.
> What, then, hath man wherein hee well may boast . . . ?
> (ll. 700–704)

The passage helps prepare for Ida's defense of her virtue at the end of this scene. Ateukin comes to woo on James's behalf, and Ida repels the assault of court on country with religious zeal:

> *Ida.*   Better, then liue vnchaste, to liue in graue.
>
> *Ateu.* Hee shall erect your state, & wed you well.
>
> *Ida.*   But can his warrant keep my soule from hell?
>
> *Ateu.* He will inforce, if you resist his sute.
>
> *Ida.*   What tho, the world may shame to him account,
>   To bee a King of men and worldly pelfe,
>   Yet hath no power to rule and guide him selfe.
>   (ll. 820–26)

Separating the two parts of this scene is a meeting between Ida and Eustace, an Englishman visiting Scotland with letters of introduction to Ida's mother. Although the countess at once invites Eustace in, he is on stage long enough to fall in love with Ida. Ateukin's approach, then, has the effect of Prince Edward's pursuit of Margaret in *Friar Bacon,* threatening the course of virtuous love. Two acts later, although James still hopes to seduce her, Ida is betrothed to Eustace in a scene containing two symbolic motifs: the betrothal itself and the welcoming to country hospitality of James's huntsmen by Ida and her mother. The two motifs are linked by parallel gifts. Ida gives Eustace a "ring, wherein my heart is set; / A constant heart, with burning flames befret, / But vnder written this: *O morte dura*" (ll. 1491–93), and the huntsmen give Ida a "Silver heart with arrow wounded" (l. 1506). Eustace immediately notes the relevance of the huntsmen's gift to himself—"This doth shadow my lament"—and later refers to it in wooing Ida (ll. 1522ff.).[42] The two emblems juxtapose Ida's hospitality to her love, identifying as moral order a social order destroyed at court but still possible in the country and represented further in the song of the huntsmen as they enter. "If mine entertainment please you," says Ida's mother, "let vs feast" (l. 1520).

Ida's insistence on her country identity helps define Dorothea's flight from court after learning that James has hired an assassin to murder her. The escape links the two women as images of virtue, while also giving Dorothea something of the quality of the royal heroines who become shepherdesses in Greene's prose works:

> What should I do? ah poore vnhappy Queen,
> Borne to indure what fortune can containe! . . .
> Oh, what auailes to be allied and matcht
> With high estates, that marry but in shewe!
>   (ll. 1385–86, 1391–92)

In this case, however, Dorothea does not become a shepherdess but disguises herself as a squire, embarking for the country accompanied by Nano, her dwarfish servant. The parallel to several of Shakespeare's comedies underlines the fact that Greene draws on traditions of romance narrative, and Dorothea's subsequent actions have many literary analogues. She beats away the hired assassin but is wounded and taken in by Sir Cuthbert Anderson, a virtuous Scot. Anderson's wife, nursing her back to health, is misled by her squire's disguise and falls in love. That complication resolved, Dorothea miraculously appears *"richly attired"* (l. 2308) in the last scene to end the war that has resulted from her supposed death, her survival described by Anderson in an elaborate beast fable resembling the mysterious prophecies of romance (ll. 2330ff.). Throughout the second half of the play, then, Dorothea is at the center of a set of highly conventional adventures that together help end the chaos that James's passion has brought to Scotland. Her entrance to the country in the middle of the play is a turning point in the movement toward romance, with the very conventionality of her story underlining the transition.

The triumph of romance is also a triumph of the attitudes represented by Ida and by Oberon and his dancing fairies. Dorothea adopts Ida's language—"to be great and happie, these are twaine" (l. 1395)—and becomes an instrument for reforming the court on the basis of detachment from it. Indeed, that the court can be reformed in itself indicates the defeat of cynicism by romance, and Dorothea is throughout the play a spokesman for an optimistic view of human nature. As Howard C. Cole says, she is Greene's "best piece of evidence against the sordid world Bohan is attempting to paint."[43] When James's courtiers lament his follies, she urges them not to desert him but to be patient with his immaturity:

> The King is young; and if he step awrie,
> He may amend, and I will loue him still.
> Should we disdaine our vines because they sprout
> Before their time? or young men, if they straine
> Beyond their reach? no; vines that bloome and spread
> Do promise fruites, and young men that are wilde
> In age grow wise.
>
> (ll. 969–75)

Dorothea sees James here just as Mamillia had seen Pharicles in
Greene's earliest work, and her love, like Mamillia's, never wavers.
She faces exile prepared to forgive James for ordering her murder,
and she refuses to sanction revenge against him because of the
identity with him that love grants:

> As if they kill not me, who with him fight!
> As if his brest be toucht, I am not wounded!
> As if he waild, my ioyes were not confounded!
> We are one heart tho rent by hate in twaine;
> One soule, one essence, doth our weale containe:
> What, then, can conquer him that kils not me?
> (ll. 1399–1404)

Dorothea resembles Mamillia in another respect: her unflagging
devotion allows no psychological definition and can be seen only in
terms of what she represents—despite the claim of many critics that
she is "the best-drawn woman figure in sixteenth-century drama
outside Shakespeare's comedies."[44] Such is also the case with James,
whose repellant behavior hardly justifies Dorothea's love and whose
reformation is as conventional as the emblematic transformations of
the heroes of morality drama and euphuistic fiction.[45] James moves
from one set of instincts to another in reforming, both sets laid out
in the inner debate of the first scene, discussed above, which establishes a mood which he shows throughout. When Ateukin suggests that the death of Dorothea would aid the pursuit of Ida, James
weighs alternatives with the same stiff formality that he had shown
earlier:

> What, murther of my Queene!
> Yet, to enioy my loue, what is my Queene?
> Oh, but my vowe and promise to my Queene!
> I, but my hope to gaine a fairer Queene:
> With how contrarious thoughts am I withdrawne!
> (ll. 1077–81)

That Ateukin guides James at this point, just as Parolles guides
Shakespeare's Bertram in *All's Well,* signifies both James's youthful
weakness and his ability to outgrow it: Ateukin objectifies qualities

that may be discarded. Thus, in his next appearance James allows Ateukin to resolve his mixed feelings about the report of Dorothea's death. "I am incenst with greefe, yet faine would ioy" (l. 1750), says James, but Ateukin talks him out of depression and rekindles his passion for Ida.

At the same time, the audience's knowledge in this scene that Dorothea is alive and that Ida is betrothed to Eustace makes James seem pathetic in his futility. His rhetoric begins to ring hollow:

> Go to mine *Ida,* tell her that I vowe
> To raise her head, and make her honours great:
> Go to mine *Ida,* tell her that her haires
> Salbe [sic] embellished with orient pearles,
> And Crownes of saphyrs, compassing her browes,
> Shall warre with those sweet beauties of her eyes.
>
> (ll. 1770–75)

Ateukin tells a servant after James's exit that James is "thine onely God on earth" (l. 1790), but the audience knows that he is merely the ruler over a corrupt court that is rapidly collapsing around him. Even the servant sees the impending fall and makes plans to desert to the English king (ll. 1797ff.). As the play moves toward its last phase, then, James's weakness and confusion grow more evident, providing an image of redeemability from which grows the restoration of earthly happiness. Indeed, James's reformation is only one in a sequence of actions that portray in the last act the victory of love over revenge, peace over war, and forgiveness over punishment.

The sequence begins with Dorothea's affirmation of continuing love for James in the first scene of act 5. Learning that her father has invaded Scotland because of her supposed death, she sends Nano to urge James's noblemen not to desert him. In describing her feelings she links her love to natural processes, opposing a definition of human need to the images of human corruption in the play:

> Ah, *Nano,* trees liue not without their sap.
> And *Clitie* cannot blush but on the sunne;
> The thirstie earth is broke with many a gap,
> And lands are leane where riuers do not runne:
> Where soule is reft from that it loueth best,
> How can it thriue or boast of quiet rest?
>
> (ll. 1906–11)

The passage defines the optimism that Nano expresses: "Couer these sorrowes with the vaile of ioy, / And hope the best; for why this warre will cause / A great repentance in your husbands minde" (ll. 1903–5). In the second scene of act 5 it is not James who repents, however, but Ateukin (ll. 1930–70). Returning to Ida now that Dorothea is thought dead, he arrives just in time to see her marriage to Eustace. Symbolic ritual surrounds the marriage: "*After a solemne seruice,*" reads the stage direction, "*enter, from the widdowes house, a seruice, musical songs of marriages, or a maske, or what prettie triumph you list.*" The ceremony recalls the opening scene, making the marriage an assertion of positive forces. Ateukin looks on in horror, his defeat encapsulated in a servant's unconsciously ironic invitation: "if you please, come in and take your part." Ateukin realizes his defeat: "What shall become of mee, if [James] shall heare / That I haue causde him kill a vertuous Queene, / And hope in vaine for that which now is lost?" Facing a fall from "the height of all [his] pompe," Ateukin reacts to failure not, as might be expected from his Machiavellian and vicelike nature, with curses and a resolve to practice villainy elsewhere, but with feelings of shame and disgust: "I know the heauens / Are iust, and will reuenge; I know my sinnes / Exceede compare." Declaring a self-abasement that anticipates the conversion of James, he leaves the stage (and the play) "Ashamde to looke vpon my Prince again, / Ashamde of my suggestions and aduice, / Ashamde of life, ashamde that I haue erde."

The third scene of act 5 presents another image of reconciliation when Lord Douglas surrenders Dunbar to the English king instead of defending it. Douglas begs that innocent subjects be spared punishment for James's sins: "Can generous hearts in nature bee so sterne / To pray on those that neuer did offend?" (ll. 1987–88). The Scots have fought only from "alleageance to our liefest liege" (l. 1999) and now appeal to the emblem that the English themselves carry: "The Roseall crosse is spred within thy field, / A signe of peace, not of reuenging warre" (ll. 1995–96). The English king relents, turning the scene into a vignette of forgiveness by symbolically withholding his upraised sword:

> This hand now reared, my *Douglas,* if I list,
> Could part thy head and shoulders both in twaine;
> But since I see thee wise and olde in yeares,

> True to thy King, and faithfull in his warres,
> Liue thou and thine.
>
> (ll. 2005–9)

After a formal debate of the causes of disorder in Scotland in the next scene, Greene returns to reconciliation and forgiveness as Dorothea learns that James has offered a reward for her. The possibility that the king's offer is a purely selfish effort to end the war is countered by Lady Anderson's assertion that "he loues her, then, I see, altho inforst, / That would bestow such gifts for to regaine her" (ll. 2141–42). Moreover, when Lady Anderson argues that Dorothea acts naively in deciding to rejoin James, Dorothea responds by declaring her pity for him:

> Ah Ladie, so wold worldly counsell work;
> But constancie, obedience, and my loue,
> In that my husband is my Lorde and Chiefe,
> These call me to compassion of his estate:
> Disswade me not, for vertue will not change.
>
> (ll. 2200–2204)

The reference to "worldly counsel" condemns the devotion to the flesh underlying James's passion for Ida and the ambitions of Ateukin and others. Dorothea's loyalty to James embodies not only her commitments but also her nature; as she says, "vertue will not change." This same scene presents another movement away from fleshly appetite when Lady Anderson learns that she has loved a disguise. Although the text is confused,[46] it makes clear that Lady Anderson awakens to her own folly, saying to herself, "Blush, greeue, and die in thine insaciat lust" (l. 2169). Her passion is transformed into higher love when Dorothea urges her to "ioy that thou hast won a friend"; she answers, "I ioy . . . more then my tongue can tell: / Though not as I desir'd, I loue you well" (ll. 2170–73).

Lady Anderson's awakening is one more anticipation of the final scene, which begins with the entrance of James, plagued again by the doubts he has felt throughout: "Twixt loue and feare, continuall is the warres: / The one assures me of my *Idaes* loue, / The other moues me for my murthred Queene" (ll. 2212–14). When the news of Ida's marriage arrives, its effect on James parallels its effect on Ateukin. Defeat reveals futility, and futility leads to despair. James scorns dependence on the "flattering tongues, by whom I was mis-

led" (l. 2240) and faces for the first time the consequences of his
actions, hearing the ghosts of Dorothea and his subjects "crying
out, woe, woe to lust!" (l. 2245). His first reaction is to strike out
at those around him, ordering the servants Andrew and Slipper
hanged. Slipper, however, is Bohan's son, and Oberon had promised
in one of the interludes to protect him; he now intercedes with his
"Antiques" to rescue Slipper—another escape from disaster (ll.
2261ff.).

When the English king enters with his troops, James attempts
to avoid battle by lying and by offering to return Dorothea's dowry.
His desperate evasions are reminiscent of Bertram's attempts to save
himself at the end of *All's Well,* and their failure prepares for a
carefully managed climax: *"Alarum sounded; both the battailes offer to
meet, &, as the* Kings *are ioyning battaile, enter* Sir Cuthbert, *to him*
Lady Anderson, *with the* Queen Dorothea *richly attired"* (l. 2308).
In interrupting bloodshed, Dorothea's appearance is a symbolic re-
capitulation of the reconciliations of the last act. "Thy foe is now
thy friend" (l. 2390), says Dorothea, presenting herself as a figure
of heavenly forgiveness. The English king, speaking of the feeling
that rises in his own breast, suggests that larger forces lie behind
what has happened: "Thou prouident kinde mother of increase, /
Thou must preuaile; ah, nature, thou must rule" (ll. 2384–85).
Dorothea says, more simply, "See what God hath wrought" (l.
2389). The mysteriousness of Dorothea's appearance adds to the
effect, for she remains disguised while Sir Cuthbert delivers an
enigmatic speech before dramatically revealing her identity. The
scene is as ritualistic as the opening scene, and Dorothea's return,
like that of Hero in *Much Ado,* permits a kind of second marriage.
Like Hero, moreover (as well as Hermione, Viola, and other Shakespearean heroines), Dorothea appears as though reborn, providing
the misguided humans around her with a second chance.[47] Her
appearance matches Oberon's use of magic to prevent Bohan's drawing his sword in the prologue, a prologue that begins, moreover,
with the awakening of a man from a tomb.

The second chance has been earned by suffering and repentance,
with social regeneration dependent on the personal regeneration that
James can at last declare (ll. 2363–69). Dorothea's forgiveness is
light in tone: "Youth hath misled,—tut, but a little fault: / Tis
kingly to amend what is amisse" (ll. 2371–72). Her reference to
James's youth, however, summarizes the emphasis on human frailty

throughout the play. Like *Friar Bacon, James IV* ends squarely in the world of experience. It too is a comic fable in which joyous conclusion follows from recognition both of weakness and of need. *James IV* first vindicates Bohan's disillusionment by presenting the corruptions of the court, but then moves beyond the court to the country, and beyond individuals to a larger symbolic world. If the purpose of satire is self-knowledge, the play exploits the satirical point of view as but one element in the acquiring of such knowledge, to be absorbed into the meanings of romantic tragicomedy. As Dorothea says, "Men learn at last to know their good estate" (l. 2451).

Chapter Four
Greene's Reputation

Wolfgang Clemen writes as follows of one of Dorothea's declarations of love in *James IV*: "This sententious preamble with its string of clichés is not merely a prefatory flourish; for Greene it serves also as a fitting substitute for the words that Dorothea ought to have spoken to express her tumult of spirit directly and unmistakably."[1] The comment illustrates some of the most interesting of the problems Greene has raised over the past four centuries. Most obviously, Clemen complains about something Greene "ought" to have done. Greene ought to have done a number of things that he did not do, according to critics through the years, beginning with living a more respectable life. "Greene deserves," said a Victorian critic, "almost unmitigated reprobation."[2] What later generations made of Greene's life has been discussed in chapter 1 and need not be reconsidered. His reputation echoes down the years as an inevitable starting point for reading his works. Indeed, reading Greene has sometimes failed to move beyond discussing his life, and many have been content to rest with Greene's attack on Shakespeare in the *Groats-worth of Wit*; the Upstart Crow has had more than his due revenge in the distraction from Greene's literary accomplishments which the attack has provided, although it took a Baconian, eager to prove that Shakespeare was not Shake-scene, to point most angrily to the "tempest of depreciation by which Shakespeare's biographers and commentators have succeeded in handing down . . . Greene's reputation as a preposterous combination of infamy and envy."[3]

To lament the energy spent on the Shake-scene passage and the nature of some of the interest in Greene's life as a whole is not to suggest, of course, that his biography does not reward study. One would not go so far as J. J. Jusserand—"as a novel writer and an observer of human nature, [Greene's] own portrait is perhaps his masterpiece"[4]—but certainly he is a compelling figure, and his life must have a role in any consideration of such topics as the profession of writing, the literary milieu, or the nature of the reading public. As Irving Ribner writes, "the vast body of his extant writings in verse and prose furnishes an excellent index of changing taste in Elizabethan letters."[5] At the same time, Greene lived in many ways a representative life. His journey from Norwich to Cambridge to London involved a variety of contemporary issues, and his works both reflect and comment on important social questions. The quantity of information known about Greene also allows us to move beyond sociological to psychological interpretations. Such approaches are perilous enough, but many of the works, and not only the confessional ones, do seem to have significant personal elements. This dimension has been largely unexplored in recent years and awaits post-Victorian commentators who can perhaps transcend attacking and defending Greene's character.

If our knowledge of Greene's life can thus open up perspectives, it has also functioned to interfere with taking the works seriously. As suggested in the preface to this study, Greene's career as a popular writer has often led to the denigration of what he wrote, a tendency marked out in Thomas Heywood's 1635 comment on Greene's reputation: "*Greene* . . . had in both Academies ta'ne / Degree of Master, yet could neuer gaine / To be call'd more than *Robin*."[6] Throughout criticism of Greene runs a kind of condescension rarely seen in readings of other writers. One notes the telling words "for Greene" in Clemen's remark: "for Greene it serves also as a fitting substitute for the words that Dorothea ought to have spoken." Such a note is struck again and again. When Greene takes colorful animal images from works of natural history but ignores their symbolism, he is "paying once again the inevitable price of his hack work," for "he was never deep in anything save wine—and debt."[7] A play with multiple plots is "a circus of many rings," and one with a variety of subject matter is written to "a recipe that has had long success in the commercial theatre and the moving picture industry."[8] The Greene of tradition is calculating in seducing his readers but careless in managing his art. Thus Louis B. Wright says of moralistic elements in Greene's prose that "for middle-class readers Greene performed a worthy service by providing them with a quantity of reading matter which furnished amusement without smelling too strongly of damnation."[9] Here Greene is demoted from writer to performer of "a worthy service," and his works become not a corpus but "a quantity of reading matter."

No purely theoretical answer to the attitude expressed by Wright can be made. It can only be set aside for an attempt to see Greene's works for what they are. Such an attempt has been made by various recent critics and it is made in chapters 2 and 3 above, with emphasis on the appreciation of Greene's use of emblematic elements. Here again Clemen's comment is indicative: Dorothea should "express her tumult of spirit directly and unmistakably," not in a "string of clichés." The speech is too conventional and too stylized, objections made by innumerable critics before and after Clemen. On the first objection, conventionality, it is useful to recall the words of G. K. Hunter: "Mere repetition revolts the modern mind, but the 'familiar and conventional' does not seem to have been equated, *per se,* with triteness in Elizabethan minds."[10] On stylization, it is useful to look to the many recent studies of emblematic literature. Removing what Alan C. Dessen has called the "Spectacles of Realism"[11] has become easier lately, and Greene's works may be more accessible as a result. The prose works in particular gain in interest as the canon laws of realism are abandoned, although, as seen in chapter 2, the effort to find in Greene a growth toward modern tastes is still a factor in criticism and an obstacle to sympathetic analysis.

Greene's plays have fared better. Often, however, admiration takes a purely historical form: Greene is appreciated for occupying a stage in evolution and read in terms of what he foreshadowed. Indeed, critics have been most comfortable when praising whatever in Greene resembles something in Shakespeare. Greene is "the first great master of plot in the English drama," his clowns are "the high-water mark before Shakespeare," *James IV* is "the most important landmark in the whole formative period of English tragicomedy," and *Friar Bacon*'s double plot achieves a "perfected form . . . for the use of future playwrights."[12] It is no small thing to be called the creator of a "stagecraft which taught 'the only Shake-scene in a country' more about the making of plays than he learned from any other predecessor" or to be seen standing "in the same relation to Romantic Comedy as [Marlowe] stands to Romantic Tragedy and History."[13] Moreover, Greene assuredly did influence Shakespeare and did set important precedents in dramatic form. Yet the emphasis on evolution and on Shakespearean analogy has led to needless debating of such questions as whether Greene's heroines are "realistic" or merely speak the clichés that Clemen deplores. Such debates go only a small way toward exploring the attempts to design a unity of theme and idea that give Greene's plays their clearest claim on our attention.

In both drama and prose, then, Greene deserves a serious reading, unbiased by his biography, his reputation as a popular writer, or his capacity to be fit into developmental schemes that celebrate modern taste as the goal of history. To grant him that reading is to find works that vary greatly in quality, originality, and significance but that repay close attention and sometimes surprise us with their complexity. Claiming for Greene a place in the small circle of our greatest writers would be pointless, but equally pointless is denying him a place in that larger circle whose merits are sufficient to inspire us to set aside the instinct to judge in favor of the need to understand.

Notes and References

Preface

1. Willard Thorp, *The Triumph of Realism in Elizabethan Drama: 1558–1612* (Princeton: Princeton University Press, 1928), 50.
2. John Clark Jordan, *Robert Greene* (New York, 1915), 52.
3. C. H. Herford, "A Few Suggestions on Greene's Romances and Shakspere," *Transactions of the New Shakspere Society, 1887–1892,* ser. 1, pt. 2, 181.
4. Norman Sanders, "Robert Greene's Way with a Source," *Notes & Queries,* n.s., 14 (1967):89.
5. G. E. Woodberry, "Robert Greene: His Place in Comedy," in *Representative English Comedies,* ed. Charles Mills Gayley (New York, 1903): 1:388.
6. Allan S. Downer, *The British Drama* (New York, 1951), 90.
7. Alexander Dyce, ed., *The Dramatic and Poetical Works* (London, 1861), 25; C. S. Lewis, *English Literature in the Sixteenth Century Excluding Drama* (Oxford: Clarendon Press, 1954), 401.
8. The best survey of the variety of Greene's poetry remains Jordan's in *Robert Greene,* 127–63.
9. Ernest A. Baker, *The History of the English Novel* (London, 1929), 90.

Chapter One

1. "I dare not trust too much to [William Winstanley in *The Lives of the Most Famous English Poets,* 1687], knowing how subject he is to take things upon Report. . . . However, for once I will venture to transcribe the following passage upon his Authority" (Gerard Langbaine, *An Account of the English Dramatic Poets* [Oxford, 1691], 241).
2. Greene is the hero, for example, of novels by Gwyn Jones (*Garland of Bays,* 1938) and Carl S. Downes (*Robin Redbeard,* 1937), and plays by J. Le Gay Brereton (*Tomorrow: A Dramatic Sketch of the Character and Environment of Robert Greene,* 1910) and Christopher Dafoe (*The Frog Galliard: A Play in One Act,* 1978). In addition, Greene plays a role in some of the many novels centering on Shakespeare, from Ludwig Tieck's *Dichterleben* (1826) to Anthony Burgess's *Nothing Like the Sun* (1964). Greene's appeal to fiction writers is perhaps summarized by a speech given him in Brereton's *Tomorrow* (Sidney: Angus & Robertson, 1910), 17: "Tomorrow all my merriment must die, / For this our life is but a barren

dream, / At best begetting shadows of evil and good, / Munch, hog, and bowse; to-morrow we must die."

3. *The Queen's Progress and Other Elizabethan Sketches* (London: T. Werner Laurie, 1904), 131.

4. All quotations (cited in the text) from Greene's prose works are from *The Life and Complete Works in Prose and Verse of Robert Greene,* ed. Alexander Grosart, 15 vols. (London, 1881–86); quotations from the plays are from *The Plays & Poems of Robert Greene,* ed. J. Collins, 2 vols. (Oxford, 1905)—hereafter cited in the text as *PP.*

5. So assumed, for example, by Storojenko (Grosart, ed., *Works,* 1:7, n.).

6. Brenda Richardson, "Robert Greene's Yorkshire Connexions," *Year's Work in English Studies* 10 (1980):165–67.

7. René Pruvost, *Robert Greene* (Paris, 1938), 16–18.

8. Ibid., 18 ("Ce tempérament fait les martyrs et les révoltés"). The Renaissance-Reformation contrast is a major theme of Pruvost's book; see, for example, 22, 40, 261, 457–58, 556ff. Related in approach is S. L. Wolff's emphasis on the strain in Greene's personality caused by his Puritan side ("Robert Greene and the Italian Renaissance," *Englische Studien,* 37 [1907]:321–74).

9. Richardson, "Yorkshire Connexions," 179.

10. Greene's university career is summarized by Collins, Pruvost, and others, including Johnstone Parr in "Robert Greene and His Classmates," *PMLA* 77 (1962):536–43, where a confusion about the date of Greene's B.A. is clarified. Kenneth Mildenberger, finding a Robert Greene who matriculated at Corpus Christi, Cambridge, in 1573 and (apparently) never took a degree, suggests that Greene may have moved from there to St. John's ("Robert Greene at Cambridge," *Modern Language Notes* 64 [1951]:546–49).

11. All matters treated in this paragraph are discussed in Parr, "Greene and His Classmates."

12. James Bass Mullinger, *The History of Cambridge from the Royal Injunctions of 1535 to the Accession of Charles the First* (Cambridge: Cambridge University Press, 1884), 2:390; *St. John's College* (London: Robinson, 1901), 66. Pruvost considers the effect of Cambridge on Greene at length (*Robert Greene,* 29ff.).

13. Charles Henry Cooper, *Annals of Cambridge* (Cambridge: Warwick, 1843), 2:360–61.

14. Alfred Harbage, *Shakespeare and the Rival Traditions* (New York: Macmillan, 1952), 98. Cf. Charles J. Sisson's suggestion that Oxford turned Thomas Lodge away from "the career marked out for him by his parents" and made him eager "to consort henceforth with Town and Court instead of City" ("Thomas Lodge and His Family," in *Thomas Lodge and*

Other Elizabethans, ed. Charles J. Sisson [Cambridge, Mass.: Harvard University Press, 1933], 82). Cf. too John Bakeless on Marlowe's desire to force "his way up through the rigid stratification of Elizabethan society" (*Christopher Marlowe: The Man in His Time* [New York: Morrow, 1937], 7).

15. See, for example, Jordan, *Robert Greene,* 77, n.; Pruvost, *Robert Greene,* 100–104; and Robert Ralston Cawley, *Unpathed Waters: Studies in the Influence of the Voyagers on Elizabethan Literature* (Princeton: Princeton University Press, 1940), 215–20.

16. Gabriel Harvey, *Foure Letters and certeine Sonnets, especially touching Robert Greene and other parties by him abused: 1592,* ed. G. B. Harrison (London: John Lane, 1923), 20.

17. Ibid.

18. Mark Eccles, *Christopher Marlowe in London* (Cambridge, Mass.: Harvard University Press, 1934), 124–26. By putting several documents together, Eccles is able to locate Em Ball and Fortunatus Greene on the same street.

19. Harvey, *Foure Letters,* 20.

20. The record was first published in J. Payne Collier, *Memoirs of the Principal Actors in the Plays of Shakespeare* (London: Shakespeare Society, 1846), xx, n.

21. See, for example, Pruvost, *Robert Greene,* 244–45; Jordan, *Robert Greene,* 1; and Collins, ed., *Plays & Poems,* 1:22.

22. Richardson, "Yorkshire Connexions," 173–74.

23. Brenda Richardson argues in a paper forthcoming in *Proceedings of the Royal Irish Academy* that the London phase of Greene's career began quite late and that throughout most of the 1580s he lived comfortably and respectably, perhaps under the patronage of wealthy friends. This view is in conflict with the traditional assumption that Greene's prodigality extended over several years and was closely linked to his career as a writer. Richardson's research, still in progress, may thus lead to a significant revision of our view of Greene.

24. Harvey, *Foure Letters,* 19–20.

25. Cooper, *Annals of Cambridge,* 2:161.

26. Harvey, *Four Letters,* 19.

27. *Henrie Chettle, Kind-Hartes Dreame 1592, and William Kemp, Nine Daies Wonder 1600,* ed. G. B. Harrison (London: John Lane, 1923), 13.

28. *Greenes Newes both from Heauen and Hell 1593 and Greenes Funeralls 1594,* ed. R. B. McKerrow (London: Sidgwick & Jackson, 1911), sig. C3^r. R. B. may be Richard Barnfield. See McKerrow's introduction, vii–x, and two articles by Harry Morris: "Richard Barnfield, 'Amyntas,'

and the Sidney Circle," *PMLA* 74 (1959):318–24, and "Richard Barnfield: The Affectionate Shepheard," *Tulane Studies in English* 10 (1960):13–38.

29. *Newes and Funeralls,* sig. A4ᵛ. For the possibility that B. R. is Barnabe Riche, see McKerrow's introduction, vii.

30. *The Second Part of the French Academie . . . by Peter de la Primaudaye,* 2d ed. (London: Bishop, 1594), sig. B1ʳ.

31. Parr, "Greene and His Classmates," 540.

32. *Strange Newes, of the Intercepting Certaine Letters,* in *The Works of Thomas Nashe,* ed. Ronald McKerrow, 5 vols. (Oxford, 1958), 1:330.

33. Ibid., 1:287.

34. Ibid.

35. Ibid.

36. Ibid., 1:271. Since the same story can be found elsewhere, both in literary works and court records, Evelyn May Albright asks whether Nashe is actually describing something he saw or simply borrowing a good anecdote ("Eating a Citation," *Modern Language Notes* 30 [1915]:201–6).

37. Ibid., 1:287.

38. *Pierces Supererogation or A New Praise of the Old Asse* (London: John Wolfe, 1593; Facsimile reprint, Menston: Scolar Press, 1970), sig. Z1ʳ.

39. Nashe, *Works,* 1:287.

40. Ibid.

41. Harvey, *Foure Letters,* 37, 41.

42. *Newes and Funeralls,* sig. A2ᵛ.

43. G. B.'s poem prefacing the second part of *Mamillia* says that the work grew in the "plat" of Cambridge (2:249). It is possible that in this early period Greene also wrote the lost (or never printed) ballad entered as "by Greene" in the Stationers' Register on 20 March 1580/81: "Youthe seeing all his waies so troublesome, abandoning Virtue and Learning to Vice recalleth his former Follies with an Inward Repentance." Certainly the subject is consistent with Greene's concerns throughout his career, and Aldo Maugeri has suggested that the ballad might have followed from the conversion in Norwich (*Greene, Marlowe e Shakespeare: Tre studi biographici* [Messina: Ferrara, 1952], 11–12).

44. Harvey's attitude toward Greene's works runs throughout the *Foure Letters,* despite his saying, "I will not condemne, or censure his workes, which I neuer did so much as superficially ouerrunne, but as some fewe of them occursiuly presented themselues in Stationers shops, and some other houses of my acquaintaunce" (41). Other contemporary attacks on Greene make use of the same image of him as author of immoral and trivial works about love. The translator of the *French Academie,* for example, castigating Greene's character and opinions, laments the fact that "this fellow in his life time and in the middest of his greatest ruffe, had the

Presse at commaundement to publish his lasciusous [*sic*] Pamphlets" (sig. B1ʳ).

45. A "Farewell to Follie by Greene" was registered on 11 June 1587 but no work of this title has survived before the *Farewell to Folly* of 1591. Since the prefaces to the latter fit it clearly into the sequence under discussion, Greene either withdrew it or never finished it in 1587, instead giving the same printer *Penelopes Web*, registered two weeks later. Pruvost suggests that Greene abandoned the *Farewell* when he abandoned his wife and draws a link between *Penelopes Web* and Greene's attitude toward women (*Robert Greene*, 249). The other old work was *Philomela*, registered 1 July 1592, which Greene offers although it was "writen long since & kept charily" as "scollers treasurs be, in loose papers" (11:109). He goes on to apologize for violating his promise in the *Mourning Garment* and the *Farewell* "neuer to busie my selfe about any wanton pamphlets again" (11:113).

46. Collins, ed., *Plays & Poems*, 1:33; Jordan, *Robert Greene*, 94. Other discussions of authenticity can be found in Pruvost, *Robert Greene*: the pamphlets do not suggest close contact with the underworld (431–43); Frank Aydelotte, *Elizabethan Rogues and Vagabonds*, Oxford Historical and Literary Studies, vol. 1 (Oxford: Clarendon Press, 1913): the pamphlets "bear on their face the stamp of truth and are the most vivid and brilliant works of the kind which the age produced" (126); James McPeek, *The Black Book of Knaves* (n.p., 1969), 101–33: Greene probably knew coney-catchers and used what he had learned from them; and Edwin Miller, *The Professional Writer in Elizabethan England*: "most of the material . . . is his own" (241). The works on which Greene draws are reprinted in A. V. Judges, *The Elizabethan Underworld* (London: Routledge, 1930).

47. Theophilus Cibber, *The Lives of the Poets of Great Britain and Ireland, to the Time of Dean Swift* (London: R. Griffiths, 1753), 1:87.

48. Nashe, *Works*, 1:271.

49. The statement is part of Collins's effort to show that Greene came to the drama very late. For reactions to this controversial idea see the reviews of Collins in the bibliography. In addition to Collins, good starting points for reviewing the many attempts to date Greene's plays are provided by Jordan, *Robert Greene*, 174–82, and *A Looking Glasse*, ed. George Clugson (New York, 1980), 48–61.

50. So argued in 1878 by R. Simpson in *The School of Shakspere* (London: Chatto and Windus, 1878), 2:352ff., and endorsed by such writers as Collins, ed., *Plays & Poems*, 1:39–43; Pruvost, *Robert Greene*, 256–58; John Bakeless, *The Tragicall History of Christopher Marlowe* (Cambridge, Mass.: Harvard University Press, 1942), 2:95–97; and Thomas Dickinson, ed., *Robert Greene* (London, 1909), xxxii–v. Dickinson provides a particularly good example of the analysis based on a definition of Greene's capacity for envy which the text goes on to note.

51. See Jordan, *Robert Greene*, 96–107; Pruvost, *Robert Greene*, 443–53; David Parker, "Robert Greene and 'The Defense of Conny Catching,' " *Notes & Queries*, n.s., 21 (1974):87–89; and three articles by Edwin Haviland Miller: " 'The Defense of Cony-Catching' (1592): The Argument of H. C. Hart," *Notes & Queries* 196 (1951):509–12; "Further Notes on the Authorship of 'The Defence of Cony-Catching' (1592)," *Notes & Queries* 197 (1952):446–51; and "The Relationship of Robert Greene and Thomas Nashe," *Philological Quarterly* 33 (1954):353–67. For denials of Greene's authorship see H. C. Hart, "Robert Greene's Prose Works," *Notes & Queries*, 10th ser., 5 (1906):84–85, and I. A. Shapiro, "An Unsuspected Earlier Edition of *The Defence of Conny-catching*," *Library*, 5th ser., 18 (1963):88–112. It is interesting that the central charge of the *Defence*—that Greene busied himself with small offenders only—is the reason for Greene's exclusion from Heaven in *Greenes Newes* (*Newes and Funeralls*, sigs. C1ʳ–C1ᵛ).

52. See W. W. Greg, *Two Elizabethan Stage Abridgements* (Oxford: Clarendon Press, 1923), esp. 127. Greg concludes, though, that Greene need not have sold the play twice (see 352–57). E. K. Chambers raises important questions about Greg's argument in his review of Greg's book in *Library*, 4th ser., 4 (1924):242–48.

53. Harvey, *Foure Letters*, 44.

54. Nashe, *Works*, 3:132.

55. Ibid., 1:303.

56. Ibid., 1:330.

57. Possibilities are reviewed in Miller, "Greene and Nashe."

58. Nashe, *Works*, 1:319.

59. Reprinted in ibid., 5:180.

60. Ibid., 3:130.

61. Ibid., 1:271.

62. Pruvost, *Robert Greene*, 546. Harvey's attack has had a way of inspiring colorful phrases. Grosart referred to Harvey's "self-conceit so malignant and malignancy so self-conceited" (*The Works of Gabriel Harvey*, D. C. L. [London: Huth Library, 1885], 3:xi), and Gayley wrote that Harvey "embalmed [the story of Greene's death] with the foul peculiar juices of his spite" (*Representative English Comedies*, 1:398). Francis Meres began the tradition by comparing Harvey's treatment of Greene to the way "*Achilles* tortured the deade bodie of *Hector*, and . . . *Antonius*, and his wife *Fuluia* tormented the liuelesse corps of *Cicero*" in *Palladis Tamia* (London, 1598; facsimile reprint, ed. Don Cameron Allen [New York: Scholar's Facsimiles and Reprints, 1938]), sig. Oo6ʳ.

63. *A New Letter of Notable Contents* . . . (London: John Wolfe, 1593; facsimile reprint, Menston: Scolar Press, 1970), sig. B4ʳ. Greene's role in the Harvey-Nashe quarrel is treated in the summaries of the quarrel

in Nashe, *Works,* 5:65–110; G. R. Hibbard, *Thomas Nashe: A Critical Introduction* (Cambridge, Mass.: Harvard University Press, 1962), 180–232; and Virginia F. Stern, *Gabriel Harvey: His Life, Marginalia and Library* (Oxford: Clarendon Press, 1979), 88–129. Greene's relations with the Harveys are the subject of Chauncey Sanders, *Robert Greene and the Harveys* (Bloomington, 1931).

64. Donald J. McGinn suggests that Greene and Nashe collaborated on the passage in the *Quip* in "A Quip from Tom Nashe," in *Studies in the English Renaissance Drama in Memory of Karl Julius Holzknecht,* ed. Josephine W. Bennett et al. (New York: New York University Press, 1959), 172–88. The idea is disputed in Hibbard, *Thomas Nashe,* 254–55.

65. G. B. Harrison calls Greene flatly the "head of the group" of "the professional writers who were paid to answer the Martin Marprelate pamphlets" (in *Pierce Penilesse, His Supplication to the Diuell (1592)* [London: John Lane, 1924], viii), but other scholars are more cautious. McKerrow writes that "if Greene had not been a prominent anti-Martinist, it seems probable that the great quarrel would never have arisen," but he recognizes the ambiguity of Nashe's account (Nashe, *Works,* 5:75–76). Chauncey Sanders finds no evidence whatever that Greene was an anti-Martinist (*Greene and the Harveys,* 13–17).

66. Harvey says in *Foure Letters* that Greene was motivated by fear (13–14), but Nashe answered that Greene honored the wishes of "a learned Doctour of Phisicke" who objected to seeing a fellow physician (John Harvey) "ill spoken of" (*Strange Newes,* in Nashe, *Works,* 1:279–80). Hibbard *(Thomas Nashe)* and Sanders *(Greene and the Harveys)* both suggest that John Harvey's death caused Greene to withdraw the passage, and R. B. Parker says that it may reflect an attack of conscience ("Alterations in the First Edition of Greene's *A Quip for an Upstart Courtier* (1592)," *Huntington Library Quarterly* 23 [1960]:181–86). Edwin Haviland Miller agrees in "Deletions in Robert Greene's *A Quip for an Upstart Courtier* (1592)," *Huntington Library Quarterly* 15 (1952):277–82; in another article Miller suggests that Greene withdrew the attack because it had been written under the influence of Nashe, who was now out of London ("Greene and Nashe").

67. Harvey, *Foure Letters,* 20.

68. George Watson Cole, "Bibliography—A Forecast," *Publications of the Bibliographical Society of America* 14 (1920):7–8. Cole first reprinted the passage, which had been lost until that time. It is also reprinted in Nashe, *Works,* 5:75–76.

69. Nashe, *Works,* 5:68, 1:282.

70. The evidence is reviewed in Philip Drew, "Was Greene's 'Young Juvenal' Nashe or Lodge?" *Studies in English Literature* 7 (1967):55–56.

71. David H. Horne argues that the evidence for Greene's friendship
with Peele is slim and that Greene may be picking well-known writers
to address merely in order to make the pamphlet attractive (*The Life and
Minor Works of George Peele* [New Haven: Yale University Press, 1952],
87–89, 127–29). Horne follows most other writers, however, in assuming
that Peele is indeed intended in the passage, although the identification
rests mainly on the use of an oath by St. George: "And thou no lesse
deseruing then the other two, in some things rarer, in nothing inferiour;
driuen (as my selfe) to extreame shifts, a little haue I to say to thee: and
were it not an idolatrous oth, I would sweare by sweet *S. George,* thou art
vnworthie better hap, sith thou dependest on so meane a stay" (12:143).
72. Treated at length in Eccles, *Marlowe in London.*
73. For evaluation of Meres's comment and for the struggles of
Peele's life generally see Horne, *George Peele,* passim.
74. For Nashe's admissions see *Works,* 1:303, 310. The Harvey
passage is in *A New Letter,* sig. C4ᵛ. For discussion of Nashe's *A Choice of
Valentines* and its context see David O. Frantz, " 'Leud Priapians' and
Renaissance Pornography," *Studies in English Literature* 12 (1972):157–72.
75. Sisson, "Lodge and His Family," 102–3; Gosson, Dedicatory
Epistle in *Playes Confuted in Fiue actions* (London, 1582; facsimile reprint,
New York: Garland, 1972). In addition to the names here reviewed, the
Robert Lee to whom the second part of *Mamillia* is dedicated may have
been an actor (and possibly a dramatist) of that name; see E. K. Chambers,
The Elizabethan Stage (Oxford: Clarendon Press, 1923), 2:328, 407. Richardson suggests, however, that he may have been a Robert Lee who was
a member of the Yorkshire circle from which several of Greene's dedicatees
came ("Yorkshire Connexions," 162).
76. The three essential starting points for reviewing this question
are Edmond Malone, "A Dissertation on the Three Parts of Henry VI,"
in *Malone's Shakespeare,* ed. Boswell (London, 1821), 18:570ff.; Peter Alexander, *Shakespeare's Henry VI and Richard III* (Cambridge, 1929); and J.
Dover Wilson, "Malone and the Upstart Crow," *Shakespeare Survey* 4
(1951):56–58. Malone uses the passage as the foundation for his famous
argument that Shakespeare began his career as a reviser of other men's
plays—thus Greene's phrase "beautified with our feathers." When Alexander showed that what had been thought Shakespeare's source plays were
not by Greene and others but bad quartos of Shakespeare's own plays, he
defined "feathers" as lines spoken by actors but written by playwrights;
Greene's complaint is that Shakespeare, as upstart crow, is an actor writing
his own plays. Wilson found a series of parallel references to borrowed
feathers to support a resurrection of Malone's reading (though conceding
Alexander's view of the texts in question). Since then, both Alexander and
Wilson have had adherents, with majority opinion favoring Alexander.

The eccentric view that Shakespeare is not, after all, the upstart crow can be sampled in C. A. C. Davis, "The Upstart Crow," *Times Literary Supplement,* 17 August 1951, 517, or William Hall Chapman, *Shakespeare: The Personal Phase* (n.p., 1920), 287–371.

    77. Social prejudice in Greene's attack is discussed by J. A. K. Thompson in *Shakespeare and the Classics* (London: Allen & Unwin, 1952), 156–62, 179–80, and by Muriel C. Bradbrook in two places: *The Rise of the Common Player: A Study of Actor and Society in Shakespeare's England* (Cambridge, Mass.: Harvard University Press, 1962), 83, and "Beasts and Gods: Greene's *Groats-worth of Witte* and the Social Purpose of *Venus and Adonis*," *Shakespeare Survey* 15 (1962):62–72. See also A. Robin Bowers's answer to Bradbrook: " 'Hard Armours' and 'Delicate Amours' in Shakespeare's *Venus and Adonis*," *Shakespeare Studies* 12 (1979):1–23.

    78. C. Elliot Brown, "Greene's 'Upstart Crow,' " *Notes & Queries,* 5th ser., 3 (1874):64. Other attempts to set the quarrel back in time include R. Simpson, "On Some Plays Attributed to Shakspere," *Transactions of the New Shakspere Society, 1875,* ser. 1, pt. 1, 155–80; Charles Speroni, "Did Greene Have Shakespeare in Mind?" *Modern Language Notes* 87 (1972):134–41; and T. W. Baldwin, *On the Literary Genetics of Shakespeare's Plays 1592–1594* (Urbana, 1959), 1–55. For critics of Simpson's generation, tracing the quarrel often meant searching for portraits of real people in plays of the period. See, for example, J. M. Brown's reading Shakespeare's Falstaff and Bottom as parodies of Greene in "An Early Rival of Shakespeare," *New Zealand Magazine,* no. 6 (1877), quoted in Grosart, ed., *Works,* 1:xviii. The identification with Bottom was around at least until 1938, when discussed by Thomas H. McNeal in "The Tyger's Heart Wrapt in a Player's Hide," *Shakespeare Association Bulletin* 13 (1938):30–39. An even more recent critic has seen Greene in Armado in *Love's Labor's Lost*: Eugene J. Kettner, "*Love's Labor's Lost* and the Harvey-Nashe-Greene Quarrel," *Emporia State Research Studies* 10 (1962):37–38. Other examples, old and new, include [Robert Cartwright], *The Footsteps of Shakespeare; or a Ramble with the Early Dramatists* (London: John Russell Smith, 1862), 146–53; F. G. Fleay, *Shakespeare Manual* (London: Macmillan, 1878), 280–302; and W. Schrickx, *Shakespeare's Early Contemporaries: The Background of the Harvey-Nashe Polemic and Love's Labour's Lost* (Antwerp: Nederlansche Boekhandel, 1956), passim.

    79. See, for example, G. M. Pinciss, "Shakespeare, Her Majesty's Players and Pembroke's Men," *Shakespeare Survey* 27 (1974):129–36. Theories have not always rested on solid evidence; for example, Shakespeare had a hand in "the boycott which almost certainly followed" the double sale of *Orlando* and which "proved the final cause of Greene's ruin" (Wilson, "Malone and the Upstart Crow," 63). And yes it has been suggested that

Greene was the rival poet of the sonnets: H. A. Shield, "Links with Shakespeare VI," *Notes & Queries* 195 (1950):206.

80. The identification is at least as old as an anonymous article from 1840—"Suppositions about Shakspere, By a *ci-devant* Comedian," *New Monthly Magazine* 60 (1840):297–99—and has been suggested more recently by Bradbrook in "Beasts and Gods," 67, and *Common Player*, 86.

81. Anthony Burgess, *Shakespeare* (New York: Knopf, 1970), 108–10.

82. Harvey, *Foure Letters*, 97–98.

83. Ibid., 13.

84. Ibid., 20–24.

85. Harvey's second letter is dated 5 September and in it he refers to Greene's "buriall yesterday" (*Foure Letters*, 22). In the *Repentance*, discussed below, a letter purporting to be written by Greene on the night before his death is dated 2 September (12:185–86).

86. Harvey, *Foure Letters*, 13–14.

87. Ibid., 39.

88. Chettle, *Kind-Hartes Dreame*, 5–7. It is here that Chettle makes a comment often taken as an apology to Shakespeare for Greene's attack. Many writers follow Storojenko in assuming that Burby wrote the account (Grosart, ed., *Works*, 1:53) but there is no evidence that he did. Charles Crawford offers the interesting theory that Nicholas Breton wrote both the account and *Greenes Funeralls*, and visited Greene on the night before he died ("*Greenes Funeralls*, 1594, and Nicholas Breton," *Studies in Philology*, extra ser., 1 [1929]:1–39).

89. Chettle, *Kind-Hartes Dreame*, 35.

90. Nashe, *Works*, 1:269.

91. Ibid., 1:289.

92. Ibid., 1:287–88.

93. Ibid., 1:153.

94. R. B.'s prayer for mercy toward Greene is ambiguous (*Newes and Funeralls*, sig. C3^r); Bowes assumes a repentant Greene but the assumption may be based entirely on the *Repentance*, which he quotes (*French Academie*, sig. B1^r).

95. Chettle, *Kind-Hartes Dreame*, 5–7. One other contemporary gives the *Groats-worth* to Greene: B. R., in *Greenes Newes*, lists it among several of Greene's works (*Newes and Funeralls*, sigs. B2^r–B2^v, C1^r).

96. The authenticity of the *Groats-worth* was attacked with thoroughness in Chauncey Elwood Sanders, "Robert Greene and His 'Editors,' " *PMLA* 48 (1933):392–417. Sanders was answered by Pruvost, *Robert Greene*, 505–25, and Harold Jenkins, "On the Authenticity of Greene's *Groatsworth of Wit* and *The Repentance of Robert Greene*," *Review of English Studies* 11 (1935):28–41; the matter was reopened by Warren B.

Austin, whose preliminary case against Greene's authorship is summarized by Louis Marder in "Greene's Attack on Shakespeare: A Posthumous Hoax?" *Shakespeare Newsletter* 16 (1966):29–30. Austin proceeded to a computer study, reporting his results in *A Computer-Aided Technique* (Washington, D.C., 1969). Marder summarized this study in "Chettle's Forgery of the Groatsworth of Wit and the 'Shake-scene' Passage," *Shakespeare Newsletter* 20 (1970):42. See also Austin's "Technique of the Chettle-Greene Forgery: Supplementary Material on the Authorship of the Groatsworth of Wit," *Shakespeare Newsletter* 20 (1970):43. Reviewers of Austin were unconvinced that his statistical methods had led to conclusive results; see T. R. Waldo in *Computers and the Humanities* 7 (1972):109–10; R. L. Widmann in *Shakespeare Quarterly* 23 (1972):214–15; and William Proudfoot in *Shakespeare Survey* 26 (1973):177–84. See also T. M. Pearce's letter and Austin's answer in *Shakespeare Newsletter* 21 (1971):4. Barbara Kreifelts's later computer-based study led her also to assign the *Groats-worth* to Chettle: *Eine statistische stilanalyse*—digested by her in *Shakespeare Newsletter* 24 (1974):49.

97. The use of the *Resolution,* called by Collins "a truly appalling work" (*Plays & Poems,* 1:46), is discussed in Edwin Haviland Miller, "Robert Parson's [sic] 'Resolution' and 'The Repentance of Robert Greene,' " *Notes & Queries,* n.s., 1 (1954):104–8.

98. Bowes, *French Academie,* sig. B1ʳ.

99. Storojenko's review of the debate up to his time (Grosart, ed., *Works,* 1:151–55) is a useful summary and notes especially the attack on authenticity in Friedrich Bodenstedt, *Shakespeare's Zeitgenossen und ihre Werke* (Berlin: R. Decker, 1860), 3:57–75. Collins was "half inclined to think that *The Repentance* may have been interpolated with passages taken from" the confession of a coney-catcher and notes "a suspiciously close resemblance" to the confessions of Ned Browne in the *Blacke Bookes Messenger* (*Plays & Poems,* 1:53, 51). Sanders developed at length what Collins suspected in "Greene and His 'Editors,' " to be answered, as for the *Groatsworth,* by Jenkins in "Authenticity." Pruvost also rejected Sanders' arguments (*Robert Greene,* 525–45). More recently, Norbert Bolz concluded from computer analysis that the "Repentance" is a forgery in *Eine statistische, computerunterstützte Echtheitsprüfung*—summarized by Bolz in "Are Robert Greene's 'Autobiographies' Fake? The Forgery of *The Repentance of Robert Greene,*" *Shakespeare Newsletter* 29 (1979):43. All of these writers take up not simply the "Repentance" but other sections of the *Repentance* as well.

100. Among discussions of the date and authenticity of the *Vision,* see especially Collins, ed., *Plays & Poems,* 1:26, n.; Jordan, *Robert Greene,* 169–70; and Pruvost, *Robert Greene,* 369–73, 378–82. Attempts to set the work precisely in the sequence of works around 1590 proclaiming a

new purpose are made by Waldo F. McNeir, "The Date of Greene's 'Vision,' " *Notes & Queries* 195 (1950):137, and D. Nicholas Ranson, "The Date of Greene's 'Vision' Revisited," *Notes & Queries*, n.s., 22 (1975):534–35. See also McNeir's "The Date of 'A Looking Glasse for London,' " *Notes & Queries*, n.s., 2 (1955):282–83.
    101. Nashe, *Works*, 1:287.
    102. *The Lives of the Most Famous English Poets* (London, 1687; facsimile reprint, ed. William Riley Parker [Gainesville, Fla.: Scholars' Facsimiles, 1963], 74). The paradox has been the center of many approaches to Greene. See Storojenko (in Grosart, ed., *Works*, vol. 1) for a classic treatment.

Chapter Two

    1. The most thorough examination of Greene's reversal of *Euphues* is contained in Jaroslav Hornát, "*Mamillia*: Robert Greene's Controversy with *Euphues*," *Philologica Pragensia* 5 (1962):210–18.
    2. Jordan, *Robert Greene*, 7.
    3. Louis Cazamian, *The Development of English Humor, Parts I and II* (Durham, N.C.: Duke University Press, 1952), 137; Howard C. Cole, *A Quest of Inquirie* (Indianapolis, 1973), 520; and Normand Berlin, *The Base String: The Underworld in Elizabethan Drama* (Rutherford, N.J.: Fairleigh Dickinson University Press, 1968), 26.
    4. David Bevington, *Tudor Drama and Politics* (Cambridge, Mass., 1968), 208.
    5. Jordan, *Robert Greene*, 204.
    6. Rosemond Tuve, *Elizabethan and Metaphysical Imagery: Renaissance Poetic and Twentieth-Century Critics* (Chicago: University of Chicago Press, 1947), 409.
    7. Robert Scholes and Robert Kellogg, *The Nature of Narrative* (Oxford: Oxford University Press, 1966), 88.
    8. Richard Lanham's discussion of rhetoric as a theme in Gascoigne, Lyly, Sidney, and Nashe is relevant to *Mamillia*: "Opaque Style in Elizabethan Fiction," *Pacific Coast Philology* 1 (1966):25–31.
    9. The failure of precepts to protect Mamillia is noted in Richard Helgerson, *The Elizabethan Prodigals* (Berkeley, 1976), 81.
    10. *A Midsummer Night's Dream* (1.1.74–78), in *The Riverside Shakespeare*, ed. G. Blakemore Evans et al. (Boston: Houghton Mifflin, 1974).
    11. Collins made the same point in an unsigned review of 1885 (*Quarterly Review* 161 [1885]:370).
    12. Greene's use of Greek romance is most thoroughly described in Samuel Lee Wolff, *The Greek Romances in Elizabethan Prose Fiction* (New York, 1912), 367–458. See also chapter 5 in Walter R. Davis, *Idea and Act in Elizabethan Fiction* (Princeton, 1969), 138–88.

13. Lewis, *English Literature,* 421.

14. Wolff, "Italian Renaissance," 367–68.

15. *The Mirror for Magistrates,* ed. Lily B. Campbell (Cambridge: Cambridge University Press, 1938), 172. The lines are from a passage cited for its relevance to drama in Douglas Cole, *Suffering and Evil in the Plays of Christopher Marlowe* (Princeton: Princeton University Press, 1962), 44.

16. Cecile W. Cary finds the same kind of connection between temperance and spiritual health in *Friar Bacon and Friar Bungay* in "The Iconography of Food and the Motif of World Order in *Friar Bacon and Friar Bungay,*" *Comparative Drama* 13 (1979):150–63.

17. *The Decameron of Giovanni Boccaccio,* trans. Frances Winwar (New York: Random House, 1955), 77.

18. Baker, *English Novel,* 113. Wolff makes the same point in virtually the same words: Greene's "combination of such a love of plot with a weak sense of motive and causal nexus, strongly inclines him to employ Fortune as the mover of his plot" (*Greek Romances,* 375). Indeed, Wolff's is the most violent of attacks on Greene's use of Fortune (see especially 381–92).

19. Ian Watt, *The Rise of the Novel: Studies in Defoe, Richardson and Fielding* (London: Chatto & Windus, 1957), 12.

20. Charles Dickens, *Hard Times,* ed. George Ford and Sylvère Monod (New York: Norton, 1966), 46.

21. The borrowings are reviewed in Pruvost, *Robert Greene,* 313–15.

22. For Longus and Greene's other sources, see Wolff, *Greek Romances,* 442–45.

23. Davis, *Idea and Act,* 178.

24. Ibid., 60.

25. Wallace A. Bacon, ed., *William Warner's Syrinx or A Sevenfold History* (Evanston, Ill.: Northwestern University Press, 1950), lxxvii.

26. The poem is based on the "Description d'Amour" of Mellin de Saint-Gelais (1534) and in it, says Richard E. Quaintance, Jr., "Greene seems to have dodged rather carefully the neutral or approving statements in Saint-Gelais' description of love" ("The French Source of Robert Greene's 'What Thing Is Love,' " *Notes & Queries,* n.s., 10 [1963]:295).

27. A. C. Hamilton, "Elizabethan Romance: The Example of Prose Fiction," *English Literary History* 49 (1982):289.

28. Shakespeare, *All's Well . . .* (5.3.6–8), in *Riverside Shakespeare.*

29. Shakespeare, *As You Like It* (5.4.36), in ibid.

30. Shakespeare, *Twelfth Night* (2.2.31) and *Measure for Measure* (5.1.439–41), both in ibid.

31. Of the many discussions of euphuistic imagery, especially relevant here is Shimon Sandbank's observation that the use of strings of

parallel images tends to make individual images "perfectly replaceable instances of highly formalized and very comprehensive logical formulas" ("Euphuistic Symmetry and the Image," *Studies in English Literature* 11 [1971]:12).

32. A link to Polonius is noted by Herford in "A Few Suggestions." Helgerson discusses parallels to other writers in *Elizabethan Prodigals*, 16–18.

33. Pruvost, *Robert Greene*, 459; Baker, *History of the English Novel*, 144.

34. See Louis B. Wright, *Middle-Class Culture in Elizabethan England* (Chapel Hill: University of North Carolina Press, 1935), 384–87 and passim, for a discussion of Greene's audience.

35. For C. S. Lewis this apology "suggests that Greene felt himself not to be essaying a new kind of excellence but to be absolved from caring how he wrote" (*English Literature*, 402).

36. He took the idea for terms, though, from the anonymous *Manifest Detection of Dice Play* (1552), which describes the Taker-Up, the Verser, the Barnard, and the Rutter. See Jordan, *Robert Greene*, 89–91.

37. The passage in the *Manifest Detection* is quoted in Pruvost, *Robert Greene*, 440, n.

38. Parallels between *Mamillia* and *The Merchant of Venice* are noted in René Pruvost, "Le 'Marchand de Venise' avant Shakespeare," *Revue Anglo-Américaine* 3 (1926):511–14, and Thomas H. McNeal, "Who Is Sylvia?—and Other Problems in the Greene-Shakespeare Relationship," *Shakespeare Association Bulletin* 13 (1938):240–54.

39. Sources are discussed in Wolff, *Greek Romances*, 395–404; Pruvost, *Robert Greene*, 162–66; Jaroslav Hornát, "Two Euphuistic Stories of Robert Greene: *The Carde of Fancie* and *Pandosto*," *Philologica Pragensia* 6 (1963):21–35; and Robert W. Dent, "Greene's *Gwydonius*: A Study in Elizabethan Plagiarism," *Huntington Library Quarterly* 24 (1961):151–62.

40. Helmut Bonheim briefly relates *Gwydonius* to Elizabethan fascination with family struggles in "Robert Greene's *Gwydonius*," *Anglia* 96 (1978):59–60, and Helgerson discusses it in terms of a "conflict between established, but abusive authority and youth" which, after *Mamillia*, came "to occupy the dramatic center of [Greene's] fiction" in *Elizabethan Prodigals*, 83–87.

41. Thus Davis notes that Gwydonius's "success unites kingdoms, lovers, families, and the two sides of his own identity" (*Idea and Act*, 143).

42. The use of euphuistic style in Susanna's story is discussed with stern disapproval by Pruvost in *Robert Greene*, 168–72.

43. Johnstone Parr, "Sources of the Astrological Prefaces in Robert Greene's *Planetomachia*," *Studies in Philology* 36 (1949):400–410.

44. Sources of the stories in *Planetomachia,* Italian and otherwise, are surveyed in Pruvost, *Robert Greene,* 218–22. For Italian sources generally, see W. W. Greg, "Giraldi Cintio and the English Drama," *Modern Language Quarterly* 3 (1900):189–90; 5 (1902):72–73, and René Pruvost, *Matteo Bandello and Elizabethan Fiction* (Paris: Champion, 1937).

45. Jordan, *Robert Greene,* 32.

46. Richardson, "Yorkshire Connexions," 178.

47. Arthur Freeman, "An Unacknowledged Work of Robert Greene," *Notes & Queries,* n.s., 12 (1965):378–79.

48. Greene's possible influence on *Troilus and Cressida* is discussed in Herford, "A Few Suggestions," 187–90; Kenneth Muir, "Greene and 'Troilus and Cressida,' " *Notes & Queries,* n.s., 2 (1955):141–42; Kenneth Muir, *Shakespeare's Sources: I. Comedies and Tragedies* (London: Methuen, 1957), 87–88; Robert Kimbrough, *Shakespeare's Troilus and Cressida and Its Setting* (Cambridge, Mass.: Harvard University Press, 1964), 34–36; and Virgil K. Whitaker, "Still Another Source for *Troilus and Cressida,*" in *English Renaissance Drama: Essays in Honor of Madeleine Doran and Mark Eccles,* ed. Standish Henning et al. (Carbondale: Southern Illinois University Press, 1976), 100–107.

49. Lewis, *English Literature,* 422; the first quotation in the sentence is from Cole, *Quest of Inquirie,* 521.

50. J. J. Jusserand, *English Novel in the Time of Shakespeare,* rev. ed., trans. Elizabeth Lee (London, 1895), 179.

51. Anthony Esler, "Robert Greene and the Spanish Armada," *English Literary History* 32 (1965):332.

52. See the chronology in A. F. Allison, *Robert Greene 1558–1592: A Bibliographical Catalogue of the Early Editions in English (to 1640)* (Folkestone, 1975), 9–14.

53. Storojenko, in Grosart, ed., *Works,* 1:119.

54. Charles Speroni compares Greene's translation to the original in *The Aphorisms of Orazio Rinaldi, Robert Greene, and Lucas Gracian Dantisco* (Berkeley: University of California Press, 1968), 22–29. In "Did Greene Have Shakespeare in Mind?" Speroni notes the relation of the "shamefast" aphorism to Greene's attitude toward drama.

55. For the relation of this story to the *Myrrour* see Hart, "Greene's Prose Works" (1905):162–64, and Pruvost, *Robert Greene,* 386, n.

56. Margaret Schlauch briefly notes some of the elements of "contemporary real life" in *Never Too Late,* in *Antecedents of the English Novel 1400–1600 (from Chaucer to Deloney)* (Warsaw: PWN, 1963), 193–94.

57. Henry Morley suggests that the three tales were to have been followed by four more to complete a treatment of the Seven Deadly Sins (*English Writers: An Attempt Towards a History of English Literature,* vol.

10, *Shakespeare and His Time: Under Elizabeth* [London: Cassell, 1893], 94–95).

58. Charles Read Baskervill, *English Elements in Jonson's Early Comedy* (Austin: University of Texas, 1911), 13.

59. Jordan warmly praises the humor of the *Disputation* (*Robert Greene,* 117–18).

60. Greene borrows the tale from Gascoigne's *Adventures of Master F. J.*, as first discussed by John Clark Jordan, "Greene and Gascoigne," *Modern Language Notes* 30 (1915):61–62.

61. See Collins, ed., *Plays & Poems,* 2:219–20, for commentary on the dedication. That Greene dedicated three works of 1591 and 1592 (*A Maidens Dreame,* Lodge's *Euphues Shadowe,* and *Philomela*) to members of Norfolk families perhaps bears on the autobiographical pamphlets soon to be published.

62. John Colin Dunlop, *History of Prose Fiction,* rev. ed. (1816; reprint, London: Bell, 1888), 2:557.

63. J. Payne Collier said of the *Quip* that "a more wholesale or barefaced piece of plagiarism is not, perhaps, to be pointed out in our literature" (*The Debate between Pride and Lowliness: By Francis Thynn* [London: Shakespeare Society, 1841], v–vi). According to Edwin H. Miller, however, only about 40 percent is based on F. T.'s poem ("The Sources of Robert Greene's 'A Quip for an Upstart Courtier' (1592)," *Notes & Queries* 198 [1953]:148–52, 187–91). Greene's use of the poem is also discussed in detail in Pruvost, *Robert Greene,* 478–85.

64. The language is seen as "the highest point in the development of Greene's prose style" by Jordan (*Robert Greene,* 124), whose enthusiasm for the *Quip* as a whole (121–26) is matched by a number of other critics, including C. S. Lewis ("the best of all Greene's pamphlets" [*English Literature,* 404]) and Harold V. Routh (Greene here "reaches his consummation" ["London and the Development of Popular Literature: Character Writing, Satire, The Essay," in *The Cambridge History of English Literature,* vol. 4, *Prose and Poetry: Sir Thomas North to Michael Drayton* (Cambridge: Cambridge University Press, 1917), 366]).

Chapter Three

1. Thomas Marc Parrott, *Shakespearean Comedy* (New York, 1949), 79.

2. Norman Sanders, "The Comedy of Greene and Shakespeare," in *Early Shakespeare,* ed. John Brown and Bernard Harris (London, 1961), 36.

3. The traditional account of the University Wits and their contributions can be sampled in Downer, *British Drama,* 73–94, or Allardyce

Nicoll, *British Drama,* 4th ed. (New York: Barnes & Noble, 1947), 73–100.

4. Werner Habicht, "The *Wit*-Interludes and the Form of Pre-Shakespearean 'Romantic Comedy,' " *Renaissance Drama* 8 (1965):73. See the discussion of Greene in Habicht's *Studien zur Dramenform vor Shakespeare* (Heidelberg, 1968).

5. The most systematic study of the relation of the plays to Greene's fiction is Allan H. MacLaine, "Greene's Borrowings from His Own Prose Fiction in *Bacon and Bungay* and *James the Fourth,*" *Philological Quarterly* 30 (1951):22–29. A useful approach to broader continuities between the two genres is R. S. White, " 'Comedy' in Elizabethan Prose Romances," *Year's Work in English Studies* 5 (1975):46–51. Emblematic elements in Elizabethan drama have received a great deal of attention in recent years, and there is no need for a list of works on the subject here. Particularly useful, however, in approaching Greene is the chapter "Emblematic Drama" in Peter M. Daly, *Literature in the Light of the Emblem: Structural Parallels between the Emblem and Literature in the Sixteenth and Seventeenth Centuries* (Toronto: University of Toronto Press, 1979), 134–67. Daly describes many emblematic motifs that have parallels in Greene's plays.

6. Parallels to *Tamburlaine* are listed in Collins, ed., *Plays & Poems,* 1:72–73, and Bakeless, *Tragicall History,* 1:248–52.

7. Werner Senn describes elements of "popular romance and fairy tale" in *Alphonsus* and notes the transition to more explicit imitation of Marlowe described below (*Studies in the Dramatic Construction of Robert Greene and George Peele* [Bern, 1973], 42–44, 72).

8. The parallel is noted in Collins, ed., *Plays & Poems,* 1:279.

9. Irving Ribner suggests that in *Alphonsus* Greene "would repeat the sensationalist elements in *Tamburlaine* and at the same time answer Marlowe's irreverence with the orthodox views dear to most Elizabethans" ("Greene's Attack on Marlowe: Some Light on *Alphonsus and Selimus,*" *Studies in Philology* 52 [1955]:165). Bevington comments on Ribner's view in *Tudor Drama and Politics,* 220–21.

10. Sanders, "Comedy of Greene and Shakespeare," 39.

11. See, for example, *Robert Greene,* ed. Dickinson, xxxvi; Thomas Marc Parrott and Robert Hamilton Ball, *A Short View of Elizabethan Drama* (New York: Scribner's, 1943), 71; Wolfgang Clemen, *Tragedy before Shakespeare,* trans. T. S. Dorsch (London, 1961), 181–82; and Una Ellis-Fermor, "Marlowe and Greene: A Note on Their Relations as Dramatic Artists," in *Studies in Honor of T. W. Baldwin,* ed. Don C. Allen (Urbana, 1958):143–45.

12. Greg, *Elizabethan Stage Abridgements,* 352–57.

13. For comparison of the play to its source see Charles W. Lemmi, "The Sources of Greene's *Orlando Furioso,*" *Modern Language Notes* 31

(1916):440–41; Peter Morrison, "Greene's Use of Ariosto in *Orlando Furioso*," *Modern Language Notes* 49 (1934):449–51; Waldo F. McNeir, "Greene's Medievalization of Ariosto," *Revue de littérature comparée* 29 (1955):351–60; and Robert G. Hunter, *Shakespeare and the Comedy of Forgiveness* (New York, 1965), 71–74.

14. Greg, *Elizabethan Stage Abridgements*, 226.

15. The disparity is treated in Norman Gelber, "Robert Greene's 'Orlando Furioso': A Study of Thematic Ambiguity," *Modern Language Review* 64 (1969):264–66.

16. William Babula sees incompatibility between Sacrepant's last words to Orlando and his last words to the audience ("Fortune or Fate: Ambiguity in Robert Greene's 'Orlando Furioso,' " *Modern Language Review* 67 [1972]: 481–85).

17. M. C. Bradbrook, *The Growth and Structure of Elizabethan Comedy* (London: Chatto & Windus, 1955), 67.

18. Ruth H. Blackburn counts about fifty known plays from 1520 to 1603 based on scripture (*Biblical Drama under the Tudors* [The Hague, 1971], 8). The playwrights' use of the book of Jonah is most thoroughly examined in Robert Adger Law, "*A Looking Glasse* and the Scriptures," *University of Texas Studies in English* (1939):31–47, and Blackburn describes the use of the other prophets in *Biblical Drama*, 167–69. Naomi E. Pasachoff explores the relation of the play to contemporary sermons in *Playwrights, Preachers, and Politicians: A Study of Four Tudor Old Testament Dramas* (Salzburg, 1975), 57–99.

19. Attempts to divide authorship are reviewed in *Looking Glasse*, ed. Clugson, 84–92.

20. Nashe, *Works*, 2:132.

21. Representative statements of the idea include: Greene "established romantic comedy as a type to be attempted by all aspiring playwrights" (Downer, *British Drama*, 89); *Bacon* is "the first well planned and skilfully executed romantic comedy in English" (Parrott and Ball, *Short View*, 71); "In the development of Elizabethan drama this play is historically significant as the first successful Romantic Comedy" (*Friar Bacon and Friar Bungay*, ed. J. A. Lavin [London, 1969], xxi).

22. In characterizing a traditional element in approaches to the play, I am not of course suggesting that other views have not been argued. See, for example, John Weld, *Meaning in Comedy: Studies in Elizabethan Romantic Comedy* (Albany, N.Y., 1975), 136–53; Albert Wertheim, "The Presentation of Sin in 'Friar Bacon and Friar Bungay,' " *Criticism* 16 (1974):273–86; and Cary, "Iconography of Food."

23. For this side of Bacon see Waldo F. McNeir, "Traditional Elements in the Character of Greene's Friar Bacon," *Studies in Philology* 45 (1948):172–79.

24. Frank Towne attacks the view that Bacon's magic is white in " 'White Magic' in *Friar Bacon and Friar Bungay?*" *Modern Language Notes* 67 (1952):9–13; he cites several earlier critics, including Robert Hunter West in *The Invisible World: A Study of Pneumatology in Elizabethan Drama* (Athens: University of Georgia Press, 1939), 133–34. West claims in a rejoinder to have been misrepresented ("White Magic in *Friar Bacon,*" *Modern Language Notes* 67 [1952]:499–500). Among more recent proponents of the black-magic view, see Wertheim, "Presentation of Sin." A. W. Ward's introduction contains a still useful summary of the historical and literary backgrounds of Greene's treatment of magic (*Tragical History of Dr. Faustus: Honourable History of Friar Bacon and Friar Bungay,* ed. A. W. Ward, 4th ed. [Oxford, 1901]).

25. On the question of precedence see Charles F. Herford, *Studies in the Literary Relations of England and Germany in the Sixteenth Century* (Cambridge: Cambridge University Press, 1886), 189–95; *Faustus and Bacon,* ed. Ward, xxi–xxvi; and W. W. Greg, ed., *Marlowe's Doctor Faustus 1606–1616* (Oxford: Clarendon Press, 1950), 7–8.

26. Collins prints this work (2:6–13), the earliest surviving edition of which is dated 1627. Its relation to the play is discussed painstakingly in Kerstin Assarsson-Rizzi, *Friar Bacon and Friar Bungay: A Structural and Thematic Analysis of Robert Greene's Play* (Lund, 1972), 24–43; see also Senn, *Dramatic Construction,* 45–51.

27. Cf. Lavin: "inconsistency" not "of a character in real life, but of an incomplete artistic integration" (*Bacon,* xxix); and Madeleine Doran: "we cannot seriously think that Greene's end in exhibiting Bacon's fascinating magical powers . . . was merely to prepare for the friar's pious abjuration of his art" (*Endeavors of Art* [Madison: University of Wisconsin Press, 1954], 98).

28. C. F. Tucker Brooke, *The Tudor Drama* (Boston: Houghton Mifflin, 1911), 264.

29. William Empson, *Some Versions of Pastoral* (London, 1935), 31–34.

30. Seltzer reviews this and other changes which darken the treatment of Bacon's magic (*Friar Bacon and Friar Bungay* [Lincoln, 1963], xii–xiii).

31. Weld argues that the sight of Ralph as leader of the courtiers duplicates the inversion of reason and folly in Edward's psyche (*Meaning in Comedy,* 138). The unmasking of Ralph as "an anticipatory mirror scene for Edward's resumption of identity" is noted in Peter Mortenson, "Friar Bacon and Friar Bungay: Festive Comedy and 'Three-Form'd Luna,' " *English Literary Renaissance* 2 (1972):199.

32. Several parallels between the two characters are described in Mortenson, "Festive Comedy," 199–201.

33. See, for example, *Friar Bacon*, ed. Seltzer, xviii ("so hyperbolic as to be amusing").

34. Ibid., xvii. The passage bears on the question of the "realism" of Greene's heroines, for Seltzer reacts against a tradition typified in Parrott's description of Margaret as "a new creation, the first girl, loving and beloved, in English comedy who is clearly perceived and realistically presented" (*Shakespearean Comedy*, 82). The tradition is attacked by Kenneth Muir ("Robert Greene as Dramatist," in *Essays on Shakespeare and Elizabethan Drama in Honor of Hardin Craig*, ed. Richard Hosley [Columbia, Mo., 1962], 53), who quotes several critics; others are quoted in *Friar Bacon*, ed. Lavin, xxv, n. For a recent defense of the older view see Dean, "Greene's Romantic Heroines."

35. See Weld's important discussion of this scene, based on his account of Christian statements of the view that "an awareness of the limitations and dangers of earthly delights enables one to appreciate them properly—without committing oneself to them" (*Meaning in Comedy*, 148).

36. The case for *James IV* as Greene's last play is reviewed in *James IV*, ed. Norman Sanders (London, 1970), xxv–xxix. An English version of a French translation of the story in *Gli Hecatommithi* that Greene may have used is printed as an appendix in Sanders's edition, and Sanders examines the relation of the play to the source in detail (xxix–xxxv). See also Marvin T. Herrick, *Tragicomedy* (Urbana: University of Illinois Press, 1955), 232–37, and Senn, *Dramatic Construction*, 51–56.

37. The authenticity of the debate scene has been questioned. Sanders reviews the issue and concludes, however, that there is no reason to doubt Greene's authorship (*James IV*, xli).

38. Ruth Hudson suggests, however, that the play may contain references to the Scottish court of Greene's day ("Greene's *James IV* and Contemporary Allusions to Scotland," *PMLA* 47 [1932]:652–67).

39. See the review of such characters in Lawrence Babb, *The Elizabethan Malady: A Study of Melancholia in English Literature from 1580 to 1642* (East Lansing: Michigan State University Press, 1951), 91–96. Also relevant is Vanna Gentili, *La recita della follia: Funzioni dell' insania nel teatro dell' età di Shakespeare* (Turin: Einandi, 1978), passim. Baskervill compares Bohan to Asper-Malicente in Jonson's *Every Man Out of His Humor* (*English Elements*, 148), and many critics compare him to Jaques in *As You Like It*.

40. The disparity between Bohan's declaration of the purpose of the play and its happy ending has inspired a good deal of comment. For A. R. Braunmuller, "Greene has created a complicated and rewarding balance between rival claims that love has fled the earth and that it cures and reconciles all passionate excess" ("The Serious Comedy of Greene's *James IV*," *English Language Review* 3 [1973]:350). What some critics see

as a lamentable breakdown of illusion (not only in the disparity between the frame and the play itself but also in such actions as Bohan's sons' entering service under characters in the play) Braunmuller sees as part of a conscious design to undermine "the audience's confidence in any 'conventional' understanding of the relation among the various actions on stage" (341). Dieter Mehl also finds the frame complex and innovative in *The Elizabethan Dumb Show: The History of a Dramatic Convention* (Cambridge, Mass.: Harvard University Press, 1966), 83–85, but Enid Welsford attacks it vigorously in *The Court Masque: A Study in the Relation between Poetry & the Revels* (London: Cambridge University Press, 1962), 280.

41. James is compared to morality heroes in *James IV*, ed. Lavin, xv–xviii; Hunter, *Comedy of Forgiveness*, 79–83; Ernest William Talbert, *Elizabethan Drama and Shakespeare's Early Plays: An Essay in Historical Criticism* (Chapel Hill: University of North Carolina Press, 1963), 92–95; and Glynne Wickham, *Early English Stages: 1300 to 1660*, vol. 2, *1576 to 1660*, pt. 1 (New York: Columbia University Press, 1963), 41–42. Murray Krieger compares James's struggles to those of Shakespeare's Angelo in "*Measure for Measure* and Elizabethan Comedy," *PMLA* 66 (1951):782.

42. See *James IV*, ed. Sanders, 78–79, for textual problems in this scene (which he believes one of the most effective scenes in the play [xliii]).

43. Cole, *Quest of Inquirie*, 539.

44. Nicoll, *British Drama*, 90. For attacks on such views see Muir, "Greene as Dramatist," especially 51–52, and Clemen, *Tragedy before Shakespeare*, 186–91. See also note 34 above.

45. Thus Sanders writes of the conclusion of the play that James's "single moment of doubt in his course of action and his final repentance are neither sufficiently strong, dramatically or poetically, to make his place in the happy ending altogether acceptable" (*James IV*, xlvii).

46. See *James IV*, ed. Lavin, 89, and *James IV*, ed. Sanders, 112–14, for attempts to solve the textual problem.

47. Sanders makes a similar point about the relation of the play to the frame: the ending, that is, answers to Bohan's cynicism by offering "a second chance for the real-life audience" (*James IV*, liii).

Chapter Four

1. Clemen, *Tragedy before Shakespeare*, 189.

2. John Addington Symonds, *Shakespeare's Predecessors in the English Drama*, new ed. (London: Smith, Elder, 1913), 436 (first published in 1884).

3. William H. Chapman, *William Shakespeare and Robert Greene: The Evidence* (Oakland, Calif.: Tribune Publ. Co., 1912), 9.

4. Jusserand, *English Novel*, 152.

5. Ribner, "Greene's Attack on Marlowe," 163.

6. Thomas Heywood, *The Hierarchie of the blessed Angells* (London: Islip, 1635).

7. John Leon Lievsay, "Greene's Panther," *Philological Quarterly* 20 (1941):303, 301.

8. Charles M. Gayley, "Critical Essay," in *Representative English Comedies* (New York, 1903), 1:428; Lily B. Campbell, *Divine Poetry and Drama in Sixteenth-Century England* (Cambridge: Cambridge University Press, 1959), 252.

9. Wright, *Middle-Class Culture*, 387.

10. G. K. Hunter, "Isocrates' Precepts and Polonius' Character," *Shakespeare Quarterly* 8 (1957):501–2.

11. Allan C. Dessen, *Elizabethan Drama and the Viewer's Eye* (Chapel Hill: University of North Carolina Press, 1977), 157–64.

12. Hardin Craig, *Shakespeare: A Historical and Critical Study with Annotated Texts of Twenty-one Plays* (Chicago: Scott Foresman, 1931), 29; Olive Mary Busby, *Studies in the Development of the Fool in the Elizabethan Drama* (London: Oxford University Press, 1923), 33; Frank Humphrey Ristine, *English Tragicomedy: Its Origin and History* (New York: Columbia University Press, 1910), 80; Downer, *British Drama*, 91.

13. *Friar Bacon*, ed. Seltzer, xxi; Collins, ed., *Plays & Poems*, 1:57.

Selected Bibliography

PRIMARY SOURCES

1. Collected Editions

The Dramatic and Poetical Works of Robert Greene & George Peele. Edited by Alexander Dyce. London: Routledge and Sons, 1861. Reprints with corrections Dyce's 1831 *The Dramatic Works of Robert Greene.*

The Life and Complete Works in Prose and Verse of Robert Greene, M. A. Cambridge and Oxford. Edited by Alexander B. Grosart. 15 vols. London: Huth Library, 1881–86. Inconsistent editorially but the only collected edition. Contains plays and all prose works except *An Oration* and the third tale in *Planetomachia.*

The Plays & Poems of Robert Greene. Edited by J. Churton Collins. 2 vols. Oxford: Clarendon Press, 1905. The standard edition, superseding Dyce and Grosart despite its flaws (two planned new editions have been abandoned in the last thirty years). Critics include W. W. Greg in *Modern Language Review* 1 (1906):238–51; Henry Bradley in *Modern Language Review* 1 (1906):208–11; Robert Adger Law in *Modern Language Notes* 22 (1907):197–99; and J. Le Gay Brereton in *Beiblatt zur Anglia* 18 (1907):46–62.

Robert Greene. Edited by Thomas H. Dickinson. Mermaid Series. London: T. F. Unwin, 1909.

2. Some Editions of Individual Works

a. *Alphonsus*

Alphonsus, King of Aragon. Edited by W. W. Greg. London: Malone Society, 1926.

b. *Ciceronis Amor*

A Critical Edition of Robert Greene's Ciceronis Amor: Tullies Love. Edited by Charles Howard Larson. Elizabethan & Renaissance Studies, no. 36. Salzburg: Universität Salzburg, 1974.

c. *Friar Bacon and Friar Bungay*

Tragical History of Dr. Faustus: Honourable History of Friar Bacon and Friar Bungay. Edited by Adolphus William Ward. 4th ed. Oxford: Clarendon Press, 1901.

Friar Bacon and Friar Bungay. Edited by W. W. Greg. Oxford: Malone
    Society, 1926.
Friar Bacon and Friar Bungay. Edited by Daniel Seltzer. Regents Renais-
    sance Drama Series. Lincoln: University of Nebraska Press, 1963.
Friar Bacon and Friar Bungay. Edited by J. A. Lavin. New Mermaids.
    London: Ernest Benn, 1969.

d. *James IV*
The Scottish History of James the Fourth. Edited by A. E. H. Swaen and
    W. W. Greg. London: Malone Society, 1921.
The Scottish History of James the Fourth. Edited by J. A. Lavin. New Mer-
    maids. London: Ernest Benn, 1967.
The Scottish History of James the Fourth. Edited by Norman Sanders. Revels
    Plays. London: Methuen, 1970.
The Scottish History of James IV: A Critical, Old-Spelling Edition. Edited by
    Charles H. Stein. Elizabethan & Renaissance Studies, no. 54. Salz-
    burg: Universität Salzburg, 1977.

e. *Looking Glasse for London and England*
A Looking-Glasse for London and England. Edited by W. W. Greg. Oxford:
    Malone Society, 1932.
A Looking Glasse for London and England: An Elizabethan Text. Edited by
    Tetsumaro Hayashi. Metuchan, N.J.: Scarecrow Press, 1970.
A Looking Glasse for London and England: A Critical Edition. Edited by
    George Alan Clugson. New York: Garland, 1980.

f. *Orlando Furioso*
The History of Orlando Furioso. Edited by W. W. Greg. Oxford: Malone
    Society, 1907.
Two Elizabethan Stage Abridgments: The Battle of Alcazar & Orlando Furioso.
    Edited by W. W. Greg. Oxford: Clarendon Press, 1923.
A Textual Study of Robert Greene's Orlando Furioso with an Elizabethan Text.
    Edited by Tetsumaro Hayashi. Ball State Monographs, no. 21. Mun-
    cie, Ind.: Ball State University, 1973.

g. *Planetomachia*
*Robert Greene's Planetomachia and the Text of the Third Tragedy: A Biblio-
    graphical Explanation and a New Edition of the Text.* Edited by D. F.
    Bratchell. Avebury, 1979.

h. *The Royal Exchange*
The Aphorisms of Orazio Rinaldi, Robert Greene, and Lucas Gracian Dantisco.
    Edited by Charles Speroni. Berkeley: University of California Press,
    1968.

SECONDARY SOURCES

1. Bibliographies

Allison, A. F. *Robert Greene 1558–1592: A Bibliographical Catalogue of the Early Editions in English (to 1640).* Pall Mall Bibliographies, no. 4. Folkestone: Dawson, 1975.

Dean, J. S., Jr. "Robert Greene: An Addendum and Supplementary Bibliography of Editions, Biography, and Criticism 1945–1969." *Research Opportunities in Renaissance Drama* 13–14 (1970–71):181–86.

Harner, James L. *English Renaissance Prose Fiction, 1500–1660: An Annotated Bibliography of Criticism.* Boston: G. K. Hall, 1978.

Hayashi, Tetsumaro. *Robert Greene Criticism: A Comprehensive Bibliography.* Metuchan, N.J.: Scarecrow Press, 1971.

Johnson, Robert C. *Elizabethan Bibliographies Supplements V: Robert Greene 1945–1965.* London: Nether P., 1968.

Nestrick, William. "Robert Greene." In *The Predecessors of Shakespeare: A Survey and Bibliography of Recent Studies in English Renaissance Drama,* edited by Terence P. Logan and Denzell S. Smith, 56–92. Lincoln: University of Nebraska Press, 1973.

Tannenbaum, Samuel A. *Robert Greene (A Concise Bibliography).* New York: S. A. Tannenbaum, 1939.

———. and Tannenbaum, Dorothy R. *Supplement to a Bibliography of Robert Greene.* New York: S. A. Tannenbaum, 1945.

2. General Accounts of Greene

Collier, J. Payne. *The History of English Dramatic Poetry to the Time of Shakespeare: And Annals of the Stage to the Restoration.* 3 vols. London: Murray, 1831. Along with comments on the works, volume 3 includes biographical conjectures that influenced later writers.

Gayley, Charles Mills. "Critical Essay." In *Representative English Comedies,* 1:397–431. New York: Macmillan, 1903. A useful summary of attitudes toward Greene in Gayley's day.

Helgerson, Richard. *The Elizabethan Prodigals.* Berkeley: University of California Press, 1976. Greene (79–104) is one of several writers treated in this important study of the relation of art to life in portrayals of prodigal figures.

Jordan, John Clark. *Robert Greene.* New York: Columbia University Press, 1915. A basic book, used by all subsequent critics. Jordan argues throughout that Greene's "real power . . . was in narrative" (33).

Pruvost, René. *Robert Greene et ses Romans (1558–1592).* Paris: Belles Lettres, 1938. The most comprehensive study of Greene's life and works. Long (578 pages) and sometimes tedious, but essential.

Storojenko, Nicholas. *Robert Greene: His Life and Works: A Critical Investigation*, translated by E. A. Brayley Hodgetts. In *Works . . . of Robert Greene*, edited by Alexander Grosart. Vol. 1. London, 1881. First published in Moscow in 1878. Careless as biography and dated as criticism, but the most thorough work on Greene before the twentieth century.

Wolff, S. L. "Robert Greene and the Italian Renaissance." *Englische Studien* 37 (1907):321–74. Surveys Italian sources, although Greene's Puritan streak is seen to have prevented his full absorption of Renaissance ideas.

3. Biography and Repentance Pamphlets

Alexander, Peter. *Shakespeare's Henry VI and Richard III*. Cambridge: Cambridge University Press, 1929. Includes an important analysis of the Shake-scene passage (seen as not an accusation of plagiarism).

Austin, Warren B. *A Computer-Aided Technique for Stylistic Discrimination: The Authorship of Greene's Groats-worth of Wit*. Project 7–G–036, Grant no. OEG 1–7–070036–4593, U.S. Department of H.E.W. Washington, D.C.: U.S. Office of Education, 1969. Denies Greene's authorship.

Bolz, Norbert. *Eine statistische, computerunterstützte Echtheitsprüfung von The Repentance of Robert Greene: Ein methodischer und systematischer Ansatz*. Frankfurt am Main: Peter Lang, 1978. Denies Greene's authorship.

Drew, Philip. "Was Greene's 'Young Juvenal' Nashe or Lodge?" *Studies in English Literature* 7 (1967):55–66. A thorough review of the evidence; it favors Lodge, but not clearly enough to justify confident identification.

Jenkins, Harold. "On the Authenticity of Greene's *Groatsworth of Wit* and *The Repentance of Robert Greene*." *Review of English Studies* 11 (1935):28–41. A vigorous point-by-point answer to Sanders's "Greene and His 'Editors,' " maintaining that Greene wrote both works.

Kreifelts, Barbara. *Eine statistische Stilanalyse zur Klärung von Autorenschaftsfragen, durchgeführt am Beispiel von Greens Groatsworth of Wit*. Cologne: University of Cologne, 1972. Chettle wrote the *Groatsworth*.

McKerrow, Ronald B. *The Works of Thomas Nashe, with corrections and supplementary notes by F. P. Wilson*. 5 vols. Oxford: Oxford University Press, 1958. Introduction and notes include discussion of the Harvey-Nashe quarrel and commentary on Nashe's various references to Greene.

Miller, Edwin Haviland. *The Professional Writer in Elizabethan England: A Study of Nondramatic Literature*. Cambridge, Mass.: Harvard University

Press, 1959. Greene's career provides evidence for a number of Miller's arguments.

————. "The Relationship of Robert Greene and Thomas Nashe (1588–1592." *Philological Quarterly* 33 (1954):353–67. Nashe was closer to Greene than he admitted. They may have collaborated on the attack on the Harveys in the *Quip*.

Parr, Johnstone. "Robert Greene and His Classmates at Cambridge." *PMLA* 77 (1962):536–43. Seeks to shed light on Greene by looking at other students of his day. Useful statement of facts and possibilities.

Richardson, Brenda. "Robert Greene's Yorkshire Connexions: A New Hypothesis." *Year's Work in English Studies* 10 (1980):160–80. The first report on research still in progress. An important article with large implications for our view of Greene's life.

Sanders, Chauncey Elwood. "Robert Greene and His 'Editors.' " *PMLA* 48 (1933):392–417. A thorough attack on the authenticity of the repentance pamphlets.

————. *Robert Greene and the Harveys.* Indiana University Studies, no. 93. Bloomington: Indiana University, 1931. Reviews the course of the antipathy and seeks to determine its causes.

Wilson, J. Dover. "Malone and the Upstart Crow." *Shakespeare Survey* 4 (1951):56–68. Answers Alexander on the Shake-scene passage.

4. Prose Works

Allen, Don Cameron. "Science and Invention in Greene's Prose." *PMLA* 53 (1938):1007–18. Greene's use of natural history.

Applegate, James. "The Classical Learning of Robert Greene." *Bibliothèque d'Humanisme et Renaissance* 28 (1966):354–68. "The most striking thing about [Greene's] use of . . . classical information is his misuse of it" (366).

Baker, Ernest A. *The History of the English Novel: The Elizabethan Age and After.* London: Witherby, 1929. Includes a generally unsympathetic survey of the prose works.

Bonheim, Helmut. "Robert Greene's *Gwydonius: The Card of Fancie.*" *Anglia* 96 (1978):45–64. A general article that considers several features of *Gwydonius*.

Davis, Walter R. *Idea and Act in Elizabethan Fiction.* Princeton: Princeton University Press, 1969. This important study of Elizabethan fiction includes a chapter on Greene in which his career is seen as moving toward the "radical dissociation of ideas from action" (189).

Dent, Robert W. "Greene's *Gwydonius*: A Study in Elizabethan Plagiarism." *Huntington Library Quarterly* 24 (1961):151–62. Detailed analysis of borrowings from Pettie and Greene's own *Mamillia*.

Esler, Anthony. "Robert Greene and the Spanish Armada." *English Literary History* 32 (1965):314–32. A general article on *The Spanish Masquerado.*

Freeman, Arthur. "An Unacknowledged Work of Robert Greene." *Notes & Queries,* n.s., 12 (1965):378–79. Description and brief analysis of *An Oration.*

Goree, Roselle Gould. "Concerning Repetitions in Greene's Romances." *Philological Quarterly* 3 (1924):69–75. Identifies a number of passages that Greene used more than once.

Hart, H. C. "Robert Greene's Prose Works." *Notes & Queries,* 10th ser., 4 (1905):1–5, 81–84, 162–64, 224–27, 483–85; 5 (1906):84–85, 202–4, 343–44, 424–25, 442–45, 463–65, 484–87, 504–6. Mainly on Greene's borrowings and repetitions.

Hornat, Jaroslav. "*Mamillia:* Robert Greene's Controversy with *Euphues.*" *Philologica Pragensia* 5 (1962):210–18. Greene "tried to enrich the literary genre which he set out to imitate" (211).

———. "Two Euphuistic Stories of Robert Greene: *The Carde of Fancie* and *Pandosto.*" *Philologica Pragensia* 6 (1963):21–35. General approaches to the two works, both of which fall into parallel halves.

Jusserand, J. J. *The English Novel in the Time of Shakespeare.* Rev. ed. Translated by Elizabeth Lee. London: T. F. Unwin, 1895. Mainly biography and plot summary, but interesting for its forthright evaluations of individual works.

Larson, Charles H. "Robert Greene's *Ciceronis Amor:* Fictional Biography in the Romance Genre." *Studies in the Novel* 6 (1974):256–67. A romance, not a novel, showing Greene's interest in narrative, not in "moral dissertations" (258).

Lievsay, John Leon. "Greene's Panther." *Philological Quarterly* 20 (1941):296–303. On Greene's uses of the panther as an image.

Lindheim, Nancy R. "Lyly's Golden Legacy: *Rosalynde* and *Pandosto.*" *Studies in English Literature* 15 (1975):3–20. *Pandosto* presents "a world of moral anarchy, where choice is balanced against choice."

McPeek, James A. S. *The Black Book of Knaves and Unthrifts in Shakespeare and Other Renaissance Authors.* N.p.: University of Connecticut, 1969. Includes chapter on the coney-catching pamphlets.

Miller, Edwin H. "The Sources of Robert Greene's 'A Quip for an Upstart Courtier' (1592)." *Notes & Queries* 198 (1953):148–52, 187–91. Greene used a number of works in addition to F. T.'s *Debate between Pride and Lowliness.*

Parr, Johnstone. "Sources of the Astrological Prefaces in Robert Greene's *Planetomachia.*" *Studies in Philology* 36 (1949):400–410. Nothing in the prefaces is original with Greene.

Sanders, Norman. "Robert Greene's Way with a Source." *Notes & Queries,* n.s., 14 (1967):89–91. Seventy passages in *Farewell to Folly* come from R. B.'s translation of *The French Academy.*

Vincent, C. J. "Further Repetitions in the Works of Robert Greene." *Philological Quarterly* 18 (1939):73–77. Repetitions listed; they show Greene "taking advantage not only of his readers, but also of his publishers" (77).

————. "Pettie and Greene." *Modern Language Notes* 54 (1939):105–11. Borrowings from Pettie in several works.

Weld, John S. "Some Problems of Euphuistic Narrative: Robert Greene and Henry Wotton." *Studies in Philology* 45 (1948):165–71. On the use of Wotton in *Mamillia.*

Wolff, Samuel Lee. *The Greek Romances in Elizabethan Prose Fiction.* New York: Columbia University Press, 1912. The section on Greene is essential for students of his sources (367–458).

5. Plays
a. Plays accepted as Greene's

Assarsson-Rizzi, Kerstin. *Friar Bacon and Friar Bungay: A Structural and Thematic Analysis of Robert Greene's Play.* Lund Studies in English, no. 44. Lund: Gleerup, 1972. A painstaking commentary on the play that includes some useful perceptions, especially concerning Greene's use of his source.

Babula, William. "Fortune or Fate: Ambiguity in Robert Greene's 'Orlando Furioso.' " *Modern Language Review* 67 (1972):481–85. Conflict between conceptions of Fortune and Fate is unresolved in the play.

Baldwin, T. W. *On the Literary Genetics of Shakspere's Plays 1592–1594.* Urbana: University of Illinois Press, 1959. Includes a lengthy commentary on the Shake-scene passage and an attempt to date Greene's plays.

Bevington, David. *Tudor Drama and Politics: A Critical Approach to Topical Meaning.* Cambridge, Mass.: Harvard University Press, 1968. Considers political and social elements in Greene's plays (passim).

Blackburn, Ruth H. *Biblical Drama under the Tudors.* Studies in English Literature, no. 65. The Hague: Mouton, 1971. Treats the *Looking Glasse,* noting especially the use of scriptural sources and the formal complexity of the play.

Braunmuller, A. R. "The Serious Comedy of Greene's *James IV.*" *English Language Review* 3 (1973):335–50. "Greene elaborately complicates two features of the play: its treatment of dramatic illusion and its handling of romantic, pastoral, and comic conventions" (337).

Cary, Cecile Williamson. "The Iconography of Food and the Motif of World Order in *Friar Bacon and Friar Bungay.*" *Comparative Drama* 13 (1979):150–63. References to food in the play reflect iconographic traditions.

Clemen, Wolfgang. *English Tragedy before Shakespeare: The Development of Dramatic Speech.* Translated by T. S. Dorsch. London: Methuen, 1961. First published in 1955. Greene's career is a miniature version of the movement away from set speeches in Elizabethan drama, although he never freed himself completely from "worn-out formulas" (186).

Cole, Howard C. *A Quest of Inquirie: Some Contexts of Tudor Literature.* Indianapolis: Pegasus, 1973. Approaches the plays through sources and traditions, with attention especially to Greene's combining of disparate elements (507–42).

Dean, J. S., Jr. "Robert Greene's Romantic Heroines: Caught Up in Knowledge and Power?" *Ball State University Forum* 14 (1973):3–12. "This essay seeks redress against the defamation of Greene's characterization"; his heroines "become romantic instruments of comic resolution" (3).

Downer, Alan S. *The British Drama: A Handbook and Brief Chronicle.* New York: Appleton-Century-Crofts, 1950. Includes an appreciative account of structure in *Friar Bacon* (89–94).

Ellis-Fermor, Una. "Marlowe and Greene: A Note on Their Relations as Dramatic Artists." In *Studies in Honor of T. W. Baldwin,* edited by Don Cameron Allen, 136–49. Urbana: University of Illinois Press, 1958. Following the unsuccessful imitation of Marlowe in *Alphonsus,* Greene's parody in *Orlando* helped free him to find his own voice in his mature plays.

Empson, William. *Some Versions of Pastoral.* London: Chatto & Windus, 1935. Includes an influential description of the love-magic analogy in *Friar Bacon* (31–34).

Gelber, Norman. "Robert Greene's 'Orlando Furioso': A Study of Thematic Ambiguity." *Modern Language Review* 64 (1969):264–66. The contrast between antifeminist passages and Angelica's virtues shows that "women must be judged as individuals" (266).

Giachino, Enzo. "Per recuperare il miracolo." In *Utopia e Fantascienza.* Turin: Giappichelli, 1975, 63–79. *Friar Bacon* in relation to science fiction.

Habicht, Werner. *Studien zur Dramenform vor Shakespeare: Moralität, Interlude, romaneskes Drama.* Heidelberg: Carl Winter, 1968. Includes discussion of Greene (and other "romantic" playwrights) in relation to native traditions.

Hudson, Ruth. "Greene's *James IV* and Contemporary Allusions to Scotland." *PMLA* 47 (1932):652–67. The fictional court of James IV is a commentary on the real court of James VI.

Hunter, Robert Grams. *Shakespeare and the Comedy of Forgiveness.* New York: Columbia University Press, 1965. *Orlando* and *James IV* are precedents for Shakespeare.

Law, Robert Adger. "*A Looking Glasse* and the Scriptures." *University of Texas Studies in English* (1939):31–47. Greene and Lodge used the Bishop's Bible, a fact which solves some textual puzzles and bears on the attribution of individual scenes.

Lawlor, John. "*Pandosto* and the Nature of Dramatic Romance." *Philological Quarterly* 41 (1962):96–113. Among the most useful of the many comparisons of *Pandosto* and *The Winter's Tale.*

Lemmi, Charles W. "The Sources of Greene's *Orlando Furioso.*" *Modern Language Notes* 31 (1916):440–41. "Practically every situation in Greene's *Orlando Furioso* has its analogue in Ariosto's" (440).

MacLaine, Allan H. "Greene's Borrowings from His Own Prose Fiction in *Bacon and Bungay* and *James the Fourth.*" *Philological Quarterly* 30 (1951):22–29. The most systematic study of this subject.

McNeir, Waldo F. "Greene's Medievalization of Ariosto." *Revue de littérature comparée* 29 (1955):351–60. On *Orlando Furioso* as "a return to the primal tradition of romance" (351).

———. "Traditional Elements in the Character of Greene's Friar Bacon." *Studies in Philology* 45 (1948):172–79. Greene sets Bacon in the tradition of the benevolent sorcerers of medieval romance.

Morrison, Morris Robert. "Greene's Use of Ariosto in *Orlando Furioso.*" *Modern Language Notes* 49 (1934):449–51. Orlando and Angelica are modeled on Ariosto's Ariodantes and Genevra.

Mortenson, Peter. "Friar Bacon and Friar Bungay: Festive Comedy and 'Three-Form'd Luna.' " *English Literary Renaissance* 2 (1972):194–207. On the progress of the characters toward true identity through holiday misrule and the association of Bacon and Margaret with the moon goddess.

Muir, Kenneth. "Robert Greene as Dramatist." In *Essays on Shakespeare and Elizabethan Drama in Honor of Hardin Craig,* edited by Richard Hosley, 45–54. Columbia: University of Missouri Press, 1962. A general approach to the plays that includes some important comments on the traditional praise of the realism of Greene's heroines.

Parrott, Thomas Marc. *Shakespearean Comedy.* New York: Oxford, 1949. Includes section on Shakespearean elements in Greene's plays (76–88).

Pasachoff, Naomi E. *Playwrights, Preachers, and Politicians: A Study of Four Tudor Old Testament Dramas.* Elizabethan & Renaissance Studies, no. 45. Salzburg: Universität Salzburg, 1975. Treats the *Looking Glasse* in relation to sixteenth-century sermons.

Pettet, E. C. *Shakespeare and the Romance Tradition.* London: Staples Press, 1949. Includes discussion of Greene's use of (and departures from) romance conventions.

Ribner, Irving. "Greene's Attack on Marlowe: Some Light on *Alphonsus* and *Selimus*." *Studies in Philology* 52 (1955): 162–71. Both plays answer Marlowe's attack on Elizabethan orthodoxy.

Sanders, Norman. "The Comedy of Greene and Shakespeare." In *Early Shakespeare,* edited by John Russell Brown and Bernard Harris, 35–53. Stratford-upon-Avon studies, no. 3. London: Arnold, 1961. Greene's kinship to Shakespeare a matter of shared comic view, not "close correspondence" between individual plays (36).

Senn, Werner. *Studies in the Dramatic Construction of Robert Greene and George Peele.* Bern: Francke, 1973. Treats several aspects of the plays, including sources. One of the few discussions of Greene to include substantial commentary on *Alphonsus.*

Towne, Frank. " 'White Magic' in *Friar Bacon and Friar Bungay?*" *Modern Language Notes* 67 (1952): 9–13. Bacon's magic is black magic, and he is saved in the end only because he repents.

Weld, John. *Meaning in Comedy: Studies in Elizabethan Romantic Comedy.* Albany: State University of New York Press, 1975. Includes an important reading of *Friar Bacon* (136–53) in the context of homiletic tradition and Elizabethan Christianity.

Wertheim, Albert. "The Presentation of Sin in 'Friar Bacon and Friar Bungay.' " *Criticism* 16 (1974): 273–86. The play has an "allegorical structure" (282) in that Bacon's necromancy leads him to "reflect in himself or foster in others each of the traditional Seven Deadly Sins" (275).

b. Doubtful plays

Born, Hanspeter. *The Rare Wit and the Rude Groom: The Authorship of A Knack to Know a Knave in Relation to Greene, Nashe & Shakespeare.* Bern: Francke, 1972.

Brooke, C. F. Tucker. *The Shakespeare Apocrypha.* 2d ed. Oxford: Clarendon Press, 1918. First published in 1908. *Locrine* and *Selimus* discussed.

Grosart, Alexander B. *The Tragical Reign of Selimus.* London: Dent, 1898.

McNeir, Waldo F. "Robert Greene and *John of Bordeaux.*" *PMLA* 64 (1949): 781–801.

Maxwell, Baldwin. *Studies in the Shakespeare Apocrypha.* New York: Columbia University Press, 1956. *Locrine* and *Selimus* discussed.

Pennel, Charles A. "The Authenticity of the *George a Greene* Title-Page Inscriptions." *Journal of English and Germanic Philology* 64 (1965):668–76.

Sykes, H. Dugdale. "Robert Greene and *George a Greene, The Pinner of Wakefield.*" *Review of English Studies* 7 (1931):129–36.

Index